John Paul II and the Jewish People

John Paul II and the Jewish People

A Jewish-Christian Dialogue

Edited by
David G. Dalin and
Matthew Levering

A SHEED & WARD BOOK

ROWMAN & LITTLEFIELD PUBLISHERS, INC.
Lanham • Boulder • New York • Toronto • Plymouth, UK

A SHEED & WARD BOOK

ROWMAN & LITTLEFIELD PUBLISHERS, INC.

Published in the United States of America
by Rowman & Littlefield Publishers, Inc.
A wholly owned subsidiary of The Rowman & Littlefield Publishing Group, Inc.
4501 Forbes Boulevard, Suite 200, Lanham, Maryland 20706
www.rowmanlittlefield.com

Estover Road
Plymouth PL6 7PY
United Kingdom

British Library Cataloguing in Publication Information Available

Library of Congress Cataloging-in-Publication Data

John Paul II and the Jewish people : a Jewish-Christian dialogue / edited by David G.
 Dalin and Matthew Levering.
  p. cm.
 Includes Index.
 ISBN-13: 978-0-7425-5998-1 (cloth : alk paper)
 ISBN-10: 0-7425-5998-X (cloth : alk paper)
 ISBN-13: 978-0-7425-5999-8 (pbk. : alk paper)
 ISBN-10: 0-7425-5999-8 (pbk. : alk paper)
 1. John Paul II, Pope, 1920–2005—Relations with Jews. 2. Catholic Church—
Relations—Judaism. 3. Judaism—Relations—Catholic Church. I. Dalin, David G.
II. Levering, Matthew

 BM535.J577 2007
 261.2'6092—dc22   2007030315

Printed in the United States of America

∞™ The paper used in this publication meets the minimum requirements of American
National Standard for Information Sciences—Permanence of Paper for Printed Library
Materials, ANSI/NISO Z39.48-1992.

Contents

PART III: BIBLICAL-SYSTEMATIC REFLECTIONS

Foreword

Persecution of Jews by Christians—including officials of the Church and even popes—is the great historical stain on the Christian conscience. This is not to suggest that all Christians or all Church officials have been anti-Semites—far from it. Indeed, many Christians—some still unsung—heroically came to the assistance of their Jewish brothers and sisters when the unspeakable evil of Nazism cast its shadow upon them. But crimes committed by professing Christians against Jews have been all too common in the history of the Church; and all too often Christians have rationalized these injustices in theological terms.

In the great document *Nostra aetate*, the fathers of the Second Vatican Council struck a powerful blow against Christian anti-Semitism by declaring solemnly that the Jews as a people are not responsible, and must not be treated as if they were responsible, for the crucifixion of Jesus. This declaration laid the foundation for the work of Pope John Paul the Great to advance the cause of reconciliation and brotherhood between Catholic Christians and the Jewish people.

When I say "brotherhood," I mean it quite literally. On April 13, 1986, the Holy Father presented himself at the Great Synagogue of Rome at the invitation of the chief rabbi, Elio Toaff. There he declared anti-Semitism to be a grave sin. But he did not stop there. He seized the opportunity to make a declaration which, in the perspective of the sad and tortured history of relations between Jews and Christians, can only be described as magnificent. He proclaimed that the Jews "are our brothers, and in a sense our *elder* brothers, in faith."

Our elder brothers in faith. The pope went beyond the condemnation of prejudice and oppression to affirm from a Christian theological vantage point the continuing validity of God's covenant with the Jewish people. While abandoning no portion of the Church's witness to Jesus as the Messiah, the pope with a single sentence destroyed the foundation of the false doctrine of supersessionism by which some Christians since the time of the heretic Marcion have attempted to sever Christianity from its Jewish roots, maintaining that God's covenant with the Jews was abolished and replaced by his new covenant with the Church.

Years later, in another magnificent moment, the pope made a profound and dramatic gesture of repentance and reconciliation toward the Jewish people while praying at the Western Wall in Jerusalem. Not only Jews and Christians but also Muslims and even unbelievers were deeply moved as they observed the (by then) aged and frail pontiff acknowledge on behalf of the Church the sins of the past and point the way to a future in which Christians and Jews truly understand each other as brothers under the divine Father whom they both worship.

The volume in your hands brings together outstanding Jewish and Christian scholars who have been inspired by the witness of John Paul the Great. His visit to the Holy Land, and the great effort of Jewish-Christian reconciliation that it symbolized and did much to advance, is the point of departure for their scholarly reflections. The authors of the essays here collected each pay to the late pope the wonderful tribute of joining him in the cause of Jewish-Christian brotherhood.

Robert P. George

Introduction

This volume explores Jewish-Christian dialogue in light of the contributions of Pope John Paul II. All of the contributors agree that John Paul's papacy marked a period of profound political and theological gains for Jewish-Christian reconciliation. Up to now, however, no scholarly volume has addressed John Paul's contributions to Jewish-Christian dialogue in a thoroughgoing fashion, and so there is the risk that John Paul's work might bear less fruit than would otherwise be the case.

This book seeks to rectify this situation. Like John Paul himself, we do not deny the irreducible particularity of the claims of Jews and Christians. Instead, we focus on three areas in which John Paul's contributions should lead to further progress in Jewish-Christian relations. First, historically and politically speaking, John Paul's frequent affirmations of solidarity with the Jewish people, his diplomatic recognition of the State of Israel, his groundbreaking visit to the Holy Land in 2000, and his agonized remembrance of the Holocaust establish his papacy as a powerful source for Christian reconciliation with the Jewish people. Second, his stance against moral relativism and for the God-given dignity and value of every human life finds a strong echo in Jewish ethical teaching. Third, his writings, both before and during his papacy, affirm a profound theological place for his "elder brothers" the Jewish people and a deep sense of the importance of the land of Israel.

As an interdisciplinary project, this book therefore approaches its topic from three perspectives: historical, ethical, and biblical-systematic. Let us briefly survey the contributions of the eight chapters.

George Weigel's "John Paul II: A Biblical Pilgrim in the World" begins with Robert Jenson's image of a world that, in the West at least, has lost the sense of a unifying "story." Many in the modern West can no longer affirm that history, or life, has any meaning beyond the daily scramble for money and pleasure. By contrast, Karol Wojtyła / John Paul II pointed to the biblical story as the true story of each human being. To make this "story" present again in the world, Weigel observes, John Paul II made a practice of going on "pilgrimage" throughout the world. In these pilgrimages, he affirmed against a variety of dehumanizing ideologies that each human person possesses the highest meaning in God's eyes. Furthermore, these pilgrimages depended upon his sense of solidarity with the Jewish people, whose story belongs integrally to the proclamation by which the world learns its true story. God's covenantal love for the Jewish people set in motion the awakening of the world to the true value of each human person. For Weigel, John Paul's pilgrimages thus attained their highest point in his pilgrimage to the Holy Land in 2000. Together, Jews and Christians have the vocation of defending the world against the pagan view of humanity, which justifies the mass death of innocents.

David G. Dalin's "John Paul II and the Jews" recounts young Karol Wojtyła's formative experiences with the Jewish community of Wadowice, Wojtyła's hometown, and in particular his lifelong friendship with Jerzy Kluger. The experiences, Dalin argues, colored Wojtyła / John Paul II's later engagement with the Jewish people. In 1979, for instance, John Paul visited Auschwitz, where Jerzy Kluger's mother, sister, and grandmother died in the gas chambers. The pope's personal knowledge of Jewish life and suffering led him to condemn anti-Semitism in all its forms, and to call repeatedly for the remembrance of the Holocaust that it might never happen again. John Paul thus oversaw the publication of the Church's first official document on the Holocaust, *We Remember: A Reflection on the Shoah*, calling upon all Christians to repent for the sins of so many Christians during the Holocaust. He also became the first pope to visit the chief synagogue of Rome, and he spearheaded the establishment of diplomatic relations between the Vatican and Israel. Dalin also notes John Paul's speech at Yad Vashem and prayer at the Western Wall as significant moments in Jewish-Christian reconciliation. Lastly, Dalin remarks upon John Paul's clear response to the recent rise of European anti-Semitism and violence against Jews.

Hadley Arkes's "John Paul II and the Moral Ground of the Polis: Reclaiming the Jewish-Catholic Ground" has in view the problem of legal positivism. The American Founders, he argues, recognized the principle of natural right or natural law, against the notion that whatever positive law proclaims is thereby veritable law. For the American Founders, positive law could not be its own justification, but must be measured against objective standards of right and wrong. In recent times, a regnant moral relativism has called into question the existence of such standards, with the resulting fruit of the mass killing of the innocent. John Paul II's great contribution in this context was to insist upon the truth of the Jewish-Christian witness to an understanding of the human person that must ground all positive law. No dictate of positive law can override the fact that human persons have a value and dignity that requires that innocent human beings must not be killed, whether by genocidal or murderous regimes, or by state-sanctioned abortions. Arkes traces John Paul's account of the human person, and especially the human person's ability to know the truth about the good, through John Paul's writings. Only by means of such an account of the human ability to know truth can a society avoid the legal positivism of "might makes right" and the resulting moral equivalence of all social structures, including Nazism and slavery. The insistence upon the integration of faith and reason stands at the center of what Arkes calls the "Jewish-Catholic ground."

David Novak's "Natural Law and Divine Command: Some Thoughts on *Veritatis Splendor*" takes up a philosophical issue within the encyclical *Veritatis splendor*, namely the status of "natural law"—an issue that bears profoundly upon Jewish-Christian dialogue. Novak begins by discussing the relationship of theology and philosophy. The former follows upon divine revelation, whereas the latter develops hypotheses on the basis of what can be learned from the world. Theology, as a witness to the particularity of divine election, cannot do without the universal claims of philosophy, because the God who elects is the Creator of all. As a second step, Novak explores the understanding of natural law put forward in *Veritatis splendor*. According to the encyclical, he argues, natural law is not in "nature" per se, but rather is the participation of rational creatures in God's eternal law and therefore is rooted in God's commands. By contrast, in Greek and Roman philosophical accounts of nature and natural law, God seems to remain aloof: "Nature," with its teleological and inexorable laws, is separated from the biblical God who commands. Novak asks whether John Paul, in seeking to unite within natural-law doctrine the commandments of the biblical God and the inexorable movement of teleological "nature," does so successfully. The key question, he suggests, is whether *Veritatis splendor*'s metaphysical understanding of the "good," as teleologically drawing the rational creature to itself, can be sustained. Answering no, Novak proposes instead to reframe the discussion of natural law around justice, whose terms allow more properly for the "negative commandments" of the natural law that John Paul seeks to promote.

Michael Novak's "The Asymmetrical Relation: Novak and Novak" addresses, in the context of friendship, the asymmetries between Christians and Jews. Jews cannot accept that Jesus was the Messiah, let alone the divine Son of the Father in the communion of the Spirit, one God in three Persons. Christians cannot accept that God's covenants with Israel were not fulfilled and transformed by Jesus as the divine Messiah who revealed the mystery of the divine unity-in-Trinity. More than this, however, Novak observes that the "asymmetry" also includes the fact that Christians, in order to be Christians, must accept nearly the whole of the Jewish faith as true, whereas the converse is certainly not the case. Christians and Jews cannot both be "Israel" or both be "the people of God." Yet, drawing upon David Novak's thought and in particular the document *Dabru Emet*, Michael Novak notes that there can be significant "overlapping commonalities," in particular as regards strictures against idolatry, murder, and sexual immorality. Christians and Jews can join hands in fighting the totalitarian state that idolatrously leaves no room for worship of God, and likewise can struggle together against liberal secularism, with its condoning of abortion and instrumentalization of sexuality. After remarking upon these "commonalities," he comments upon an even deeper bond, namely that the two communities can also unite in a desire for the living God's accomplishment of the awe-inspiring mystery of eschatological fulfillment, where friendships will be perfected.

Matthew Levering's "John Paul II, Maimonides, and Aquinas: Reflections on Divine Providence" suggests that the poetry of John Paul II about the Holy Land provides a lens for renewed examination of Jewish and Christian teachings about Divine Providence. Jews and Christians are united by commitment to trust in God's guiding care. John Paul II, however, was deeply aware that many modern individuals and societies no longer recognize Divine Providence, but instead understand human nature as a human construct, and human history as having no lasting, fulfilling *telos* or goal. In this context, the very existence of the "Holy Land" serves as a Jewish and Christian witness to the living God's care for human beings, whom God desires to "meet" in human history. Lacking this witness, the notion that human power is unrestricted by objective standards of right and wrong prevails. Yet, what kind of care is this, if God permits so much violence and barrenness, even in the Holy Land? To gain insight into this question, Levering explores a medieval example of Jewish-Christian dialogue, namely Maimonides' understanding of Divine Providence as later engaged by Thomas Aquinas. Levering emphasizes that the "meeting" of God and human beings requires that human persons, afflicted by pride and desire for autonomy, learn receptivity to divine guidance.

Bruce D. Marshall's "Elder Brothers: John Paul II's Teaching on the Jewish People as a Question to the Church" asks what it means for Christians to call Jews their "elder brothers." If the Jews are Christians' "elder brothers," how should this bond be further articulated? Marshall rejects the idea that the special bond requires weakening the distinctive mysteries of Christian faith, such as the Incarnation, the Trinity, and so forth. If it truly is a bond, then its inner dynamism will not be manifested by denying key elements of Christianity, but rather such key elements will be found to be in accord with the special bond. Indeed, Marshall proposes that it will be through meditating upon the special bond with Jews that Christians will better understand the key elements of Christian faith. He adds that John Paul considers the "elder brothers" to be not merely biblical Judaism, but the contemporary Jewish people, whose covenantal election remains in force. As an alternative perspective, Marshall brings forward the theology of the Jews and Judaism taught by Jacques Maritain and Charles Journet earlier in the twentieth century. While Maritain and Journet have a high view of the Jews, they have a low view of postbiblical Judaism. By contrast, recent pluralist thinkers, such as Paul Knitter, hold a low view of the Jews (specifically of the doctrine of election) and a high view of Judaism as a path to God. Is it possible, Marshall asks, to spell out what it might mean to hold, with John Paul II, a high view of both Jewish election and postbiblical Judaism? How can the irrevocable election of the Jewish people, which seems to require the permanence of the practice of Judaism, be squared with Christ's universal saving work as carried out sacramentally in the Church's universal mission? Without seeking here to resolve this question, Marshall evaluates three answers that have been put forward: the "two-covenant" model, the "fulfillment" model, and the "Messianic Judaism" approach.

Lastly, Gregory Vall's "'Man Is the Land': The Sacramentality of the Land of Israel" explores John Paul II's theology of the land of Israel as the "meeting place" of God and human beings, the place where God reveals Himself. Given this significance of the Holy Land, Vall inquires whether the land might be thought of as a "sacrament" that spiritually signifies the holy humanity of Jesus Christ. In dialogue with the research of W. D. Davies, Waldemar Janzen, and Robert L. Wilken, Vall asks whether this reading of the land of Israel spiritualizes Israel's conception of her land. He suggests that the danger of overspiritualization is avoided by means of attention to the physical reality of Christ's body. In this regard, he argues that Scripture, including the Torah, envisions an ongoing process of spiritualization, but as the sacramental indwelling of God rather than as an idealism. He first shows that the "land" is connected always with "revelation," with the presence of God. Second, he explores the ways in which the fruits of the land are "spiritualized" by connection with the wisdom embodied by the Torah. Third, he observes how the land of Canaan serves as an "efficacious sign" marking, and making possible, the vocation of the people of God. Fourth, he notes that the Old Testament itself contains imagery that spiritualizes or sacramentalizes (in a nonidealist manner) Jerusalem and Mount Zion by depicting them as God's heavenly dwelling. Turning to the New Testament, Vall shows that the same kind of spiritualization or sacramentalization pertains to the early Christians' understanding of the physical body of Jesus Christ as the incarnate and risen Son, and he also treats similar themes in the presentation of the Virgin Mary. He concludes with a reading of the Letter to the Hebrews, often thought to be the pinnacle of spiritualization but in fact committed to a profound sacramental realism regarding Christ's crucified and glorified body. In short, as John Paul II would expect of the great "meeting place," the material dimension of Israel's land is never left behind.

This book thus draws together historical, philosophical, and theological perspectives from various Jewish and Christian points of view, united by a desire to explore and to develop the contributions of Pope John Paul II's political and theological ventures in Jewish-Christian dialogue. John Paul challenges Jews and Christians to think together about the existence of truth, good and evil, the meaning of the Holocaust, the nature of the human person, Divine Providence, and the history and *telos* of God's covenantal love.

Part I

HISTORICAL REFLECTIONS

Chapter One

John Paul II:
A Biblical Pilgrim in the World

George Weigel

Some twelve years ago, the distinguished Lutheran theologian, Dr. Robert Jenson, wrote a brilliant essay for *First Things* with the provocative title, "How the World Lost Its Story."[1] Dr. Jenson's purpose was to sketch a strategy for the Christian church in the distinctive cultural circumstances of the postmodern world, but his central image—the idea of a world bereft of a "story"—may help us understand one important facet of the life and ministry of Pope John Paul II.

While it was primarily an essay in ecclesiology, Jenson's article was also an acute analysis of the contemporary situation of both Jews and Christians under the conditions of postmodernity. We live, he writes, in a culture of incoherence. The more generous postmodern theorists may concede that there are truths around us that can be grasped, although the postmodernist is most likely to describe such discoveries as a matter of "your truth" or "my truth." What cannot be admitted is that whatever fragments of truth may be found can be fit into a coherent narrative or story. And a world without a storyline, Dr. Jenson goes on to observe, is a world bereft of dramatic texture: no story, no drama; no drama, no dramatic resolution. A world without a story, a world without drama, is a world without a sense of promise, a world that, as Jenson puts it, "cannot entertain promises."[2] Little wonder that this is a cultural circumstance in which people of biblical faith often feel acutely uncomfortable.

The Western world once had a story, Jenson observes. It was a story learned from many sources. But its essential narrative line was preeminently the byproduct of biblical faith. Rodney Stark has made a parallel point in his recent study, *The Victory of Reason*: It was biblical faith—or, more explicitly, the Christian development of the faith of the people of Israel—that gave Western civilization its linear concept of history, its future-orientation, its belief in both spiritual and moral progress.[3] Thus it was biblical faith that gave the West its sense of what we might call the world's "narratability."

Forty years ago, prior to the social and cultural upheavals responsible for what we now style "postmodernity," I was taught one way to tell the world's story; it was a story that many of you were taught as well; and in its most intellectually sophisticated form, you can still find it in weighty books like William H. McNeill's *The Rise of the West*.[4] According to this rendering of the world's story, the key chapter headings read something like this: Ancient Civilizations, Greece and Rome, the Dark Ages, the Middle Ages, Renaissance and Reformation, the Age of Reason, the Age of Revolution, the Age of Science, the Space Age. Now this was, to be sure, a largely secular telling of the world's story; still, it was a rendering of the story that was not hostile to, but was in fact dependent on, the concept of a linear story, a human story oriented toward the future. And that, I suggest, was because this way of telling the world's story—which even in its secular form acknowledged the accomplishments of both Judaism and Christianity in forming that unique civilizational enterprise known as "the West"—remained tethered, if by a rather long and perhaps frayed umbilical cord, to a deeper storyline: a storyline whose chapter headings read Creation, Fall, Promise, and Prophecy; Incarnation, Redemption, Sanctification, the Kingdom of God. The story of the West that I was taught in school was a story that skated perhaps too comfortably across what Christopher Dawson would have called "the surface of history."[5] But, in Jenson's terms, it was in fact a coherent story because its narratability rested on the foundations of that deeper biblical storyline to which it was tethered.

Over the past several generations, though, that tether has been broken. History texts may still tell the world's story in more-or-less linear fashion, beginning with ancient civilizations and finishing up with the space age. But that, one suspects, is because the textbook publishers, influenced by the market (which means school boards), have not yet become completely enthralled by the gospel of incoherence proclaimed by the prophets of postmodernism. In large sectors of Western high culture, however, a sense of the narratability of the world has been completely lost, because the tether between the world's story and the deep narrative of that story as proclaimed by the Hebrew Bible and the New Testament has been cut. And the result is the world that we dub "postmodern": the world of the nonstory, the unnarrative, the world of fragmented knowledge and incoherence, the world cut off from a true knowledge of the past and skeptical about any notion of the future that speaks of promise.

When he was elected the 264th bishop of Rome in 1978, Karol Wojtyła brought to the Office of Peter a sharp intuition about this problem, which he had honed in his work in the late 1960s and early 1970s with doctoral candidates in philosophy at the University of Lublin. Before the first decade of his pontificate was completed, he seems to have come to the judgment that the problem of postmodernity—the problem of a world that had lost its story—would (and sooner rather than later) replace the Marxist misconstrual of reality as the principal challenge to a biblical understanding of human nature, human community, human origins, and human destiny. History would not end with the communist crack-up; but the very idea of something called "history" might well be lost, were postmodernism to triumph.

Wojtyła also brought to the papacy a settled conviction that the world's story and the biblical story were not stories running on parallel tracks. Rather, the biblical story—the story, to repeat, whose chapter headings are Creation, Fall, Promise, and Prophecy; Incarnation, Redemption, Sanctification, and the Kingdom of God—*is* the world's story: the story whose surface features are conventionally labeled Ancient Civilizations, Greece and Rome, the Dark Ages, the Middle Ages, Renaissance and Reformation, and so forth and so on. The biblical story is the world's story read in its deepest dimension and against its most ample horizon. The biblical story is, if you will, the story inside the conventional story of history, the depth story that gives the surface story its narratability and, ultimately, its coherence.

Let me put this in another, if related, way: John Paul II believed, with Hans Urs von Balthasar, that the human story is not the story of man's search for God, but rather the story of God's search for us and our learning to take the same path through history that God takes. That is what the biblical story teaches and that, John Paul II was convinced, was the story the world must learn anew (or, in some instances, for the first time), if the world were to recover a sense of its nobility and possibility—which is to say, if the world were to recover its story and its destiny. And it was in that conviction that John Paul II became a pilgrim to the world: a biblical pilgrim, telling the world its true story—the story of Abraham, the story of Moses, the story of Jesus—so that, as he put it at the United Nations in 1995, "a century of tears might give birth to a new springtime of the human spirit."[6]

It was neither an accident nor a curiosity of the Vatican's sometimes arcane terminology that John Paul II always referred to his travels—as did the Vatican's press releases and other official documents—as "pilgrimages." This was not tourism. This was not "travel." On 250 occasions over twenty-six years, John Paul left Rome and went on pilgrimage to a foreign country or a particular local church in Italy, to remind the people of those unique places that their story was part of the deep narrative of the world's story, the story of creation and redemption. Thus John Paul II's biblical pilgrimage throughout the world and through contemporary history was a pilgrimage intended to restore a sense of history as His-story: the story, to repeat, of God's search for man and our learning to take the same path through history that God is taking.

That twenty-six-year-long pilgrimage had certain moments of the highest drama. There was John Paul II's first Polish pilgrimage in June 1979. There, by speaking truth to and about power, and by giving back to his people the truth about their identity and their culture, John Paul ignited a revolution of conscience in Poland and throughout east-central Europe. That revolution of conscience, in turn, was a critical factor, and perhaps *the* critical factor, in shaping the nonviolent political resistance that eventually produced what we now know as the Revolution of 1989 and the collapse of European communism. As Yale historian John Lewis Gaddis has noted in his recently published history of the Cold War, the slow retreat of the communist plague from the lands behind the iron curtain began in earnest when John Paul II, biblical pilgrim, came home and reminded his people that to exclude the God of the Bible from the history of man was an offense against humanity and against true humanism.

There was John Paul's March 1983 pilgrimage to Nicaragua, a long-suffering land then being led by a gang of adolescent Marxists known as Sandinistas, who were given to careening around the nation's capital in sports cars, brandishing AK-47s, when they were not locking up their political opponents and harassing the heroic archbishop of Managua, Miguel Obando Bravo, a true man of the people. The Sandinistas tried to interrupt the papal Mass with shouts of "power to the people"; John Paul demanded "Silence!" and the Sandinistas more or less obeyed. The ruling party loaded the area in front of the papal Mass platform with their stooges; John Paul, seeing the faithful Catholic people of Nicaragua penned into enclosures more than a hundred yards away, stood at the front of the Mass platform, grasped his silver crosier-crucifix by its base, and waved it back and forth across the sky in salute to those who had come to Mass to pray. That remarkable scene was televised all over El Salvador, Guatemala, Honduras, Nicaragua, and Panama— and slowly, over the ensuing months and years, the Sandinista plague also began to recede, and with it the dream of a communist Central America.

There was John Paul's historic visit in April 1986 to the Synagogue of Rome, which was a pilgrimage of another sort, the continuation of a personal pilgrimage that had begun more than sixty years before in Wadowice, the small Polish town where Karol Wojtyła had grown up. As he drove across the Tiber and up the Lungotevere to the great synagogue into which no previous bishop of Rome had ever set foot, he carried with him memories of friendships with his Jewish classmates, of his father's teachings about tolerance, of the town pastor's gospel-based condemnations of anti-Semitism, of his loss of friends in the *Shoah* and his own experiences of life under Nazi occupation. He had, among senior churchmen, a unique sense of the drama of modern Jewish life and a unique appreciation of Jewish pain. But he had come to the Synagogue of Rome, he said, not only to remember and to repent of whatever needed repentance, but to mark a new beginning: a moment in which Jews and Catholics, mindful of their "common heritage drawn from the Law and the Prophets" undertook "a collaboration in favor of man," in defense of life and in defense of the dignity of the human person.[7] Jews and Catholics, collaboratively, had to remind the world of its true story, from which men and women learned the truth about their dignity.

Then there was John Paul II's pilgrimage to Denver and World Youth Day 2003. Most of the bishops of the United States, like most bishops throughout the West, had given up on young people: They funded youth ministry offices in their dioceses, but without any real hope that they would produce much of anything. John Paul II had a very different view, based on his own extensive experience as a young priest, when he was one of the most dynamic and effective university chaplains in the world. His magnetic presence had brought to Denver more than three times the number of young people the U.S. bishops' conference had expected; and at his last meeting with them, at a great Mass in Cherry Creek Park, he laid down a challenge—a challenge to tell the world the truth of its story. The world could not wait for these committed young souls to become its leaders in some vague future; it needed their witness now. And so he challenged them: "Do not be afraid to go out on the streets and into public places, like the first apostles who preached Christ and the good news of salvation in the squares of cities, towns, and villages. This is no time to be ashamed of the Gospel. . . . It is the time to preach it from the rooftops."[8]

John Paul made a different kind of pilgrimage to the United States two years later, when he came to the symbolic center of worldly power, the great marble rostrum of the General Assembly of the United Nations, to defend the universality of human rights against postmodern skeptics, east Asian autocrats, Islamists, and the world's remaining communists, all of whom regarded the idea of "universal human rights" as (to quote from the mummy at the University of London, Dr. Jeremy Bentham) "nonsense on stilts." A world without a story of human tragedy and aspiration, John Paul suggested, was a world in which genuine human conversation was impossible. A world that had forgotten the moral truths inscribed in the human heart—truths that could be known by reason—was a world condemned, not simply to incoherence, but to dangerous incoherence, of the sort Nietzsche had foretold in his speculations about the triumph of the will to power. Perhaps that was why, the pope proposed, there was something strange afoot at the end of the second millennium:

It is one of the great paradoxes of our time that man, who began the period we call "modernity" with a self-confident assertion of his "coming of age" and "autonomy," approaches the end of the twentieth century fearful of himself, fearful of what he might be capable of, fearful of the future. . . .

In order to ensure that the new millennium now approaching will witness the flourishing of the human spirit, mediated through an authentic culture of freedom, men and women must learn to conquer fear. We must learn not to be afraid, we must recover a spirit of hope and a spirit of trust. . . . Hope and trust are . . . nurtured in that inner sanctuary of conscience where "man is alone with God" [*Gaudium et spes*, no. 16] and thus perceives that he is not alone amid the enigmas of existence, for he is surrounded by the love of the Creator.[9]

The politics of nations could never ignore the deep narrative of the world's story; to do so meant "harming the cause of man and the cause of human freedom."[10] That was why he had come to the summit of the Mars Hill of the postmodern world; he had come "as a witness: a witness to human dignity, a witness to hope, a witness to the conviction that the destiny of all nations lies in the hands of a merciful Providence."[11]

On the night of December 24, 1999, Pope John Paul II opened the holy door of St. Peter's Basilica, symbolically opening the Great Jubilee of 2000. The door had been knocked open on previous jubilees, as the pope rapped on a loosened brick with a white and gold hammer and set loose a cascade of masonry that, when settled, revealed an open door. John Paul chose a different method on Christmas Eve 1999: the masonry that sealed the door between jubilees was already removed, and the pope inaugurated the Great Jubilee by gently pushing on the door with both hands—a symbol of the gently welcoming embrace of divine mercy, which John Paul wanted the Church and the world to experience anew, so that the Church might be reminded of the story it must proclaim to the world and the world might be reminded of the truth about itself.

Then there were the dramas at the end: John Paul II on pilgrimage to Lourdes in August 2004, a "sick man among the sick," teaching with his example that suffering embraced and transformed by grace is part of the true story of the world. And there was John Paul in his last nine weeks, teaching a last priestly lesson in the truth that he had taught for decades from the most visible pulpit in the world—that self-giving, not self-assertion, is at the heart of the world's story.

John Paul II's Holy Land pilgrimage of March 2000 has a privileged place among the dramatic highlights of his pilgrim's progress through the last quarter of the twentieth century and the first half-decade of the twenty-first. He had first broached the idea of a pilgrimage to the Holy Land shortly after his election: Where else should a pope spend his first Christmas but in Bethlehem? When the traditional managers of popes had been revived, they adduced all sorts of reasons why it was impossible: The Holy See had no diplomatic relations with the contending states in the area, the politics were a minefield, there was no time to prepare, the security situation would be impossible, and so on and so forth. For once, John Paul agreed not to follow his own instincts, and for the next twenty-one years, whenever the question of the Holy Land came up in the pope's conversations with his diplomats, he would ask, "Quando mi permetterete di andare?" (When will you let me go?). In *Tertio millennio adveniente*, his 1994 apostolic letter outlining plans for the Great Jubilee of 2000, he floated the idea of a great biblical pilgrimage through the principal sites of salvation history: Ur, Sinai, the Holy Land itself, and Damascus, site of the conversion of St. Paul and the symbolic starting point of the Christian mission *ad gentes*.[12] Five years later, in early 1999, the traditional managers of popes were privately suggesting that it was a lovely dream, but one that would remain just that—a dream.

They did not reckon with John Paul II, who on June 29, 1999, simply announced that he was going, adding Athens and the Areopagus—for John Paul, a powerful metaphor of the Church's encounter with the postmodern world—to the itinerary. Plans to begin in Ur of the Chaldees were scotched by the manipulations and intransigence of the Iraqi government of Saddam Hussein, so on February 23, 2000, John Paul conducted a "virtual pilgrimage" to the land of Abraham, whom the Roman Canon names "our father in faith," in the Paul VI Audience Hall of the Vatican, which had been transformed by oak trees (reminiscent of the terebinths of Mamre), a primitive uncarved stone (evoking the sacrifice of Isaac and the many altars Abraham had built in his wanderings), and a reproduction of Andrei Rublev's great icon of the three angels visiting Abraham. Abraham, he said, was the archetype of the person who grasps the meaning of the story of God's search for man in history, "someone [who] is heading toward a promised land that is not of this world," a destination reached, as Abraham had reached the land of the promise, "through the obedience of faith."[13] The next day, John Paul flew to Egypt, and on February 26 he came to Mt. Sinai, where he spoke of the liberating power of a divine law "written on the human heart as the universal moral law" before it was written on tablets of stone.[14] A wind still blew from Sinai, the pope proposed, and that wind reminds us that the Ten Commandments are the "law of freedom: not the freedom to follow our blind passions, but the freedom to love, to choose what is good in every situation, even when to do so is a burden."[15] That law of freedom is bound up with human fulfillment, for, as John Paul said, "in revealing Himself on the Mountain and giving his Law, God revealed man to man himself. Sinai stands at the very heart of the truth about man and his destiny."[16] Sinai is a privileged place in the depth narrative that is the world's story, rightly understood.

John Paul II finally arrived in the Holy Land of his imagination and his desire on March 21, 2000. Over the next five days, he went to Bethlehem and to Galilee, where he visited Nazareth, stood in Capernaum outside the house of Peter, his predecessor, and preached to tens of thousands of young people on the Mount of Beatitudes. Fittingly enough, however, it was in Jerusalem that John Paul's jubilee pilgrimage saw its most dramatic moments: the pope, at Yad Vashem on March 23, calling the world to reflect on the lethal consequences that result from following a false story; the pope praying at the Western Wall on March 26, in an embodiment of the divinely mandated entanglement of Christians and Jews that spoke far more powerfully than any interreligious manifesto; and later that day, the pope at Calvary and the Church of the Holy Sepulchre. He had been there, formally, in the morning, where he had celebrated Mass at the traditional site of Christ's tomb before going to pray at the Western Wall. Then, later in the afternoon, during the luncheon at the apostolic nuncio's residence that was the last event on the schedule, John Paul II quietly asked whether he might be permitted to return to the Church of the Holy Sepulchre, in private. The traditional managers of popes could not believe it, but the Israeli authorities agreed to honor the wish of the man their security services had code-named "Old Friend." So the pope went back. And there, this old man, crippled by disease, climbed the steep, stone steps to the eleventh and twelfth stations of the cross—because the man who had called the world to fearlessness on October 22, 1978, had to spend more time in prayer at the place where, he believed, the eternal Son had taken all the world's fear upon himself and, by offering himself to the Father in an act of perfect obedience, made it possible for the sons and daughters of God to live beyond fear.

John Paul's June 1999 letter "Concerning Pilgrimage to the Places Linked to the History of Salvation," one of the most lyrical documents of his papacy, was also perhaps his clearest statement of his intentions in undertaking a pilgrimage to the Holy Land—which was nothing less than to remind the world of its lost story. "To go in a spirit of prayer from one place to another," he wrote, "in the area marked especially by God's intervention, helps us not only to live our life as a journey, but also gives us a vivid sense of a God who has gone before us and leads us, who Himself set out on man's path, a God who does not look down on us from on high, but who became our traveling companion."[17] That was why he had to go on pilgrimage to "the places where God had pitched his 'tent' among us"[18]—because in doing so, he was bearing witness in an unmistakable way to the world's true story, the story whose chapter headings are Creation, Fall, Promise, and Prophecy; Incarnation, Redemption, Sanctification, and the Kingdom of God.

If the pope's pilgrimage to the Holy Land of March 2000 marked the dramatic high point of his extraordinary, 720,000-mile pilgrimage throughout the world, it was also of a piece with John Paul's approach to Jewish-Catholic dialogue over the previous two decades. It is striking that, given all the criticism of this or that facet of the pontificate, virtually no one outside the fever swamps has had a bad word to say about John Paul II's initiatives and accomplishments in this field. Yet one has to ask whether either Jews or Catholics have ever really grasped the pope's deepest intentions here. It seems virtually certain that most members of the interreligious dialogue establishment missed the deeper point, and, one suspects, so did many ordinary, faithful Catholics and Jews. And what was the deeper point? John Paul hinted at it during his historic 1986 visit to the Synagogue of Rome, when he spoke of a Jewish-Catholic "collaboration in favor of man."[19] By which I take it he meant that the people who take Abraham as their "father in faith," the people who worship the God who revealed his Name to Moses on Mt. Sinai, the people who share the same Ten Commandments as their basic moral code, the people who live in a covenant relationship with God, must be, collaboratively, lights to the nations, defenders of the dignity of human beings created in the image and likeness of God, and promoters of authentic freedom. And that collaboration is only possible, John Paul seemed to suggest over twenty-six years, if faithful Jews and faithful Catholics reconvene the conversation—the *theological* conversation—that was broken off about A.D. 70, when what became the Christian movement and what became rabbinic Judaism were decisively separated.

That separation, as we know all too well, had terrible consequences over time. After the most terrible of those consequences took place in the mid-twentieth century, some may have thought that a renewed theological encounter between Jews and Catholics was beyond the realm of the possible. John Paul, who knew all about those terrors and knew about them in his bones, had a different view: A world that had lost its story would remain a killing field, in one form or another, unless those called to be lights to the nations were in serious conversation with each other about how they might, individually and collaboratively, fulfill that awesome responsibility—which is nothing less than witnessing within the world to the world's true story.

John Paul's pilgrimage through history was, in this sense, a pilgrimage in search of a twenty-first-century understanding of Romans 9–11. In the late pope's view, the dialogue between Jews and Catholics, and their "collaboration in favor of man," was a dialogue and a collaboration with the weightiest authority behind it: God willed this, and if we, like St. Paul in those three dense chapters of Romans, cannot grasp the fullness of the divine purpose here, we can at least know that it is the will of God that we not only keep the conversation going but also deepen it. The ultimate justification for the dialogue, then, is that this is what God requires of us.

John Paul was also acutely aware of the urgency of a renewed and deepened theological encounter between Jews and Catholics because of his sense of the dangers of the present moment in history. Milton Himmelfarb, who died recently, once suggested that the essence of Jewish witness in the world could be captured in one sentence: "Judaism is against paganism."[20] John Paul would have agreed, and would have said that, as for Judaism, so for its child, Christianity. Our "collaboration in favor of man" is a collaboration against paganism.

Robert George suggested some years ago that the one, infallible way to recognize paganism in its protean array of disguises is to find where innocents are being slaughtered. Paganism, in whatever form, requires the death of innocents; that is what false gods do, and that is what their false stories require. That was true of Moloch, and it has been true of Moloch's successors down to our own time, including the National Socialist Moloch and the Marxist-Leninist Moloch. But a world without a story can be just as lethal as a world built on a false story. The false story of the imperial, autonomous self has, in a sense, filled the narrative gap in a postmodern world-without-a-story, and that false story has, predictably, had exceptionally lethal consequences, with the death of innocents from abortions over the past thirty years now tolling in the hundreds of millions around the world.

The first decade of John Paul's papacy witnessed his successful campaign against the false god of communism and its distinctive form of paganism; the entire pontificate, however, saw the late pope challenging the false gods of the postmodern culture of death by constantly preaching the God of Abraham, Moses, and Jesus as the Lord of life. As creatures of the Lord of life, human beings are endowed with an inalienable dignity; it is in the book of that dignity that we read the strongest account of what we call "human rights." Thus the task of the people who have been claimed by the Lord of life as his own, and who have entered into a covenant relationship with Him, is to be witnesses to and messengers of the truth about who we are as human beings— and in doing so, to build a culture of life that takes its orientation from the Lord of life, the ultimate source of our dignity and our rights.

On March 20, 2000, shortly after his arrival in Jordan, Pope John Paul II went to the Memorial of Moses on Mt. Nebo and looked across the Jordan Valley at the land he had first visited during the Second Vatican Council—the land to which he had wished to return for so long, the land he had frequently visited in his imagination and his prayer. Some, pondering that dramatic scene, thought of the elderly pope as a different kind of Moses: a prophet and lawgiver rich in years who would, in fact, manage to make it over Jordan into the Promised Land. But perhaps another image was more apt. John Paul II, biblical pilgrim in the postmodern world, was, rather, Joshua, constantly pressing Joshua's challenge at Shechem: "Choose . . . whom you will serve" (Jos 24:15). The Lord of life, the God of Abraham and Moses and Jesus? Or

Moloch in one of his many costumes? The Lord of life, who summons his human creatures to an even nobler life of covenant fidelity, indeed of covenant communion with him? Or Moloch, who always demands the blood of innocents? That was the challenge, and those were the questions, that John Paul II put before faithful Jews and faithful Christians alike. And the answer to those questions would determine whether John Paul's proposal at the Synagogue of Rome in 1986—that Jews and Catholics be "collaborators in favor of man"—would remain merely a pious vision, or would begin to transform the world-without-a-story into a world that has rediscovered its story, and thus its true dignity and its eternal destiny.

The early results, we have to say, have been mixed. As I indicated above, it is not at all clear that the dialogue professionals, who have dominated the institutionalized Jewish-Catholic dialogue since the Second Vatican Council, ever really grasped the radical nature of John Paul's proposal, and it seems unlikely that the reconvened theological conversation for which John Paul hoped will emerge from those quarters. On the other hand, we have *Dabru Emet*, and while none of us—especially its Jewish authors—has been entirely satisfied with the response to that remarkable statement, perhaps we can see *Dabru Emet* as a seed: a seed whose flowering may come later than we might have hoped, but a seed that is there, planted in the soil of the postmodern world, fructifying slowly. I think we can be certain that John Paul's worthy successor, Pope Benedict XVI, will do everything in his power to hasten that fruition, because he, too, knows that the stakes are very high. As he put it at the Synagogue of Cologne this past August, it was "neo-paganism" that gave birth to the "insane, racist ideology" that planned and carried out the *Shoah*; when "the holiness of God was no longer recognized . . . contempt was shown for the sacredness of human life."[21] In the face of new threats to human dignity, the pope concluded, a "sincere" Jewish-Catholic dialogue which aims "above all, to make progress toward a theological evaluation of the relationship between Judaism and Christianity" is an imperative.[22] This is the kind of dialogue to which John Paul the Great, biblical pilgrim in the postmodern world, tried to point us.

NOTES

1. Robert Jenson, "How the World Lost Its Story," *First Things* 36 (1993).

2. Jenson, "How the World Lost Its Story."

3. Rodney Stark, *The Victory of Reason: How Christianity Led to Freedom, Capitalism, and Western Success* (New York: Random House, 2006).

4. William H. McNeill, *The Rise of the West: A History of the Human Community* (Chicago: University of Chicago Press, 1992).

5. Christopher Dawson, *Religion and the Rise of Western Culture: The Classic Study of Medieval Civilization* (1950; New York: Doubleday, 1991), 27.

6. John Paul II, address to the Fiftieth General Assembly of the United Nations Organization (October 5, 1995), no. 18, http://www.vatican.va/holy_father/john_paul_ii/speeches/1995/october/documents/hf_jp-ii_spe_05101995_address-to-uno_en.html.

7. John Paul II, address to the Jewish community of Rome (April 13, 1986), no. 6, http://www.bc.edu/research/cjl/meta-elements/texts/cjrelations/resources/documents/catholic/johnpaulii/romesynagogue.htm.

8. John Paul II, homily at Cherry Creek State Park for VIII World Youth Day, Denver (August 15, 1993), http://www.vatican.va/holy_father/john_paul_ii/homilies/1993/documents/hf_jp-ii_hom_19930815_gmg-denver_en.html.

9. John Paul II, address to the Fiftieth General Assembly of the United Nations Organization (October 5, 1995), no. 16, http://www.vatican.va/holy_father/john_paul_ii/speeches/1995/october/documents/hf_jp-ii_spe_05101995_address-to-uno_en.html.

10. John Paul II, address to the Fiftieth General Assembly of the United Nations Organization (October 5, 1995), no. 16.

11. John Paul II, address to the Fiftieth General Assembly of the United Nations Organization (October 5, 1995), no. 16.

12. John Paul II, *Tertio millennio adveniente*, no. 24.

13. John Paul II, homily "Commemoration of Abraham" (February 23, 2000), no. 1, http://www.vatican.va/holy_father/john_paul_ii/homilies/2000/documents/hf_jp-ii_hom_20000223_abraham_en.html.

14. John Paul II, homily at Mt. Sinai (February 26, 2000), no. 3, http://www.vatican.va/holy_father/john_paul_ii/travels/documents/hf_jp-ii_hom_20000226_sinai_en.html.

15. John Paul II, homily at Mt. Sinai (February 26, 2000), no. 4.

16. John Paul II, homily at Mt. Sinai (February 26, 2000), no. 4.

17. John Paul II, letter "Concerning Pilgrimage to the Places Linked to the History of Salvation" (June 29, 1999), no. 10, http://www.vatican.va/holy_father/john_paul_ii/letters/documents/hf_jp-ii_let_30061999_pilgrimage_en.html.

18. John Paul II, letter "Concerning Pilgrimage to the Places Linked to the History of Salvation" (June 29, 1999), no. 11.

19. John Paul II, address to the Jewish community of Rome, no. 6.

20. Milton Himmelfarb, *Jews and Gentiles* (New York: Encounter Books, 2007), 61.

21. Benedict XVI, address at the synagogue of Cologne (August 19, 2005), http://www.vatican.va/holy_father/benedict_xvi/speeches/2005/august/documents/hf_ben-xvi_spe_20050819_cologne-synagogue_en.html.

22. Benedict XVI, address at the synagogue of Cologne (August 19, 2005).

Chapter Two

John Paul II and the Jews

David G. Dalin

More than any other pope, John Paul II was the twentieth century's greatest papal friend to and supporter of the Jewish people. Indeed, John Paul II's extraordinary relationship with the Jews was an important chapter in the historic legacy of his pontificate, which has had profound implications for Catholic-Jewish relations in our time.

John Paul II had a special relationship with Jews not enjoyed by any other pope. John Paul is the only pope to have counted several Jews among his childhood and lifelong friends. Growing up in the small Polish town of Wadowice, where Jews and Catholics mingled with relative ease, Karol Wojtyła "had Jewish playmates and classmates with whom he enjoyed easy camaraderie."[1] John Paul's closest friend was Jerzy Kluger, whose father was a prominent local attorney and president of the local Jewish community and its synagogue. About fifteen hundred Jews, more than 20 percent of Wadowice's population lived in the town during Karol Wojtyła's childhood.[2] When Karol was a teenager, the town's synagogue, which had had a full-time rabbi for many years, hired its first cantor, who was renowned for his splendid cantorial voice. On the festival of Yom Kippur, the Jewish Day of Atonement and the holiest day in the Jewish year, Karol was taken to the synagogue by his father to hear the Kol Nidre, the central prayer of the Yom Kippur worship service, chanted by the new cantor. In later years, Karol Wojtyła, as bishop and pope, would often remark on how moved and inspired he was by the memorable Yom Kippur service he attended as a teenager in his hometown of Widowice. John Paul II is the first modern pope to attend synagogue worship services while growing up, an experience that shaped his relationship to both Jews and Judaism. It may be, and probably is, more than coincidence that as pope he would become the first pontiff to attend worship services at the Great Synagogue in Rome.

As Carl Bernstein and Marco Politi have pointed out, "since the time of the Apostle Peter, no Roman pontiff has ever spent his childhood in such close contact with Jewish life."[3] The Woytylas' landlord, Chaim Balamuth, was Jewish, as were several of the Wojtyła family's other neighbors on Zatorska Street in Wadowice. Through the Wojtyła family's friendship with these Jewish neighbors, including the Klugers, Wojtyła learned firsthand about many of the Jewish religious festivals, such as Yom Kippur, Succoth—the Jewish Feast of Tabernacles—and Chanukah. He and his family were invited into the homes of their Jewish friends to join in celebrating some of these Jewish festivals as well. Across the courtyard from the Wojtyła home, Karol would watch the traditional Succoth booths set up by the family of his friend and classmate Regina Beer, and he would see the menorah in their window during the Chanukah festival. Karol Wojtyła's father had offered her family the use of his balcony for a Succoth booth.[4]

Karol Woytyła's friendship with Jerzy Kluger and his family was especially close. They had both been in the same class in the local high-school gymnasium since they were eleven years old; Jerzy Kluger would remain one of his closest friends throughout his life. The poignant story of their lifelong friendship, vividly and movingly recounted in Darcy O'Brien's book *The Hidden Pope: The Personal Journey of John Paul II and Jerzy Kluger*, is unique in the history of papal-Jewish relations in modern times.[5]

Karol Woytyła and Jerzy Kluger excelled at soccer and played together in the Wadowice high school, where soccer was the most popular sport. It is especially relevant that "while the Wadowice high-school boys formed separate Catholic and Jewish soccer teams," Karol Woytyła was always ready to play for the Jewish team.[6] "In most places, this would have been insignificant," but in the Poland of the early 1930s "it carried real meaning," shaping and defining Woytyła's ecumenical personality and philo-Semitic attitudes for the future.[7] The Jewish experience in pre–World War II Wadowice, which was relatively free of the open anti-Semitism characterizing many other Polish towns and cities, together with Karol's youthful friendships with Jerzy Kluger and several other Jews, were among the influences shaping his evolving view of Jews and Judaism; they would be central to his future role as champion of religious tolerance and Catholic-Jewish dialogue and understanding as bishop of Cracow and as pope. Indeed, his lifelong friendship with Jerzy Kluger— from their childhood in Wadowice and separation at the beginning of World War II, to their reunion almost thirty years later and their much closer personal friendship throughout the years of his pontificate—helped to influence and shape his understanding of Jews and Judaism, and of contemporary issues of Jewish concern, as well as his unprecedented commitment to furthering Catholic-Jewish dialogue and cooperation throughout the world. Jerzy Kluger was the first person to be granted a private audience by the new pope follow-ing John Paul II's election to the papacy in 1978.[8] In the two decades and more since, Kluger and his English-born wife Renee were John Paul II's frequent luncheon and dinner guests at the Vatican and at the pope's summer residence at Castel Gandolfo. It was, for example, his friend and confidant Jerzy Kluger who would advise and actively encourage John Paul II to make his historic visit to the Synagogue of Rome in 1986, and to establish diplomatic relations with the State of Israel several years later.[9] Indeed, it can be said without ex-aggeration that their extraordinary personal friendship over more than sixty years, a friendship unique in the history of papal-Jewish relations, has made a profound impact on the course of Catholic-Jewish relations in our time.

John Paul II was the first to stress that his youthful experience and Jewish friendships in Wadowice helped to influence and shape his understanding of Jews and Judaism and were the source of his unprecedented commitment as pope to furthering Catholic-Jewish dialogue and cooperation throughout the world. The local priests in Wadowice, such as Father Leonard Prochownik, were committed to religious toleration. Father Prochownik, "who had served in Wadowice since 1915 and who officially became the town's pastor in 1929," would be remembered for many decades "as someone whose promo-tion of interreligious tolerance was responsible for the town's relative lack of anti-Semitism."[10] The Wadowice of Karol Wojtyła's childhood was also, as George Weigel has noted, "a place where the Polish poet Adam Mickiewicz's description of Jews as the 'elder brothers' of Christians was taken seriously by many local Catholics."[11] As pope, John Paul II would remember his Wad-owice parish priest, Father Prochownik, preaching in church that "anti-Semi-tism is anti-Christian" and his high school Polish literature teacher quoting from Adam Mickiewicz's 1848 *Manifesto for a Future Slave State Constitu-tion* that "all citizens are equal—Israelites too."[12] Karol Wojtyła would later write that he "vividly [remembered] the Jews who gathered every Saturday at the synagogue behind our school. Both religious groups, Catholics and Jews, were united . . . by the awareness that they prayed to the same God."[13]

His memory of Wadowice, and the families of his Jewish friends from Wad-owice who had lost their lives during the Holocaust, was especially com-pelling when he visited Auschwitz in June 1979. While paying tribute to the millions of Jews, and non-Jewish Poles, whose lives were destroyed in the Nazi death camp at Auschwitz, he remembered and prayed for his friends' rel-atives who had died in the gas chambers of Auschwitz—the mother of his childhood friend Regina Beer and the mother, grandmother, and sister of friend Jerzy Kluger. After kneeling and praying at the stark Wall of Death, one of the locations at Auschwitz that Nazi leaders had selected for the murder of Polish intellectuals and priests, John Paul delivered one of the most powerful and poignant homilies of his pontificate, condemning the inhumanity and anti-Semitism that made Auschwitz possible. Calling Auschwitz a "place where human dignity was appallingly trampled underfoot," a place "built on hatred of, and contempt for humanity," he invoked the memory of the six million Jews who died in the crematoria of Auschwitz and other Nazi death camps solely because they were Jews, reminding his fellow Catholics that their memory must never be forgotten. As Father John Oesterreicher noted in his very poignant "Reflections on Pope John Paul's Pilgrimage to Auschwitz," published by Seton Hall University's Institute of Judaeo-Christian Studies in 1984, "Pope John Paul spoke with great feeling, like one who had experienced the torments Hitler's victims had had to endure, who felt their pain as his own."[14] Pope John Paul II's June 1979 homily at Auschwitz was broadcast throughout the world.

On May 9, 1989, having ordered the placement of a commemorative tablet at the site of the Wadowice synagogue destroyed by the Nazis, the pope wrote Jerzy Kluger that it would honor the memory of Jews from nearby who were exterminated during the Holocaust. To Kluger he wrote:

> Many of those who perished, your co-religionists and our fellow countrymen, were our colleagues in our elementary school and, later, in the high school where we graduated together, fifty years ago. All were citizens of Wadowice, the town to which both you and I are bound together by our memories of childhood and youth. I remember very clearly the Wadowice synagogue, which was near our high school. I have in front of my eyes the numerous worshippers who during their holidays passed on their way to pray there.

Addressing the Warsaw Jewish community on June 9, 1991, during his fourth papal pilgrimage to Poland, the pope said: "Man lives on the basis of his own experience. I belong to the generation for which relationships with Jews was a daily occurrence." Reminiscing in February 1994 about his Wadowice childhood, John Paul II remarked that "there were so many Jews there" that "the house where we lived was owned by a Jewish family," and that "it is from there that I have this attitude of community, of communal feeling about the Jews. . . . It all comes from there."

JOHN PAUL II AND THE PAPAL
CONDEMNATION OF ANTI-SEMITISM

Throughout his pontificate, John Paul II reached out to the Jewish community as no other pope before him. From his election as pope in 1978, as George Weigel has noted, John Paul II "invested enormous energy in building a new conversation between Catholics and Jews."[15] At his very first meeting with representatives of Rome's Jewish community, on March 12, 1979, John Paul noted that "our two religious communities are connected and closely related at the very level of their respective religious identities."[16] Jewish-Catholic dialogue, from a Catholic perspective, was a *religious* obligation. Addressing representatives of the German-Jewish community of Mainz in November 1980, John Paul II (who, more than any other pope before him, has made it a practice to meet with representatives of Jewish communities wherever possible in his extensive travels), spoke of "the depth and richness of our common inheritance bringing us together in mutually trustful collaboration."[17] Imbued with a deep understanding of Judaism and of the Jewish people, unique among modern pontiffs, he described Judaism as a "living" legacy that must be understood by Christians, and he spoke of a dialogue between "today's churches and today's people of the covenant concluded with Moses."[18] In this speech to the Jews of Mainz, the pope addressed the Jewish community with full respect as "the people of God and of the Old Covenant, which has never been revoked by God," and emphasized the "permanent value" of both the Hebrew Scriptures and the Jewish community which witnesses to those Scriptures as sacred texts.[19]

In subsequent addresses, he deplored the terrible persecutions suffered by the Jewish people—indeed, in Australia in 1986, he was to call acts of discrimination and persecution against Jews "sinful"—and called for Christians and Jews to hold more in-depth exchanges based on their own religious identities. "Our common spiritual heritage is considerable," he noted, "and we can find help in understanding certain aspects of the Church's life by taking into account the faith and religious life of the Jewish people."[20]

No other pope of the twentieth century was as forthright and unequivocal in his condemnation of anti-Semitism generally and the Nazi Holocaust in particular. This abhorrence, as Eugene Fisher has noted, "was not simply theoretical. John Paul II lived under Nazism in Poland and experienced personally the malignancy of the ancient evil of Jew-hatred."[21] In his first papal audience with Jewish leaders, following his election as pope on March 12, 1979, he reaffirmed the Second Vatican Council's repudiation of anti-Semitism "as opposed to the very spirit of Christianity" and "which in any case the dignity of the human person alone would suffice to condemn."[22] John Paul II often repeated this message in meetings with Jewish leaders at the Vatican and in country after country throughout the world. Speaking at Auschwitz four months later, in a homily commemorating the six million Jews who perished during the Holocaust, he called on Catholics to remember "in particular, the memory of the people whose sons and daughters were intended for total extermination."[23] From the intensity of his own personal experience, the pope was able to articulate the *uniqueness* of the Jewish experience of the *Shoah* while never forgetting the memory of Nazism's millions of non-Jewish victims. The pope would, as Eugene Fisher has aptly noted, agree unreservedly with the formulation of Elie Wiesel: "Not every victim of the Holocaust was a Jew, but every Jew was a victim."[24]

Throughout his pontificate, as George Weigel has aptly noted, John Paul "persistently, vigorously, and unambiguously condemned the Shoah, the Holocaust of the European Jews during the Second World War."[25] Indeed, no other pope of the twentieth century was as forthright and unequivocal in his condemnation of the Nazi Holocaust as was John Paul II. Meeting with Jews in Paris on May 31, 1980, John Paul made a point of mentioning the great suffering of the Jewish community of France "during the dark years of the occupation," paying homage to them as victims, "whose sacrifice, we know, has not been fruitless."[26] In April 1983, speaking as a Pole and as a Catholic on the fortieth anniversary of the uprising of the Warsaw Ghetto, the pope termed "that horrible and tragic event" a "desperate cry for the right to life, for liberty, and for the salvation of human dignity."[27] On the twentieth anniversary of *Nostra aetate*, in October 1985, the pope stated that "anti-Semitism, in its ugly and sometimes violent manifestations, should be completely eradicated."[28] Speaking to the leadership of Australia's Jewish community, in Sydney, Australia, on November 26, 1986, John Paul II intensified his condemnation of anti-Semitism and, recalling that "this is still the century of the *Shoah*," declared that "no theological justification could ever be found for acts of discrimination or persecution against Jews. In fact, such acts must be held to be sinful."[29] Perhaps the most eloquent papal statement condemning the Holocaust came at a meeting with Jewish leaders in Warsaw, on June 14, 1987, when he described the Holocaust as a universal icon of evil:

> Be sure, dear brother, that . . . this Polish church is in a spirit of profound solidarity with you when she looks closely at the terrible realization of the extermination—the unconditional extermination—of your nation, an extermination carried out with premeditation. The threat against you was also a threat against us; this latter was not realized to the same extent, because it did not have time to be realized to the same extent. It was you who suffered this terrible sacrifice of extermination: one might say that you suffered it also on behalf of those who were in the purifying power of suffering. The more atrocious the suffering, the greater the purification. The more painful the experience, the greater the hope. . . . [Because] of this terrible experience . . . you have become a warning voice for all humanity, for all nations, all the powers of this world, all systems, and every person. More than anyone else, it is precisely you who have become the saving warning. I think that in this sense you continue your particular vocation, showing yourselves still to be the heirs of that election to which God is faithful. This

is your mission in the contemporary world before all the peoples, the nations, all of humanity, the Church.[30]

In the years following this dramatic statement, John Paul worked to keep the memory of the *Shoah* alive. Addressing the leaders of the Jewish community of Strasbourg in 1988, the pope said: "I repeat again with you the strongest condemnation of anti-Semitism," which is "opposed to the principles of Christianity."[31] At Saint Peter's Square on April 18, 1993, in commemorating the fiftieth anniversary of the uprising in the Warsaw Ghetto, he spoke of the *Shoah* as "a true night of history, with unimaginable crimes against God and humanity."[32]

The following year, on April 7, 1994, John Paul II hosted a Holocaust memorial concert in the Paul VI Audience Hall of the Vatican. The Royal Philharmonic Orchestra was conducted by Gilbert Levine, a Brooklyn-born American Jew whom John Paul had befriended after Levine became musical director of the Cracow Philharmonic in 1987.[33] On this occasion, the pope sat in the audience hall side by side with the chief rabbi of Rome, Elio Toaff, himself a Holocaust survivor, and Italian President Oscar Luigi Scalfero. Rabbi Toaff "had brought his congregation with him, the first time that many had been inside the Vatican except as tourists. Two hundred Holocaust survivors from twelve different countries attended, along with diplomats from all over the world."[34]

The occasion for this Holocaust memorial concert was the fiftieth anniversary of the Warsaw Ghetto uprising. The day of this concert, April 7, 1994, as John Paul's biographers have pointed out, was a "unique and unprecedented moment" in the history of the Catholic Church and of John Paul II's personal mission to keep the memory of the Holocaust alive in the center of world Catholicism.[35] In addition to hosting the Holocaust memorial concert, the pope also arranged for the traditional Jewish prayer for the dead—the Kaddish—to be recited and for six candlesticks of the menorah to be lit in his presence at the Vatican.[36] In so doing, "the pope chose to publicly honor the memory of those Jews who died in the name of freedom" during the Holocaust—in a way that "the [Catholic] Church had never done before."[37]

Throughout the 1990s, moreover, at John Paul II's instruction, the Vatican's Commission on Religious Relations with the Jews was engaged in preparing an official Catholic document on the Holocaust—*We Remember: A Reflection on the Shoah*—that was published in March 1998. A historic document, the Holy See's first official statement on the Holocaust, *We Remember* described the *Shoah* as an "unspeakable tragedy" and a "horrible genocide" before which "no one can remain indifferent, least of all the Church, by reason of her very close bonds with the Jewish people and her remembrances of the injustices of the past." *We Remember*, which included a lengthy (and controversial) footnote defending Pope Pius XII's actions during the war, also urged that Christians who had risked their lives to rescue Jews during the Holocaust not be forgotten. The fact that some resisted, however, the document suggested, did not change the fact that "the spiritual resistance and concrete action of other Christians was not that which might have been expected from Christ's followers." The *Shoah* and the failure of Christian witness during it had left a "heavy burden of conscience" on Christians today that required making "an act of . . . *teshuvah*," or profound repentance, "since, as members of the Church, we are linked to the sins as well as the merits of all her children." Finally, the Church wished "to turn awareness of past sins into a firm resolve to build a new future in which there will be no more anti-Judaism among Christians or anti-Christian sentiment among Jews, but rather a shared, mutual respect, as befits those who adore the one Creator and Lord and have a common father in faith, Abraham." In John Paul's preface to *We Remember*, a letter to Edward Cardinal Cassidy, chairman of the Holy See's Commission on Religious Relations with the Jews, the pope described the *Shoah* as an "unspeakable iniquity" and an "indelible stain on the history of the century that is coming to a close," and he expressed the "fervent hope" that *We Remember* "will indeed help to heal the wounds of past misunderstandings and injustices."

John Paul II's relationship to Jews, and to the Jewish community of Rome, was historic in other ways as well. In April 1986, John Paul II became the first pope in history to visit Rome's chief synagogue. His much-heralded and unprecedented visit to Rome's synagogue was a historic event in Catholic-Jewish relations. Throughout the previous nineteen hundred years, no pope had ever set foot in the synagogue. Pope John XXIII had once stopped (in his car) to bless the Roman Jews leaving their Sabbath worship services.[38] And, yet, even John XXIII, who was revered in the Jewish community for convening the Second Vatican Council (which publicly repudiated anti-Semitism and had expunged from the Catholic liturgy the insulting reference to the Jews as "perfidious"), had never actually entered Rome's Great Synagogue. In becoming the first bishop of Rome to go to the Great Synagogue of Rome "to meet the Roman Jewish community at their own place of worship," John Paul II changed history.[39]

Yet this historic event goes completely unmentioned in the books of liberal papal critics such as Daniel Jonah Goldhagen. Goldhagen's anti-Catholic diatribe *A Moral Reckoning: The Role of the Catholic Church in the Holocaust and Its Unfulfilled Duty of Repair*, actually attributes anti-Semitism to John Paul II.[40] Goldhagen writes that "neither John Paul II nor any other pope has seen fit to make . . . a direct and forceful public statement about Catholics' culpability and the need for all the members of the Church who have sinned during the Holocaust to repent for their many different kind of offenses and sins against Jews."[41] In fact, however, John Paul II made just such a public statement during his visit to Rome's synagogue. After the chief rabbi of Rome, Elio Toaff, welcomed the pope, John Paul II responded with an eloquent address in which he publicly acknowledged, and apologized for, the Church's sins against the Jews during the Holocaust and in the centuries that preceded it. Insisting that there was no theological justification for discrimination against Jews, John Paul II declared that the Church condemned anti-Semitism "by anyone"—"I repeat: By anyone." He did precisely what Goldhagen claims he never did: He admitted, in public, the Church's "culpability."[42] Moreover, time and again, the pope cited the Thirteenth International Catholic-Jewish Liaison Committee meeting held in Prague, with its call for Christian *teshuvah* (repentance) for anti-Semitism over the centuries and its statement that anti-Semitism is "a sin against God and humanity."[43]

John Paul II's historic visit to the Great Synagogue of Rome was, in a sense, as George Weigel has aptly noted, "the culmination of a journey that had begun in Wadowice sixty years before," when the young Karol Wojtyła had attended Yom Kippur worship services at the Wadowice synagogue with his friend Jerzy Kluger and his family. As he drove to the Synagogue of Rome,

> John Paul carried with him his boyhood friendships with Jews, his father's lessons of tolerance, his old pastor's teaching that anti-Semitism was forbidden by the Gospel, his experience of the Nazi occupation, and his knowledge of the Holocaust. He had developed, among churchmen, a distinctive sensitivity to Jewish pain and the drama of twentieth-century Jewish life.[44]

The pope concluded his address to Rome's Jewish community by noting that his presence in the Synagogue of Rome marked the beginning of a new era in Catholic-Jewish relations. John Paul II's visit to Rome's Great Synagogue was one of the historic legacies of his pontificate.

JOHN PAUL II AND THE ESTABLISHMENT OF DIPLOMATIC RELATIONS BETWEEN THE VATICAN AND ISRAEL

Also, during his pontificate, the Vatican for the first time established full diplomatic relations with the State of Israel, another historic legacy of his pontificate. When John Paul II visited the Synagogue of Rome in April 1986, Rome's chief rabbi, Elio Toaff, had asked him to establish diplomatic relations between the Vatican and the State of Israel. Six years later, over the objections of some of the bureaucrats in the Vatican's Secretariat of State, which was waiting for the government of Israel to first reach an accord with the Palestinians, John Paul II personally took the initiative to do so. In 1994, the Vatican established full diplomatic relations with Israel.[45] In taking this unprecedented initiative, once again John Paul II changed history and radically transformed the Vatican's relationship to Zionism and the Jewish state. In 1904, Pope Pius X had told the founder of Zionism, Theodore Herzl, that the Holy See could not "encourage" the Zionist movement in its goal of establishing a Jewish state.[46] No previous pope had ever referred publicly to the State of Israel, as did John Paul II in his official pronouncements and correspondence.[47] Indeed, even Pope Paul VI, during his visit to Jerusalem in 1964, had refrained from referring publicly to the "State of Israel," managing "with pointed omission never to speak the name of Israel," talking officially only of the Holy Land or Palestine.[48] Nor had any of John Paul's papal predecessors ever seriously contemplated establishing diplomatic relations with the Jewish state.

And, yet, from the earliest days of his pontificate, John Paul II was aware, from conversations with his friend Jerzy Kluger and many others, "that the absence of full diplomatic relations was regarded by Israelis and by Jews throughout the world as a depreciation of the State of Israel and as a failure to fulfill the promise of a new Jewish-Catholic relationship envisioned by the Second Vatican Council," to which John Paul II was passionately committed.[49] According to Jerzy Kluger, as early as 1981 John Paul II had authorized his old friend "to initiate private, informal discussions with Israeli diplomats in Rome to clarify issues involved in moving toward full diplomatic relations. Kluger, an Italian citizen, was also authorized by the government of then Israeli Prime Minister Menachem Begin to speak on its behalf."[50] One immediate result of these early discussions was a papal telegram of good wishes to the president of Israel on Rosh Hashanah, the Jewish New Year, in October 1981.[51] This holiday telegram was historically unprecedented: No such communication had ever previously been sent by a pope to an Israeli head of state. John Paul, by Kluger's account, "also used his old friend and Wadowice classmate as a continuing sounding board for thinking out loud about the history of relations between Catholics and Jews and the relationship of that history to the question of establishing diplomatic relations."[52]

John Paul's own actions during the 1980s, "including his regular meetings with Jewish groups in Rome and elsewhere on his pastoral pilgrimages, his condemnations of terrorist attacks on synagogues in Vienna and Rome, his 1982 meeting with Israeli foreign minister Yitzchak Shamir . . . his historic visit to the Synagogue of Rome in 1986," and his 1987 Vatican statement that there were "no theological reasons in Catholic doctrine that would inhibit full diplomatic relations between the Holy See and Israel"—all helped to further lay the foundation for the actual diplomatic negotiations that would, in the early 1990s, result in the historic establishment of diplomatic relations between the Vatican and Israel.[53]

At the culmination of the lengthy negotiations, on December 30, 1993, representatives of the Holy See and the State of Israel signed in Jerusalem the *Fundamental Agreement* that would lead the way to full diplomatic "normalization" of relations between the two.[54] On August 16, 1994, in Jerusalem, Archbishop Andrea Montezemolo presented his credentials to President Chaim Herzog of the State of Israel as the first ambassador of the Holy See to the Jewish state. The following month, in Rome, Shmuel Hadas presented his credentials to Pope John Paul II as the first ambassador of the State of Israel to the Holy See.

As the *Fundamental Agreement* establishing diplomatic relations acknowledged, "this was not just a moment of international diplomacy between two tiny Mediterranean states."[55] It was, rather, as Eugene Fisher has noted, a historic and "theologically significant moment in the nearly two-millennia-long history of the relationship between the Jewish people and the Catholic Church."[56] In taking the unprecedented initiative to bring this moment about, John Paul II had changed history. As George Weigel has pointed out, the *Fundamental Agreement* "was widely regarded as one of the diplomatic master strokes of John Paul II's pontificate and a historic turning point in Catholic-Jewish relations."[57] (The establishment of diplomatic relations between the Holy See and Israel, brought about at the personal initiative of Pope John Paul II, ushered in a new era in Catholic-Jewish dialogue and cooperation as well.)

A POPE IN THE HOLY LAND: JOHN PAUL II'S HISTORIC VISIT TO ISRAEL

In his historic visit to Israel in March 2000, moreover, John Paul II continued to condemn anti-Semitism, while continuing his personal mission—and one of the great missions of his pontificate—of furthering and consolidating a new era in Catholic-Jewish relations. Jews and Catholics alike were profoundly moved by John Paul's tearful meeting with Holocaust survivors from his hometown in Poland and by the sight of the pope saluting an Israeli flag, listening to the solemn playing of "Hatikvah," the Israeli national anthem, and being welcomed as an honored guest by the Jewish state.[58]

These were unique and unprecedented moments in the history of Catholic-Jewish relations, as was the pope's prayer at the Western Wall, one of Judaism's holiest sites, in Jerusalem. For nearly two millennia, Jews have prayed at the Western Wall, all that was left of the Jerusalem Temple compound after the Romans destroyed the city following the second Jewish revolt. Now came the bishop of Rome, the successor of Saint Peter, to pray at the Western Wall, as a humble pilgrim acknowledging the full validity of Jewish prayer, on its own terms, at this most holy of Jewish sites.[59] The Western Wall is for Jews the central physical remnant of biblical Israel, "the central symbolic referent for Jews as a people and for Judaism as a four-to-five-thousand-year-old faith tradition."[60] As Eugene Fisher has noted, in praying at the Western Wall, there was no hesitation in the pope's religious affirmation of Judaism, no political, theological, or social caveat.[61]

Profoundly moving, especially—and perhaps the highlight of John Paul's Israel visit—was the pope's impassioned and emotional talk in the Hall of Remembrance at Israel's Holocaust memorial, Yad Vashem. After observing a moment of prayerful silence, John Paul began speaking at Yad Vashem by saying:

> In this place of memories, the mind and heart and soul feel an extreme need for silence. Silence in which to remember. Silence in which to try to make some sense of the memories which come flooding back. Silence because there are no words strong enough to deplore the terrible tragedy of the *Shoah*. My own personal memories are of all that happened when the Nazis occupied Poland during the war. I remember my Jewish friends and neighbors, some of whom perished while others survived.[62]

Remembrance, he continued after a moment, must be in the service of a noble cause: "We wish to remember for a purpose," he said, "to ensure that never again will evil prevail, as it did for the millions of innocent victims of Nazism." And knowing that evil's victory during the Nazi Final Solution had ensnared too many Christians, he then made what no one listening could doubt was a heartfelt statement of repentance:

> As bishop of Rome and Successor of the Apostle Peter, I assure the Jewish people that the Catholic Church, motivated by the Gospel law of truth and love and by no political considerations, is deeply saddened by the hatred, acts of persecution, and displays of anti-Semitism directed against the Jews by Christians at any time and in any place.[63]

At the conclusion of the pope's address, many Israelis in attendance, Holocaust survivors and politicians, religious leaders and army officers alike, cried. In his own address which followed, Israeli Prime Minister Ehud Barak, himself a former army general not given to sentimentality, movingly thanked John Paul for doing more for Jewish-Catholic relations than any pope in history. "You have done," Barak asserted, "more than anyone else to bring about the historic change in the attitude of the Church toward the Jewish people . . . and to dress the gaping wounds that festered over many bitter centuries."[64]

There is much evidence to substantiate the historical accuracy of Barak's assertion. After the pope had prayed at the Western Wall and had spoken as he did at Yad Vashem, Catholic-Jewish relations could and would never be the same. Both changed the history of Catholic-Jewish relations in our time, and for all time, as did (during the same week) the pope's unprecedented meeting in Jerusalem with the two chief rabbis of Israel. "It was," as one Catholic commentator accurately pointed out, "a meeting of dialogue not diatribe, a meeting of Catholic-Jewish reconciliation after centuries of alienation. It was a meeting that neither the pope's nor the chief rabbis' parents could have dreamed to be possible in their wildest imaginations."[65] In initiating this historic meeting, Pope John Paul II "had seized the opportunity not just of a lifetime but of the millennium."[66]

A LONELY VOICE IN THE WILDERNESS: JOHN PAUL II VERSUS THE NEW MUSLIM ANTI-SEMITISM

Throughout the 1980s, John Paul II "issued strong statements of condemnation of acts of terrorism against synagogues and Jewish communities" in Vienna and Rome, "sending messages of sympathy for their victims."[67] He condemned, for example, the August 29, 1981, bomb-throwing attack on a synagogue in Vienna, Austria, as "a bloody and absurd act, which assails the Jewish community in Austria and the entire world," and warned against a "new wave of that same anti-Semitism that has provoked so much mourning throughout the centuries."[68] During the October 1985 seizure by Muslim Palestinian terrorists of the Italian cruise ship *Achille Lauro*, in which a Jewish passenger was singled out for killing, the pope condemned what he called "this grave act of violence against innocent and defenseless persons."[69]

John Paul II always condemned European anti-Semitism. But other European leaders have been less willing to take a stand against the resurgent Muslim anti-Semitism that is part of what has been called the "Islamization of Europe."[70] This is especially true in France, where Muslims make up about 10 percent of France's population and outnumber French Jews ten to one.[71] Between 2000 and 2003, Yasser Arafat and his Palestinian Authority were implicated in the bombing of French synagogues and other acts of anti-Semitic violence and terrorism against Jewish communal leaders and institutions in France. The year 2000 witnessed an alarming eruption of anti-Jewish violence carried out almost exclusively by Arab Muslims.[72] During the last three months of 2000 alone, violence aimed at French Jews included forty-four firebombings, forty-three attacks on synagogues, and thirty-nine assaults on Jews as they were leaving their places of worship.[73] Between January and May 2001, there were more than three hundred attacks against Jews. Synagogues were destroyed, school buses stoned, and even innocent Jewish children assaulted. Yet very few of the incidents were reported in the French media, which has an evident pro-Palestinian bias.[74]

On January 12, 2001, Palestinian journalist Raymonda Hawa-Tawil (whose daughter Souha was Yasser Arafat's wife) spoke out on the public radio station French Culture, attacking the "racism of the Jews of France" and the "influence of the Jewish lobby."[75] During 2002 and 2003, the violent anti-Semitic attacks against French Jews continued to increase. In December 2003, a young Jewish disc jockey was killed by his Muslim neighbor, who "slit his throat and mutilated his face." Returning to his apartment, the murderer reportedly said: "I killed my Jew. I will go to heaven."[76]

In face of this resurgence of Islam-inspired, French anti-Semitism, John Paul II often seemed to be a lonely voice in the wilderness, consistent and unequivocal in his condemnation of Europe's new anti-Semitic, post-Christian Left, while other European leaders and intellectuals—politicians, journalists, and leftist religious activists alike—chose to remain silent. Often alone among European leaders, Pope John Paul II issued strong statements condemning acts of Islamic terrorism against synagogues and other Jewish communal buildings and institutions in France and elsewhere, calling these incidents un-Christian and reprehensible. On April 3, 2002, moreover, Bishop Jean-Pierre Ricard, president of the French Conference of Catholic Bishops, issued a forceful condemnation of French anti-Semitism. Speaking in the spirit of John Paul II's many vocal protests against anti-Semitism, Ricard declared:

> In recent days, attacks were committed against several synagogues in France, in Lyons, in Marseilles, and in Strasbourg. The Jewish communities are deeply struck in their most precious places of worship. Such acts of violence make one fear the worst. . . . To strike a community, whichever it is, in its religious sensibilities and faith, is a particularly grave act, which affects our democratic life with full force. In condemning these attacks with the greatest firmness, the Catholic Church in France expresses its profound sympathy and solidarity with the Jewish communities.[77]

While almost all French politicians and liberal journalists were silent or equivocating concerning the wave of arson and violence against French synagogues and other Jewish institutions, the French bishops were the only French leaders—religious or political—to unequivocally condemn the new anti-Semitism resurgent in France. As Michel Gurfinkiel pointed out, the response of France's liberal, political elite to these and other anti-Semitic incidents that occurred on a daily basis in 2000 and 2001 was "minimal or mute."[78] Not so that of the Vatican, the Conference of French Bishops, and the Church leadership in France. As Jewish leaders have appreciatively noted, their response has been forthright and forceful.

CONCLUSION

Pope Benedict XVI, like Pope John Paul II, is known to be a staunch friend of the Jewish people and the State of Israel, and a vocal critic of anti-Semitism. As Joseph Cardinal Ratzinger, Pope Benedict wrote of "the gift of Christmas" as "the heritage of Abraham"[79] and condemned both Christian anti-Semitism and the Nazi Holocaust, which, he noted accurately, was "perpetuated in the name of anti-Christian ideology, which tried to strike the Christian faith at its Abrahamic roots in the people of Israel."[80] Shortly after succeeding to the papacy, in a history-making visit to the Community Synagogue of Cologne, Germany, which had been destroyed by the Nazis in 1938 and rebuilt after World War II, Pope Benedict called Nazism "an insane racist ideology" and denounced "the rise of new signs of anti-Semitism."[81] Pope Benedict's visit to the Cologne Synagogue in August 2005, which took place during his first papal trip to his native Germany, "was the second ever by a pope to a Jewish house of worship," following Pope John Paul II's 1986 visit to the Great Synagogue of Rome.[82] The president of the Central Council of Jews in Germany, Paul Spiegel, welcomed the pope's visit, describing it as a "historic event."[83]

Jewish leaders, including Abraham H. Foxman, director of the Anti-Defamation League, have praised Pope Benedict, saying that "he has shown the sensitivity [to Jews and the Holocaust] countless times, in meetings with Jewish leadership and in important statements condemning anti-Semitism and expressing profound sorrow for the Holocaust."[84] Rabbi David Rosen of the American Jewish Committee said that as Cardinal Ratzinger the new pope had been "supportive of the establishment of full [diplomatic] relations between the Holy See and Israel, and he cares deeply about the welfare of Israel."[85]

John Paul II was the heir and exemplar of a long and venerable philo-Semitic tradition within papal-Jewish relations, a tradition of papal friendship and support for the Jewish people that has continued with John Paul II's successor, Pope Benedict XVI.[86] John Paul II's historic role and accomplishments as the twentieth century's greatest papal friend of the Jewish people, accomplishments that have had such profound implications for the course of Catholic-Jewish dialogue and reconciliation in our time, are among the historic and enduring legacies of his pontificate that should be remembered and cherished by Jews and Catholics alike.

NOTES

1. Tad Szulc, *Pope John Paul II: The Biography* (New York: Scribner, 1995), 68.

2. Carl Bernstein and Marco Politi, *His Holiness: John Paul II and the Hidden History of Our Time* (New York: Doubleday, 1996), 30.

3. Bernstein and Politi, *His Holiness*, 30.

4. Bernstein and Politi, *His Holiness*, 30–31.

5. Darcy O'Brien, *The Hidden Pope: The Untold Story of a Lifelong Friendship That Is Changing the Relationship Between Catholics and Jews—The Personal Journey of John Paul II and Jerzy Kluger* (New York: Rodale Books, 1998).

6. Szulc, *Pope John Paul II*, 68.

7. Szulc, *Pope John Paul II*, 68.

8. O'Brien, *The Hidden Pope*, 8.

9. As Darcy O'Brien has noted, "the idea of visiting" a synagogue in Rome "first came up at a breakfast meeting" between the pope and Kluger on January 5, 1984. O'Brien, *The Hidden Pope*, 356.

10. George Weigel, *Witness to Hope: The Biography of Pope John Paul II* (New York: HarperCollins Publishers, 1999), 24.

11. Weigel, *Witness to Hope*, 24.

12. Weigel, *Witness to Hope*, 68–69.

13. Weigel, *Witness to Hope*, 24.

14. John Oesterreicher, *Martyrs of the Decalogue: Reflections on Pope John Paul's Pilgrimage to Auschwitz* (South Orange, NJ: Institute of Judaeo-Christian Studies, Seton Hall University, 1984).

15. David G. Dalin, *The Myth of Hitler's Pope: How Pope Pius XII Rescued Jews from the Nazis* (Washington, DC: Regnery Publishing, 2005), 147.

16. Eugene J. Fisher and Leon Klenicki, eds., *Pope John Paul II: Spiritual Pilgrimage—Texts on Jews and Judaism, 1979–1995* (New York: Crossroad Publishing, 1995), xxii.

17. Geoffrey Wigoder. *Jewish-Christian Relations Since the Second World War* (Manchester, England: Manchester University Press, 1988), 87.

18. Wigoder. *Jewish-Christian Relations*, 87.

19. Wigoder. *Jewish-Christian Relations*, 87.

20. Wigoder. *Jewish-Christian Relations*, 87.

21. Eugene J. Fisher, "Pope John Paul II's Pilgrimage of Reconciliation—A Commentary on the Texts," in Fisher and Klenicki, eds., *Pope John Paul II*, xxxvii.

22. Fisher, "Pope John Paul II's Pilgrimage of Reconciliation," xxxvii.

23. Fisher, "Pope John Paul II's Pilgrimage of Reconciliation," xxviii.

24. Quoted in Fisher, "Pope John Paul II's Pilgrimage of Reconciliation," xxciii.

25. Weigel, *Witness to Hope*, 823.

26. Fisher, "Pope John Paul II's Pilgrimage of Reconciliation"; and Pope John Paul II, "Meeting with Jews in Paris, May 31, 1980," in Fisher and Klenicki, eds., *Pope John Paul II*, 9.

27. Pope John Paul II, "Address on the Fortieth Anniversary of the Warsaw Ghetto Uprising, April 25, 1983," in Fisher and Klenicki, eds., *Pope John Paul II*, 27–28.

28. Fisher, "Pope John Paul II's Pilgrimage of Reconciliation," xxviii.

29. Pope John Paul II, "Address to the Jewish Community of Australia, November 26, 1986," in Fisher and Klenicki, eds., *Pope John Paul II*, 82–83.

30. Weigel, *Witness to Hope*, 823.

31. Avery Dulles, S.J., "Commentary on the Holy See's Document *We Remember*," in *The Holocaust, Never to Be Forgotten: Reflections on the Holy See's Document* We Remember (Mahwah, NJ: Paulist Press, 2001), 53; and Pope John Paul II, "Address to Leaders of the Jewish Community in Strasbourg," in Fisher and Klenicki, eds., *Pope John Paul II*, 128.

32. Pope John Paul II, "Today We Recall Warsaw Uprising" (April 18, 1993), *L'Osservatore Romano* (English), April 21, 1993, no. 3.

33. Weigel, *Witness to Hope*, 823.

34. Weigel, *Witness to Hope*, 823.

35. Szulc, *Pope John Paul II*, 454; and Weigel, *Witness to Hope*, 823.

36. Szulc, *Pope John Paul II*, 455.

37. Szulc, *Pope John Paul II*, 454.

38. Weigel, *Witness to Hope*, 484.

39. Weigel, *Witness to Hope*, 484.

40. Daniel Jonah Goldhagen. *A Moral Reckoning: The Role of the Catholic Church in the Holocaust and Its Unfulfilled Duty of Repair* (New York: Knopf, 2002). For a critique of Goldhagen's book *A Moral Reckoning*, see David G. Dalin, "History as Bigotry: Daniel Goldhagen Slanders the Catholic Church," *Weekly Standard*, February 10, 2003, 41; and Dalin, *The Myth of Hitler's Pope*, 3–6 and 111–12.

41. Goldhagen. *A Moral Reckoning*, 224.

42. Goldhagen. *A Moral Reckoning*, 221.

43. Dalin, *The Myth of Hitler's Pope*, 151.

44. Weigel, *Witness to Hope*, 484.

45. The signing of the "Fundamental Agreement between the Holy See and the State of Israel," in December 1994, which established diplomatic ties between the Vatican and Israel for the first time, is discussed in illuminating detail in the recent book edited by Marshall J. Breger, which brings together essays that analyze the legal, historical, theological, and political meaning of the accords: Marshall J. Breger, ed., *The Vatican-Israel Accords: Political, Legal, and Theological Contexts* (Notre Dame, IN: University of Notre Dame Press, 2004).

46. Weigel, *Witness to Hope*, 700. Pius X's 1904 meeting with Theodore Herzl is also discussed in Pinchas Lapide, *Three Popes and the Jews* (New York: Hawthorn Books, 1967); David I. Kertzer. *The Popes against the Jews* (New York: Alfred A. Knopf, 2001), 225; and Sergio I. Minerbi, *The Vatican and Zionism: Conflict in the Holy Land* (New York: Oxford University Press, 1990).

47. Weigel, *Witness to Hope*, 700.

48. O'Brien, *The Hidden Pope*, 11. As Geoffrey Wigoder has also pointed out, during Pope Paul VI's brief 1964 visit to Jerusalem, "he succeeded in never once uttering the word 'Israel.'" Wigoder, *Jewish-Christian Relations*, 109.

49. Weigel, *Witness to Hope*, 700.

50. Weigel, *Witness to Hope*, 701.

51. Weigel, *Witness to Hope*, 701; and O'Brien, *The Hidden Pope*, 300.

52. Weigel, *Witness to Hope*, 701.

53. Weigel, *Witness to Hope*, 702.

54. Weigel, *Witness to Hope*, 709.

55. Eugene J. Fisher, "Pilgrimage of Reconciliation: From Wadowice to the Wailing Wall," in *New Catholic Encyclopedia, Jubilee Volume: The Wojtyła Years*, 96.

56. Fisher, "Pilgrimage of Reconciliation," 96.

57. Weigel, *Witness to Hope*, 697.

58. George Weigel, "The Holy Father in the Holy Land," *Weekly Standard*, April 10, 2000.

59. Fisher, "Pilgrimage of Reconciliation," 97.

60. Fisher, "Pilgrimage of Reconciliation," 97.

61. Fisher, "Pilgrimage of Reconciliation," 97.

62. Weigel, "The Holy Father in the Holy Land."

63. Weigel, "The Holy Father in the Holy Land."

64. Fisher, "Pilgrimage of Reconciliation," 96.

65. Fisher, "Pilgrimage of Reconciliation," 96.

66. Fisher, "Pilgrimage of Reconciliation," 96.

67. Fisher, "Pope John Paul II's Pilgrimage of Reconciliation, xxx.

68. Fisher, "Pope John Paul II's Pilgrimage of Reconciliation, xxx.

69. Fisher, "Pope John Paul II's Pilgrimage of Reconciliation, xxx.

70. David Pryce-Jones, "The Islamization of Europe," *Commentary* 118 (December 2004): 29–33.

71. Gabriel Schoenfeld, *The Return of Anti-Semitism* (San Francisco: Encounter Books, 2004), 60.

72. Meir Weintrater, "France," in *American Jewish Year Book*, vol. 102, eds. David Singer and Lawrence Grossman (New York: American Jewish Committee, 2002), 334.

73. Kenneth R. Timmerman, *Preachers of Hate: Islam and the War on America* (New York: Three Rivers Press, 2004), 213.

74. Marie Brenner, "France's Scarlet Letter," in *Those Who Forget the Past: The Question of Anti-Semitism*, ed. Ron Rosenbaum (New York: Random House, 2004), 212.

75. Weintrater, "France," 334.

76. Timmerman, *Preachers of Hate*, 325.

77. Bishop Jean-Pierre Ricard, president of the French Conference of Catholic Bishops, statement, April 3, 2002.

78. Michel Gurfinkiel, "France's Jewish Problem," *Commentary* 114 (July–August 2002), quoted in Dalin, *The Myth of Hitler's Pope*, 156.

79. Joseph Cardinal Ratzinger, "The Heritage of Abraham: The Gift of Christmas," *L'Osservatore Romano* (English), December 29, 2000.

80. Ratzinger, "The Heritage of Abraham."

81. Michael Paulson, "Pope Denounces Nazism in Synagogue Visit," *Boston Globe*, August 20, 2005.

82. Jennifer Siegel, "Pope Denounces Anti-Semitism during Synagogue Visit," *Forward*, August 25, 2005.

83. Bernadette Sauvaget, "Pope Benedict Warns of Growing Anti-Semitism During German Visit," *Ecumenical News International*, August 19, 2005.

84. David Brinn, "New Pope Hailed for Strong Jewish Ties," *Jerusalem Post*, April 19, 2005.

85. Brinn, "New Pope Hailed for Strong Jewish Ties."

86. I have discussed and documented the history of this philo-Semitic tradition within papal-Jewish relations in chapter two of my book *The Myth of Hitler's Pope*, "Popes in Defense of the Jews," 17–43.

Part II

ETHICAL REFLECTIONS

Chapter Three

John Paul II and the Moral Ground of the Polis: Reclaiming the Jewish-Catholic Ground

Hadley Arkes

In 1995 John Paul II made a memorable visit to the United States, and that visit provided the occasion for the media to take surveys of opinion among American Catholics. One survey revealed a willingness of many Catholics to see women admitted to the priesthood. Whether the priesthood represented merely a convention or whether it had the standing, rather, of a *sacrament* was apparently one of those matters too refined to take up in a survey, even among Catholics. But putting that to the side, it was striking that most Catholics in the survey were under the impression that the pope, standing at the apex of the Church in Rome, had sufficient authority to bring about or at least engineer the change. My friend Russell Hittinger took the survey as a telling sign of the way in which even Catholics in America had absorbed the reigning premises of "positivism" in the law: People seemed to assume that the law governing the Church emanated from a hierarchy of officialdom, of men invested with "authority." And to be invested with authority was to be invested with the power to proclaim judgments that would have the force of law. It seemed to have escaped the notice of these American Catholics that John Paul II did not himself think that *he* possessed any such authority to bring about this change in the priesthood. He was in a position to sustain and impart a law not of his own making, a law that he was not free to change. That law emanated from Christ himself, and it was deepened by a teaching bound up with what the Congregation for the Doctrine of Faith referred to as the "economy of nature." The priest stood in the place of Christ himself, and in order to do that, he would take advantage of natural signs—in this case, the meaning signified by the presence of a man. For if God had become incarnated, God had to be, in the economy of nature, either a man or a woman.

But that is to say again that the character and the laws of the Church did not emanate simply, in the style of positivism, from those orders "posited," proclaimed, set down by people in power, with the power to issue orders and have them treated with the force of law. And yet, to recall in this way the moral ground of the law is to get clear again on the moral ground that must underlie any rightly constituted political order, as Aristotle understood the matter at the very beginning of political philosophy, and it would restate the understanding that had been incorporated quite explicitly, quite consciously, by the American Founders as they set about the task of shaping a new political order. Jefferson had famously remarked that there was nothing above the majority, or the vote of the people governing themselves—nothing, he said, except the moral law. The majority had to recognize, in the moral law, the limits on what they could reasonably will in their standing as a majority. That was the difference, after all, between a criminal mob and a people constituted as a political people, claiming the authority to govern one another.

James Wilson, in his lectures on jurisprudence, was prepared to make the audacious claim, running contra Blackstone, that the standing law could indeed incorporate a principle of revolution. Such, in fact, he insisted, had been incorporated in the American law, because the American law began with the understanding that there could indeed be an unjust or unlawful law—a law that was passed and proclaimed with all of the trappings of legality but lacked the substance of lawfulness and justice. The American law could have that rare and distinct character because the American Founders began explicitly with an understanding of natural right or natural law. They began, in other words, with the recognition of a law outside themselves: a body of principles on the things that were objectively right or wrong, just or unjust. Which is to say, the American law would begin with that recognition, at the root of moral reasoning, that power is not the source of its own justification. It had to be possible at all times to measure the positive law, the law proclaimed in any place, against some independent standards of right and wrong, apart from the law itself and quite apart from the power of those men who presumed to give laws to the community.

These understandings were once the staple of political men and women in America, and they were diffused widely among our people, even among people distant from the political centers of the country. These understandings were diffused widely because they had been planted deeply, even before the Founding, as part of a moral tradition that was as much Jewish as Christian. Michael Novak has pointed up the Hebrew metaphysic of the American Founding, as reflected notably in the Declaration of Independence: We were endowed with rights by our Creator, the Author of the nature that stamped human beings as equal in the sense of sharing a community of nature (as Locke put it), in contradistinction to the things that were subhuman and superhuman.[1] The God of the Declaration was also the Supreme Judge and the searcher of hearts. Other commentators have shown how a certain Hebraic understanding ran through the writings of Christian clerics in the period of the Founding. In the first case to elicit a set of opinions from the Supreme Court, James Wilson made it clear that, before the judges could cite any case or statute—before they could begin any project in law—they had to reject all species of moral skepticism, or what we would call moral relativism. No project in law was intelligible or defensible if one began by calling into question the very possibility of rendering judgments on the things that were right or wrong, just or unjust.[2]

But these are understandings that have faded in our own time, and have fled from the memory even of the educated. Anyone who knows the state of our colleges and universities knows that, quite regardless of the religion in which our students have been nominally raised, they have absorbed no moral premises as deeply as the premises of moral relativism. In this vein, I recalled for my own students a passage I found in the library of my late father-in-law, a biblical commentary by Meyer Waxman on that passage in 1 Kings where Elijah is lodged in Mt. Horeb. God tells Elijah to journey to Damascus and anoint Hazael as king over Aram (1 Kgs 19:15). In Waxman's account, the story dates from about the ninth century B.C., and he takes it as a sign of how early the Jews were committed to monotheism. This came as a bit of news to me, I must admit, for I have identified the very emergence of a Jewish people with the people committed to the one God. Still, I put the question to the students: What was the connection between this passage in 1 Kings and monotheism? The God who can order a prophet to cross the lines of a polity and install the ruler of another place was clearly not one of those local gods known to antiquity. This was a God with a universal jurisdiction, and did it not make sense? The same God who authored a universal law of physics would not legislate separate moral laws for Zimbabwe and Jersey City. And after all, were those Ten Commandments merely municipal regulations to govern the environs of Mt. Sinai, or were they were understood as commands universal in their reach? The question soon following, of course, was to ask how many of the students were raised in households they would describe in their religious definition as Christian, Jewish, or Muslim. Almost all of them were, and so the final question is this: How do you account for the fact that the doctrine of cultural relativism has a far deeper hold on you than the logic of that monotheism in which you were nominally raised?

Against that background—or against that sense of the current state of things—it is more than curious, it is wondrous, in a way, that it seemed to fall to John Paul II to take up the task of restoring, with explicit teaching, the moral premises that have receded from the understanding of the political class even in the United States. And in doing that, he has had to state again the Jewish-Christian perspective on the problem of moral judgment and the political-juridical order. Even justices of the Supreme Court have grown hazy on this matter involving the ultimate ground of the law. There was a time when judges were expected to act as "republican school masters," in reminding people of the moral premises that underlay their own freedom. But even conservative judges in our own time have felt the pull and even the romance of legal positivism. Two friends of mine among conservative jurists have made a show of political detachment by affirming that, if the people, through their legislatures, enacted liberal policies on abortion, the judges would enforce those laws in an earnest, dutiful way. From a construction of that kind, one can break out only with an appeal to principles of lawfulness outside the positive law. And in our time, as I say, the task of offering that teaching was taken up by a man in no judicial office, and certainly no office of legal standing in the United States.

It may be that the distinct moral mission was made all the clearer by the fact that it was undertaken by a man who claimed no political role strictly understood. He was drawn to the problem by the bloody crises of his own day—the murderous regime of the Nazis, the repression of communism, and then, finally, with the fall of the Soviet Union, the flourishing of abortion, and the killing of the most innocent, the most vulnerable, in previous centers of what had been called the "free world." It was a dramatic example of the detachment of freedom from the moral ends to which freedom was rightly directed, the ends that justified the use of freedom and measured its rightful and wrongful use. John Paul II rightly observed at one point that the Church, as a Church, has no distinct interest in the *forms* of democratic life. Whether a community rules itself with a legislature of two chambers or one, whether it has independent judges or executives—all of this, he said, may vary with the experience unfolded with time and in different settings.[3] The concern of the Church has run rather to the root of the matter, to the deep principles that underlie a "regime based on the consent of the governed." No one has been clearer in bringing out that root of the matter in the understanding of "the human person" and in the equality before God that would characterize all human beings. James Wilson observed, in that first case to elicit opinions from the Supreme Court (*Chisholm v. Georgia*), that the law in America would not begin, in the style of positivism, with a sovereign issuing commands. In America, said Wilson, "the Sovereign, when traced to his source, must be found in the man."[4] It would be found, that is, in a natural person, tendering his consent to the terms on which he is governed.

My dear friend Antonin Scalia remarked in the Cruzon case in 1990 that the nine members of his court know no more about life and death—about the beginning of life or whether life becomes "worthless" and untenable to preserve—and they had no sounder judgment to render on these matters, he said, than nine people picked at random from the Kansas City phone book.[5] He would detach judges from the authority to impose a decision not merely because he doubted that judges had any special knowledge here, but because he rather doubted that there was a firm knowledge on this matter that could be detached from opinion. Scalia has made it clear, in several ways, that he distrusts appeals to natural law, precisely because those appeals simply foster more controversy and claim no consensus. The answer, in other words, has to be found in the domain of opinion, or in the concurrence of opinion, quite apart from whether the opinion eliciting the concurrence can be judged, in any strictness, to be true or false, plausible or implausible.

As anyone who knows him knows, Scalia's arguments here have been animated by the concern for judges who themselves profess no moral truths, yet nevertheless insist on imposing their own version of truth on others. Standing against that strange combination of relativism and arrogance, he has mainly sought to reclaim for ordinary people the right to govern themselves, in redeeming the promise of the American Founding, the promise secured again by Abraham Lincoln at a blood price. But in these moves, reflecting so much the currents of thought of our own age, even a conservative jurist has detached himself, subtly but decisively, from those root premises that John Paul has sought to restore. When Scalia says that judges cannot pronounce on the beginning of human life, he would return that question to the people in the states, with their legislatures. And yet, who are the kinds of creatures suited to serve in a legislature? Or to vote for the individuals who will make up a legislature? May the dolphins, intelligent and formidable animals that they are, vote in Massachusetts? Or is it simply the case that the very notion of laws, of framing principles and giving reasons, is an enterprise suited for a very distinct kind of creature? As Aristotle carefully explained, the polis is a distinct emanation from the nature that is distinctively human; only a certain creature is destined for political life. Only a certain kind of creature makes political life comprehensible.

In other words, every path of explanation or justification for the political order leads back, as John Paul II has tried to explain to us, to the understanding of that "human person." Our own age has found many curious and subtle paths for disguising that central, decisive point, and along the way has managed to teach itself to overlook the layers of meaning that are folded into that remarkable thing, a human person. And so, as John Paul II sought to teach again about the human person, he had to state again the things that human beings are capable of "knowing," far more than other kinds of creatures. If reason had no truths to know or declare, then a creature of reason would have no special standing, for he could claim to know nothing of moral consequence.

For John Paul II, the ensemble has held together as a whole. To speak seriously of the human person is to be moved to the serious things he is capable of knowing. And to take seriously the prospect of inquiring and knowing is to reject the curious insistence on truncating that inquiry by ruling out in advance the prospect of inquiring into the highest things we can know: They are questions about the origin of things, and as John Paul II has put it, the enduring questions: Why are we here? What is the purpose to which we, and everything else, is directed? There has been nothing trivial about this set of problems, which he addressed in a concentrated and yet economical way. I will take it as my own task here to try to sketch in the way in which he sought to impart this teaching.

John Paul II rather cut to the bone in *Centesimus annus* when he noted the tendency, quite confirmed in our own time, "to claim that agnosticism and skeptical relativism are the philosophy and the basic attitude which correspond to democratic forms of political life."[6] That understanding has been celebrated these days as the mark of liberation and a modern sensibility. But John Paul II quickly connected that point to the upshot almost never noticed: that moral skepticism, in the understanding of democracy, simply offers a high-sounding rationale for what is an appeal once again, in the end, to raw power. As the Holy Father put it, "if there is no ultimate truth to guide and direct political activity, then ideas and convictions can easily be manipulated for reasons of power."[7] For if there is no truth, Justice Holmes's formula takes hold: The decisive test is whether any idea succeeds in the marketplace—which is to say, whether it gains the vote of majority. As John Paul II observed, people who are convinced that there are anchoring, objective truths become suspect, because they refuse to accept the vote of the majority as the definitive test for the truth of any proposition. This is of course not an idle matter, for it has vexed our politics for years, here and abroad. In recent days, Israel has come under severe criticism because it has barred Jerusalem to the electioneering of Hamas, and it has refused to accept Hamas as part of a legitimate election because Hamas is committed to the very destruction of Israel. But in the modern temper, we have been told again and again that we have democracy and elections because there is no monopoly on truth.

Nearly thirty years ago, when I was involved in the debate over the American Nazis seeking to march through a community of Jewish survivors of the Holocaust, David Hamlin of the American Civil Liberties Union remarked that "we must be free to hear the Nazis because we must be free to choose the Nazis." In this construction democracy begins with the understanding that there is no truth on matters of moral consequence, that there is no idea so base that it cannot be regarded as legitimate, and as a legitimate object of choice by a voter in a democracy. And so we may have parties that reject, at the root, the premise that "all men are created equal"—as the Nazis emphatically did. The democratic citizen is then invited to incorporate the understanding that the very premise of his own freedom, the anchoring premise for a regime of consent—that proposition, as Lincoln called it, "all men are created equal"— is not in fact, as Lincoln and the Founders thought, a truth. It is merely an opinion, no more or less likely to be true than any other opinion sounded in the landscape. This was, of course, precisely the same issue that was presented during the debate with Lincoln and Douglas, as the American people were encouraged to be pro-choice on the matter of slavery. As Lincoln rightly saw, Douglas was inviting citizens in a democracy to accept the notion that there was nothing that may not be rightly chosen through the instrument of democracy, as long as the decision were made with the vote of a majority. In this view, democracy was all process and no substance: We would be equally free to choose genocide or slavery through the scheme of voting. But if there were no truths, then there were no truths that established the rightness of democracy itself, or the rule of majority, or of a government restrained by law. Who was a rightful member of that majority, eligible to vote? There were no principles to tell us, any more than there were principles to measure the rightness or wrongness of the policy enacted through the vote of a majority. As John Paul II caught the whole thing in a quick connection, the rejection of grounding truths for a democracy simply gives us a high-sounding formula for installing the rule of the strong.

Of course, in our own time nothing has demonstrated more dramatically the willingness of democracies to accept the principle of the rule of the strong than the issue of abortion. And in John Paul II's understanding, no issue has marked more profoundly the current crisis of democracy than the issue of abortion. Even people with college degrees seem to have noticed no particular problem about the proposition that a dependent child in the womb—a child who cannot survive yet on its own—is somehow less of a human being, or less of a being with any rights that the rest of us need respect. In other instances, we do not seem to assume that when people fall ill, or become dependent, their weakness does anything more than call forth the care of those who are in a position to provide it. Their weakness or dependence is not taken as a condition that works to extinguish their rights or their very standings as beings who are bearers of rights. In 1998 the redoubtable Nik Nikas was defending in federal court the law passed in Arizona to bar what have been called "partial-birth abortions." Nikas argued that the purpose of the legislature was to erect a "firm barrier against infanticide." Judge Richard Bilby regarded the argument as interesting, but now rather late. Twenty-five years after *Roe v. Wade*, it seemed to Bilby that a legislature could not erect barriers indecorously firm against infanticide if it would inhibit abortions.[8] And the

Supreme Court in *Stenberg v. Carhart* would take essentially the same line—
that even the killing of a child at the point of birth may be acceptable if the
refusal to allow the procedure might—just might—cause even incidental
trouble for the health of a pregnant woman.[9]

Infanticide was no longer to be regarded as a "big deal." But infanticide
could not cease to be a big deal unless homicide ceased to be as big a deal as
it has been. And that could be the case only if we were less certain about what
it is that constituted a human being and whether one required the most demanding of justifications before one could ever intentionally take a human
life—to say nothing of an innocent human life. James Wilson had declared
that the American law would begin with the notion of a "man," with a human
being—a being capable of giving and understanding reasons over matters of
right and wrong, a being capable of understanding, then, a law outside himself. But in elaborating and defending and deepening the laws on abortion, the
judges were giving us a jurisprudence now radically detached from the understanding of a human person. Just what constituted a human person—the
subject and object of the law—did not rest on any objective standard. Just
who or what would be recognized as a human being is a decision to be made
by people holding power (perhaps in legislatures, perhaps in courts, but perhaps simply in having control over another being, in the way that a woman
has control over the child in her womb). And that decision as to who is a human being would not be tested by any standards—by any objective truths—
apart from the truths declared by power itself. But in detaching ourselves
from the understanding of the human person, the courts have made power itself the source of its own justification.

Jefferson had famously remarked that everything was changeable in human
affairs—everything, that is, except the unalienable rights of mankind. Those
would not change either because they were rooted in something enduring in
human nature or in the principles of right themselves. Several years ago,
when I was visiting at Princeton University, I met early on a graduate student
in history. When I asked about her concentration, she told me that her special
interest was in America in the nineteenth century. Ah, I said, I suspect that we
are divided already. For I do think, I told her, that Lincoln had it quite right
when he argued that "all men are created equal" was indeed, as Jefferson
thought, an abstract truth "applicable to all men and all times." To which she
replied, "Well, he thought it was true at the time." For the historians, and for
most of what we call, these days, the educated classes, "all men are created
equal" is not in fact a moral truth applicable to all men and all times, for they
have lost their confidence that there are truths of that kind. Or they think it
particularly gauche even to suggest that there are. Nor do they seriously profess to think any longer that there is an enduring nature of human beings,

which forms the ground of distinctly human rights, in all places where that nature remains the same. They may speak of "human rights," but they are rights only of positive law: They are the rights declared or set down in international conventions, containing people like themselves, drawn from the best schools and the most liberal circles. But across the board, across the division of Left and Right in our politics, the language of truth has given way to the language of "belief." Lincoln, in a rhetorical move, reiterated his "ancient faith" that all men are created equal. But Lincoln regarded "all men are created equal" as an axiomatic truth, much as the Founders themselves regarded it. My own students would find it queer if anyone remarked that he "believed" that the square of the hypotenuse of the right triangle was equal to the sum of the squares of the two adjacent sides. And they would find it equally inapt if anyone said that he had been "indoctrinated" in the Pythagorean theorem. The Founders would have found it just as queer if anyone suggested that it was merely a matter of "belief" that beings who can give and understand reasons over matters of right and wrong deserved to be ruled with a rendering of reasons, and that they may not be ruled in the way that humans rule dogs and horses. As I have had the occasion to point out more than once, even in this age of animal liberation we do not sign labor contracts with our horses or cows, or seek the informed consent of our household pets before we authorize surgery upon them. But when we recognize in this way, as the Founders did, the most consequential gradations in nature, we are not operating on the basis of beliefs or fancies of the most subjective nature.

And so we find ourselves with this paradox: The leading sections of the political class in America profess to be secular in their outlook. They disclaim any sectarian notions as the ground of any laws they would enact and in any account they would offer of the regime of freedom they have come to celebrate. But in offering this account of the goodness of the regime and their own policies, they have no confidence that they can appeal to anything more than *beliefs*, which take on their dignity as they are firmly held and widely shared, with no claim to their truth. In contrast, it is mainly within the Catholic Church, and mainly through the teaching of John Paul II, that the moral case for a democratic regime has been placed on a foundation of reason. As John Paul II has understood—and explained—it is principally through reason, the reason accessible to creatures of reason, that the principles of a government by consent can plausibly be regarded as universal in their reach. But this paradoxical split—between the beliefs of the secular and the appeal of the religious to reason—this difference is bound up with the package of confusions that afflict us now in our law on the meaning of religion and its place in our political life. Those confusions may finally extend even to the kinds of issues that may be raised—or, on the other hand, emphatically screened from the education of the young in a republic.

The package of confusions could be opened, revealing the issues that run to the core, in almost any of the cases that have fed our litigation over the Establishment Clause. And so, as a notable example, under the laws of the United States and Arizona, young James Zobrest, as a deaf student in Tucson, had a right to receive certain aids, such as the services of a sign-language interpreter in helping with his studies. Those services, supported with public funds, were available to him in schools, public or private, but then again not all private schools. For the purpose of filling in the religious component of his education, James's parents arranged his transfer for the ninth grade to the Salpointe Catholic School. At that point, the public aid flowing to him ceased. For the county attorney concluded that he could not receive that aid at a religious institution without violating the Establishment Clause of the U.S. Constitution, as that clause had been elaborated, and notably altered, in the case law of the Supreme Court. Eventually, however, the Supreme Court would overturn that decision, but for reasons that remained less than clear in their principled dimension. In supplying what is missing here, we could note that there is no evident obligation for the government at any level to furnish aid to private schools or to students afflicted with deafness. But if the government does extend such aid and create a kind of right to receive that aid, we would presume on the face of things that the right would be equally available to the student at the Andover Academy in Massachusetts as at the Salpointe Catholic School. If the aid is withdrawn solely because the student switches to a Catholic school, it would appear that the law has now displaced a right with a disability, and that the disability pivots solely, decisively, on the religion of the student or the religious character of the school.

Now, delivered from the clichés that have sprung up on this matter, we could ask the original, naive question as to why there could be any such justified difference. After all, both schools are legitimate establishments. Neither one is like Fagin's School of Pickpocketry. If there was anything wrongful in the teachings and practices of Catholicism, anything that would run afoul of the laws, a Catholic school might be regarded as an illegitimate school. Or, the unlawful parts could be screened from the practices of the Church, as polygamy had been purged from Mormonism by the laws of the United States. And at that point, the Catholic Church would stand as the Mormon Church stands now, as a fully legitimate entity under the laws. In that event, on what ground would we assume that there is anything less wholesome, or less fitting for a republic, in the ethic that pervades a Catholic school, as compared with the liberal ethic that pervades a school such as Andover?

One common reflex, elevated to a common slogan in our own day, is that the religious school indoctrinates students into beliefs and dogmas, while the secular school instructs by teaching science and things accessible to reason.

And yet, that venerable cliché has not caught up with the ruling doctrines of our own time, for we are told at every turn that our knowledge on matters of moral consequence cannot find its ground in reason. We have been told persistently by the descendants of David Hume, in their various sects, that reason is mainly the handmaid or instrument of the passions, that our moral judgments are really woven out of emotions, feelings, and beliefs. It would appear that none of the so-called secular schools professes any higher claim for the ethic it would represent in the world than the *beliefs* in which its judgments are finally anchored. But if reason has nothing to declare on matters of moral consequence, and if the character of any school finds its ground finally in beliefs, then we have a serious epistemological question: On what ground could it be claimed now that the "beliefs" of the religious, as beliefs, stand on any lower epistemic plane than the "beliefs" of the secular? As beliefs, they are no more than beliefs; they are, at best, imperfect opinions. If any beliefs stand on a higher plane, with a higher claim to our credit, then the standard of judgment must rest on something other than belief. It must rest on some other understanding that bears a closer correspondence to what we used to call "the truth."

It would seem to me then that if we strip back these arguments to their root claims, our jurisprudence on church and state, on the separation of religion from politics, has been grounded in incoherence. It has been grounded in a serious mistake about the meaning of religion or theology itself. This is by no means a recent mistake; its origins run back rather far. And yet, one way or another, the mistake has preserved a critical lie about religion and the religious tradition. As John Paul II reminds us, in the classic origins of philosophy in Greece, the knowledge of the gods, or what could be known about divine things, was readily encompassed in philosophy, in the discipline of inquiring into what we were capable of *knowing*. Anyone with the slightest acquaintance with Aquinas or with the Schoolmen of the Middle Ages knows that the canons of logic were engaged in the most demanding way by the disputants, concentrating their forensic skills on the doctrines that were summoning and dividing the community of Christians. And anyone who has seen Talmudic scholars in dispute knows that there is nothing less than strenuous in their flexing of reason. As John Paul II had so arrestingly put it, the Church has always moved with two wings, with reason and faith. And as he managed to explain, the connection was not factitious or a matter of style, but quite indispensable from the beginning. When St. Paul undertook his mission to Athens, he entered into discussions with "certain Epicurean and Stoic philosophers." When he reached outside the circle of Jews, he could not appeal to Moses and the prophets. He had to appeal to an understanding more widely accessible; as John Paul II recalled, he had to appeal to "the natural knowledge of God and to the voice of conscience in every human being."[10] Here the Fathers of the Church would build on the achievements of the Greek philosophers. For Greek religion had been polytheistic, with a persisting inclination then, as John Paul II noted, to "divinizing natural things and phenomena."[11] But it was the considerable service of the "fathers of philosophy to bring to light the link between reason and religion":

> As they broadened their view to include universal principles, they no longer rested content with the ancient myths, but wanted to provide a rational foundation for their belief in the divinity. This opened a path which took its rise from ancient traditions but allowed a development satisfying the demands of universal reason. . . . Superstitions were recognized for what they were and religion was, at least in part, purified by rational analysis. It was on this basis that the Fathers of the Church entered into fruitful dialogue with ancient philosophy, which offered new ways of proclaiming and understanding the God of Jesus Christ.[12]

Greek philosophy became a powerful lever in fending off sophistry, and so it could become, as John Paul II recalled, "the hedge and protective wall around the vineyard" of the Church.[13] As the Holy Father put it so tellingly in *Fides et ratio*, a faith deprived of reason runs the risk of falling into feeling and sentiment, and "so runs the risk of no longer being a universal proposition." It was an illusion then, he said, to "think that faith, tied to weak reasoning, might be more penetrating; on the contrary, faith then runs the grave risk of withering into myth or superstition."[14] However, reason deprived of revelation may take sidetracks, as he says, carrying the risk of diversion and the danger of losing sight of its ultimate goal.

But what of revelation itself and its claims? Revelation is usually taken as the thing that reason itself cannot explain or refute, and yet that puts the landscape in a different order. My late professor Leo Strauss insisted on the durability of revelation, standing beyond refutation, and he argued at the same time that the Bible contained no teaching about nature. His student, and my friend, David Novak has argued with proper reverence for our former teacher that the Bible had to presuppose many things about the very nature of those beings fitted to receive revelation. If they were beings invited to make a covenant with the God of Israel, they had to be beings capable of understanding what it means to enter a covenant, tender a promise, and bear an obligation. John Paul II, in *Fides et ratio*, seemed to encompass that understanding and suggested something a bit more when he observed that "the truth conferred by Revelation is a truth to be understood in the light of reason. It is this duality alone which allows us to specify correctly the relationship between revealed truth and philosophical learning."[15] Consider what we must understand about the souls, or the understanding, of those creatures fitted to receive the revelation. What is it that impresses them with the conviction that the revelation, offered in the name of God, is plausible in its teaching? What if they were not instructed to cleave to their spouses and avoid coveting the wives of other men? What if they were enjoined to throw over their promises to their wives and lie down with the wives of other men, or even with the animals in the field? The situation might resemble that scene with Woody Allen's guerrilla leader now elevated to become the leader of a small country in Latin America. Among his first proclamations upon attaining power, he announces that from now on "all girls under sixteen will be over sixteen." The comedy works as comedy because the writer can rely on the reason, or moral sense, of those beings fitted to receive comedy. I think that David Novak and John Paul II were relying on the same, settled moral competence of those beings fitted to receive the law at Mount Sinai and the Sermon on the Mount. We hear in John Paul II the voice of the serious philosopher when he writes that "a theology without a metaphysical horizon could not move beyond an analysis of religious experience, nor would it allow the *intellectus fidei* to give a coherent account of the universal and transcendent value of revealed truth."[16]

John Paul II recalled the First Vatican Ecumenical Council, arguing against the divorce between reason and revelation: "Even if faith [were] superior to reason," the council declared that "there can never be a true divergence between faith and reason, since the same God who reveals the mysteries and bestows the gift of faith has also placed in the human spirit the light of reason. This God could not deny Himself, nor could the truth ever contradict the truth."[17] What could be offered to the world, then, was a teaching, and a claim, that would cut across all divisions of locale and culture: "With the richness of the salvation wrought by Christ, the walls separating the different cultures collapsed. God's promise in Christ now became a universal offer: no longer limited to one particular people, its language and its customs, but extended to all as a heritage from which each might freely draw."[18] Reason and revelation would be joined. As John Paul II put it, the truth revealed in Christ could not be "opposed to the truths which philosophy perceives. On the contrary, the two modes of knowledge lead to truth in all its fullness. The unity of truth is a fundamental premise of human reasoning, as the principle of non-contradiction makes clear": "Revelation renders this unity certain, showing that the God of creation is also the God of salvation history. It is the one and the same God who establishes and guarantees the intelligibility and reasonableness of the natural order of things upon which scientists confidently depend."[19]

The principle of noncontradiction serves as the anchor, or to switch the figure, the touchstone, of those things that can be claimed in the domain of reason. And as John Paul II recognized, with a force that should not be overlooked, "to argue according to rigorous rational criteria is to guarantee that the results attained are universally valid."[20] Perhaps the argument here, strikingly clear, was somehow muffled in the artful weave, for it bore a teaching that should have come as notable news even to many Catholic jurists: namely, that the natural law would find its ground in "the laws of reason," and the laws of reason find the test of their first principles, or necessary truths, in the propositions that cannot be contradicted without falling into contradiction. Even many seasoned Catholic lawyers have fallen into the familiar mistake that natural law hinges on claims about the command of the Lawgiver, the Author of the moral law, and that it is hostage to all of the grand and implausible claims made by people who affect to know the will of God even as it bears on the most prosaic issues of our own day.

Or, people fall into the mistake of assuming that natural law finds its ground in generalizations about the nature of human beings, as commentators try to take the measure of that "human nature" from which their judgments may be derived. This latter construction opens itself to the curious claims, offered by the enemies of natural law, that infanticide and incest must be in accord with natural law because these practices seem to be part of an intractable record of our species. As the argument runs, these things seem to spring from something embedded in human nature. And yet here Immanuel Kant got it quite right when he warned against the tendency to deduce principles of moral judgment from "the particular natural characteristics of humanity" or the "particular constitution of human nature."[21] Through certain ties of nature and affection, people are understandably attached to their own children, or they would prefer the interests of their own children over others. And yet, some parents abandon, kill, or order the abortions of their own offspring. I would not want to claim that John Paul II was coinciding with Kant in all critical respects, but I would point out that the Holy Father saw no strain in finding the ground of moral reasoning, as Kant did, in the laws of reason, anchored in the law of contradiction. Perhaps it is no strain because John Paul II understood the laws of reason as part of the same "nature," emanating from the Author of that comprehensive nature. As the pope put it, in *Fides et ratio*, "the same God who reveals the mysteries and bestows the gift of faith has also placed in the human spirit the light of reason."[22]

Of course, the unfolding laws of reason would not exhaust the understanding of the natural law, but this bit of news may deliver even many learned Catholic lawyers from their lingering dubiety about the natural law. Justice Scalia, for one, has not been particularly shy in conveying his own reservations about natural law. His main complaint is that, as a body of doctrine, it seems irredeemably hazy, that the only thing reliable about it is the controversy that is certain to arise when it is invoked. And yet, if we follow the main

lines offered by John Paul II, we would find that this project in moral reasoning is not so inscrutable, that indeed it has things to teach, on matters of
consequence, without the least trace of fogginess.

This is not exactly the time to take on this large demonstration of the natural law, but the point here can be shown in a compressed and gentle way by
taking as the simple point of entry that understanding, shared widely in common sense, of those many things people regard, quite rightly, as attributes
wholly wanting in moral significance. Height, weight, color of hair or skin, the
fluency of speech or stuttering, acuteness in faculties, or the presence of disabilities such as deafness—all of these things may elicit our attraction or aversion, and yet when we say that these are attributes without moral significance,
we understand that we can draw no moral inferences from them. A man may
be tall or short, stout or slim, fluent or halting—and from these things we cannot draw the inference that we are dealing with good men or bad, with people
who deserve either rewards or punishments. These things we seem to grasp as
a matter of common sense. The philosopher might fill in the account by explaining that none of these attributes exerts a "deterministic" control over the
moral conduct or character of any person. The recognitions of common sense
are anchored in the problem of freedom and determinism, quite central to any
scheme of casting praise or blame, of holding people morally responsible for
their own acts. We would seem to recognize, then, to take just one example,
that from a person's disability we can draw no inference about his character.
To know that he is deaf or confined to a wheelchair tells us nothing of the kind
of man he is, whether he has a life barren of moral consequence—whether he
has a life worth living or whether in fact he deserves to die. These simple
propositions are simply embedded in the laws of reason. And yet they furnish
precise guidance in questions of assisted suicide or euthanasia in addressing
the question of whether we would be justified in ending the life of any person
simply on the strength of the evidence that he is afflicted with these disabilities. But as John Paul II points out, "to argue according to rigorous rational criteria is to guarantee that the results attained are universally valid."[23] If this
judgment about disabilities—or the moral inferences we may not rightly draw
from the presence of disabilities—is indeed anchored in the laws of reason,
then we should expect the same judgment to hold in every place where the
laws of reason hold. We may not be, in this human species, uniformly civilized
or thoughtful, but everywhere under the laws of reason it will be wrong to
judge a man unworthy on account of his deafness and, for the same wrong reason, judge him unfit to live. That sense of things would be, in a phrase of Lincoln's, "applicable to all men and all times." Now if I ventured out of the
framework of moral reasoning and took note of the temper of people around
me, my own guess is that this proposition about deafness and the ending of life

would not inspire any deep disagreements, even among lawyers. And if that is the case, it should be apparent that there are many other judgments, of like nature, that we can draw from the same ground in the laws of reason.

It has been said that Judaism is a "religion of reason," and some of us have leaned on that claim. And yet, there has been a noticeable hedging or holding back. The story was relayed to me of some scholars at the Jewish Seminary in New York, seeing Leo Strauss in action, doing his line-by-line analysis of a text, and lamenting that such a fine mind was wasted in philosophy. That mind could have been devoted, it was thought, with a richer yield, to exegesis of the Talmud. The work of reason is not apparently the work of philosophy, nor is reason expected to be universal in its reach. What is commanded for the Jews may not mark off the moral code that holds for all people in all places. Nor is it entirely clear that belief must be tested against the claims of reason and evidence. In a conference just last year in Princeton, I was a bit surprised to find the academic William Galston interpreting the Jewish perspective on the law and invoking the Talmudic line that the embryo, in the first forty days, is mainly water. Michael Pakuluk raised the direct, pertinent question of whether Galston regarded that line as *true*. Whatever merit it may have as metaphor, the findings of embryology would be sufficient to show that this line does not have a shred of plausibility as an account of the actual state of the embryo. To the extent that people are willing to take this aphorism seriously—to treat it, as Galston was willing to treat it, as a deep belief, an expression of faith, safely insulated from any test of empirical evidence—a serious question would be raised about the state of Jewish teaching. And I think it is necessary that we break away here from a certain sentimentality and face the question seriously: Are we really bringing forth claims of faith, which are to be regarded as true mainly because they are traditional—because they have been intoned, with the voice of authority, by rabbis in the past? David Novak has insisted to me that the line has a certain poetic quality, and a ceremonial bearing, but that it is not regarded as a serious teaching about the nature of the human embryo. I hope that he is right. And yet, the fact that a scholar could offer that line seriously, to illustrate intractable differences in the understanding and treatment of the embryo, may merely confirm the point that there is no central authority that claims the standing of the decisive authority in the ranks of Jewish scholars. In contrast, it goes virtually without saying that any Catholic offering that line as an opinion would not have even the slenderest claim to have that opinion treated as plausible in the Church. (That is not to say, of course, that we will not find certain Jesuits writing in favored journals and contending that what the Church has claimed to settle is not so settled after all.) In case anyone was innocent enough to raise doubts about the authoritative teaching, he could soon be presented not only with a definitive statement on the point but also with a scholarly commentary, offered by the Congregation for the Doctrine of Faith, laying out the reasons in detail, with references both biblical *and* philosophic. One dear friend, with the closest ties among Catholics and Jews, has offered a sober test here: Both traditions reject the sham of relativism, and both are willing to offer judgments on the pressing moral issues of the day, whether abortion or euthanasia or same-sex marriage. But then the question may properly be put as to the way in which each tradition is willing to deal with scientific or empirical evidence in explaining and justifying the judgments that are finally reached on these vexing matters. When the stakes and the passions are running high, as they are on matters like abortion or homosexuality, will the Jewish scholars fall back on tradition? Or would the Jewish commentators be prepared to offer reasons, to meet the empirical evidence on its own terms? That is, would they be moved to show that the traditional moral teaching has a claim to our credence because it can be shown to be compelling quite apart from whether it has been spoken again and again across the generations? To put it another way, is the teaching good because it is traditional, or could we show that it has been traditional because it has been enduringly true?

In *Fides et ratio*, John Paul II realized that he had to lean against the currents of misunderstanding, of mistakes and clichés long accumulated, by teaching again that the Church and the moral tradition have not depended solely on faith and sentiment, that the teaching has always been firmly grounded as well in the canons of reason. But then what of that other part? He had pointed out that revelation could be received only by creatures of reason, and that revelation itself had to be understood in the light of reason—though at the same time revelation conveys what reason itself cannot convey to us. As John Paul II noted, "Faith . . . has no fear of reason, but seeks it out and has trust in it. Just as grace builds on nature and brings it to fulfillment, so faith builds upon and perfects reason": "Illumined by faith, reason is set free from the fragility and limitations deriving from the disobedience of sin and finds the strength required to rise to the knowledge of the Triune God."[24] Again, the two are not disconnected. As John Paul II puts it directly, "Revelation clearly proposes certain truths which might never have been discovered by reason unaided, although they are not of themselves inaccessible to reason."[25] And what might they be?

> Among these truths is the notion of a free and personal God who is the Creator of the world, a truth which has been so crucial for the development of philosophical thinking, especially the philosophy of being. There is also the reality of sin, as it appears in the light of faith, which helps to shape an adequate philosophical formulation of the problem of evil. The notion of the person as a spiritual being is

another of faith's specific contributions: the Christian proclamation of human dignity, equality, and freedom has undoubtedly influenced modern philosophical thought. . . .

Among the objective elements of Christian philosophy we might also place the need to explore the rationality of certain truths expressed in Sacred Scripture, such as the possibility of man's supernatural vocation and original sin itself. These are tasks which challenge reason to recognize that there is something true and rational lying far beyond the straits within which it would normally be confined. These questions in fact broaden reason's scope for action.

In speculating on these questions, philosophers have not become theologians, since they have not sought to understand and expound the truths of faith on the basis of Revelation. They have continued working on their own terrain and with their own purely rational method, yet extending their research to new aspects of truth. It could be said that a good part of modern and contemporary philosophy would not exist without this stimulus of the word of God.[26]

Fr. Stanley Jaki has shown us the way in which scientists have been affirmed in their work by the confidence, borne of religious conviction, that there were universal laws to be discerned, for they emanated from the Author of the laws governing the universe, in the workings of matter *and* morals. But we might take as a certain test here that "proposition," as Lincoln called it, "all men are created equal." As an empirical truth, that proposition must ever be placed in doubt by the evident inequality of human beings in the things that matter—their intelligence and rectitude, their virtue and vice. It is notably less than self-evident that all human beings deserve to have reasons given to them or that their souls are in a condition to receive those reasons. Human beings have the unique aptitude for moral reasoning, and yet we know that gift is not present in all members of our species. Some of them have not yet filled out their capacity for reason, some have diminished capacities, and some have fallen into conditions in which they are not in command any longer of their memories. And yet, we hold to the conviction that their infirmities have not diminished their standing as human beings or the dignity that attaches to that standing. Exactly why that is the case is a matter that is evidently perplexing our law and causing serious strains over the ending of human life. But until reason can supply a more compelling account, our political practice seems to have been firmed up by that conviction, rooted in our tradition, that these beings were made in the image of something higher. The common sense of the matter was concentrated in that simple line, recalled again by John Paul II, that our equality inhered in the fact that we were all, even in our various conditions, the children of God.[27] In *Veritatis splendor*, John Paul II remarked that "God provides for man differently from the way in which He provides for beings which are not persons." He cared for man, "not 'from without,' through the laws of physical nature, but 'from within,' through reason, which, by its natural knowledge of God's eternal law, is consequently able to show man the right direction to take in his free actions."[28] And it went without saying that when John Paul II spoke about "man," he spoke, without question, about "all men," or all mankind.

In this reading, the anchoring premises of a regime of consent, or the premises of any moral order of politics, are found in the depth of our religious understanding, an understanding that has evaporated from a large portion of the citizenry, even as the original vocabulary has remained. The moral resonance remains, even when people cannot explain any longer just why that resonance lingers or what it actually means. And along with this fading of memory has come a drawing in of the horizon of politics, or, to put it another way, we have found a critical truncating or diminishing of the questions that come into sight any longer in our politics. John Paul II raised the question of just what difference revelation would make, and part of the answer was that the awareness of revelation imparted the conviction to face the highest, most demanding questions, the questions that are largely left to the side, and certainly are put out of the political arena in our own modern political regime. John Paul II put it in this way:

> As a theological virtue, faith liberates reason from presumption, the typical temptation of the philosopher. Saint Paul, the Fathers of the Church, and, closer to our own time, philosophers such as Pascal and Kierkegaard reproached such presumption. The philosopher who learns humility will also find courage to tackle questions which are difficult to resolve if the data of Revelation are ignored—for example, the problem of evil and suffering, the personal nature of God, and the question of the meaning of life or, more directly, the radical metaphysical question, "Why is there something rather than nothing?"[29]

Some political philosophers have argued that the American Founders were working in the tradition of "modernity" begun by Machiavelli and Hobbes, and as part of that new politics, they were scaling down the ends of political life. Instead of a political life directed to the highest questions—about the highest ends of human life—this new politics would be built on "low but solid ground." It would begin by seeking mainly to secure the rights of persons to preserve their own lives and the freedom to pursue their own legitimate interests. Others have become persuaded that the American Founders had never really detached themselves from the classic tradition, running back to both Athens and Jerusalem. If we follow John Paul II, I think he would be arguing to us that those highest questions cannot be purged from our political life or decorously put aside, any more than they can be put aside from any plausible moral life—which is to say, any life of serious reflection.

Now I set down these words at a time when large portions of the political class in this country seem to be suffering the vapors, and creating the appearance of a real crisis in our law, over the rather innocent prospect of teaching in the public schools the argument over intelligent design and evolution. The remarkable scenes played out in local governments and the federal courts reveal a depth of passion—one might call it the fanaticism or the religious passion of the irreligious. What is revealed is a certain brittleness, a sense of feeling under threat, if students are simply invited to consider an alternative hypothesis to the theory of evolution. The argument has been that the movement for intelligent design is fueled by those who actually think that there is a design in the universe, and that a design implies a Designer. With those hints of—gasp!—religious conviction, people have sounded some rather desperate alarms about the violation the Establishment Clause in its modern reading. For in that reading, it becomes important to purge any trace of religiosity from our common, civic life. Here we have had, in a confined theater, the evidence of real panic when public institutions, even schools, raise some of those highest questions about the presence or absence of a telos or ordering purpose in the universe—for those kinds of questions point outward, of course, to questions about the very purpose of human life. That those questions elicit a panic even among the most educated people is itself a chilling sign of our current condition.

What makes it worse is that there is no need to pose the problem as a religious question in the first place. As Frank Beckwith and others have shown, the question posed in intelligent design is a distinctly scientific and philosophic question:[30] As in other inquiries in the sciences, we ask the question of whether the events or patterns we are trying to explain could have arisen plausibly by chance, as random happenings. When we find, for example, that certain events are likely to occur by chance only one time in a thousand, we usually take that as a plausible measure of statistical significance. Even without saying anything about the identity of that Designer, or that First Cause in the universe, that question of randomness and design is a question quite intelligible on its own without any appeal to matters of faith or religious doctrine. For people who are truly scientific, with a scientific spirit, it would be hard to see why any challenges of this kind would ever be out of season. One would think that the challenges would be welcomed, if only as devices for teaching, for the posing of the question offers the chance for science to vindicate its own pretensions by explaining again the ground on which it claims to know anything with confidence. Indeed, simply as a pedagogic device, it is hard to see why a scientist would not be willing to draw the interest of his students by posing the challenge, as a distinct, intelligible question arising out of our religious tradition, but a question that would of course be addressed with the same canons of reason and evidence that we employ everywhere else, including the sciences.

It betrays, again, the most curious defensiveness and brittleness that people should be so alarmed that the question may even be raised. We have, after all, a vast body of writing, distinctly philosophic, in which the question of a First Cause in the universe has been argued for as a matter solely of "first principles." The case for that First Cause can be made without implying anything about the God who negotiated with Abraham over Sodom and Gomorrah, or about the God who died on the cross. At the same time, philosophers like Richard Swinburne at Oxford could write *The Existence of God*, offering a forceful case simply on the basis of reckonings of probability.[31] If it is regarded without question, at Oxford, that people may argue about God, or about the existence of design in the universe, by arguing mainly in terms of probabilities, it is hard to see why that kind of approach should be ruled as somehow illegitimate for schools in Pennsylvania. It seems even more bizarre that this subject should actually be struck down as an illegitimate part of a public education, in a recent judgment by a federal judge in Pennsylvania.[32]

Fr. Frank Canavan, as wise and savvy as he is learned, once remarked that one might try to keep religion out of the public schools, but it is virtually impossible to keep religion out of education. It may be possible to banish religion from the young if it were possible to purge the young of any wonderment: wonderment about the origin of things, of how they or anyone else came to be, or of where everything is heading, and about how we would know, and whether we would see someday in another place even the dearest ones who have died. If we can imagine children never induced to wonder about things of this kind, we would settle in with an education quite comfortable not only in avoiding those questions but actually in forbidding youngsters from even thinking about them, as though in thinking about them they were venturing into a religious life that was bound to be unsettling, and at least unwholesome, for the life of a republic.

Aristotle raised the question of educating the young as he neared the end of the *Ethics*, as the prelude to the *Politics*, for he was quite clear that the education of the young was bound up with the laws. It would be shaped inevitably by the moral understanding that pervaded the community and found expression in the laws. And indeed we are seeing the connection made today as people argue that these questions that John Paul II marked off, the highest questions, must be barred from the education of the young precisely because their inclusion would violate principles that were set down at the very top of our political order, in our Constitution. Of course we are left with the problem of whether a system of education that rules out questions of that kind can plausibly call itself a system of education in any serious sense.

But if we follow John Paul II we are also left with the question of whether those questions can be banned from any plausible political or moral life. Ronald Knox once mulled in print over the tendency to name certain "laws" in science after the one who discovered them. And so we hear people talk about "Boyle's Law." But as Knox said, we seem to suggest that these accomplished men invented these laws they discovered. And yet, if it took some rather formidable minds to have discovered these laws, he asked, wouldn't it figure that it took a rather accomplished Mind to have put them there in the first place? If you could imagine a life in which that kind of wit or that kind of question is never expressed, it would be a diminished life; but do we earnestly think that it is even imaginable? As we have seen of late, our capacity to stir panic in the face of serious questions, and to insist on ruling them out, is a capacity highly cultivated by the educated and the resourceful in our own time. But if we follow John Paul II, I think we would find that these questions are opened whenever we are led to reflect again on the meaning of "the human person"—of that being who is both the subject and object of our laws. The most ordinary questions of politics keep bringing us back to that meaning of the "human person," and we find that we cannot inquire into the nature of human beings without being led again into the many layers that constitute our being. When we do that, we find, as John Paul II said, the light of reason put there by the Author of that nature, and we come again into the presence of the Mind that put everything there in the first place. From whatever point we begin, we find ourselves led back, as John Paul II reminded us, to Him "who is the same yesterday and today and forever."[33]

NOTES

1. See Michael Novak, *On Two Wings* (San Francisco: Encounter Books, 2002).

2. See Wilson in *Chisholm v. Georgia*, 2 Dallas 419 (1793), at 453–54. Before Wilson would invoke the authority of any case at law or any commentator on matters jural, he would invoke the authority of "Dr. [Thomas] Reid, in his excellent inquiry into the human mind, on the principles of common sense, speaking of the skeptical and illiberal philosophy, which under bold, but false pretensions to liberality, prevailed in many parts of Europe before he wrote." Wilson would begin then by rejecting "skepticism," as the fount of all forms of relativism in morality and law.

3. John Paul II, *Centesimus annus* (1991), no. 43: "The Church has no models to present; models that are real and truly effective can only arise within the framework of different historical situations, through the efforts of all those who responsibly confront concrete problems in all their social, economic, political, and cultural aspects, as these interact with one another." And John Paul II cites here, in support: Second Vatican Ecumenical Council, Pastoral Constitution on the Church in the World of Today, *Gaudium et spes*, no. 36; Paul VI, apostolic letter *Octogesima adveniens*, nos. 2–5.

4. *Chisholm v. Georgia*, 458.

5. See *Cruzon v. Director, Missouri Department of Health*, 497 U.S. 261 (1990), at 293.

6. John Paul II, *Centesimus annus* (1991), no. 46.

7. John Paul II, *Centesimus annus* (1991), no. 46.

8. For an analysis of this case, see my *Natural Rights and the Right to Choose* (Cambridge: Cambridge University Press, 2002), 135–38, and the larger chapter in which it is contained, "Antijural Jurisprudence," 112–46.

9. 530 U.S. 914 (2000).

10. John Paul II, *Fides et ratio*, no. 36.

11. John Paul II, *Fides et ratio*, no. 36.

12. John Paul II, *Fides et ratio*, no. 36.

13. John Paul II, *Fides et ratio*, no. 38, quoting Clement of Alexandria, *Stromata* I, 20, 100, 1 (*SC* 30, 124).

14. John Paul II, *Fides et ratio*, no. 48.

15. John Paul II, *Fides et ratio*, no. 35.

16. John Paul II, *Fides et ratio*, no. 83.

17. John Paul II, *Fides et ratio*, no. 53, citing First Vatican Ecumenical Council, Dogmatic Constitution on the Catholic Faith, *Dei Filius*, IV (*DS*, no. 3017).

18. John Paul II, *Fides et ratio*, no. 70.

19. John Paul II, *Fides et ratio*, no. 34.

20. John Paul II, *Fides et ratio*, no. 75.

21. See Immanuel Kant, *Fundamental Principles of the Metaphysics of Morals*, trans. Thomas K. Abbott (1785; Indianapolis: Bobbs-Merrill, 1949), 42 and 58. And for a fuller discussion of this problem, see my own book, *First Things* (Princeton: Princeton University Press, 1986), 68–70 and passim.

22. John Paul II, *Fides et ratio*, no. 53.

23. John Paul II, *Fides et ratio*, no. 75.

24. John Paul II, *Fides et ratio*, no. 43.

25. John Paul II, *Fides et ratio*, no. 76.

26. John Paul II, *Fides et ratio*, no. 76.

27. See, for example, John Paul II, *Centesimus annus*, no. 22: "In situations strongly influenced by ideology, in which polarization obscured the awareness of a human dignity common to all, the Church affirmed clearly and forcefully that every individual—whatever his or her personal convictions—bears the image of God and therefore deserves respect."

28. John Paul II, *Veritatis splendor* (1993), no. 43.

29. John Paul II, *Fides et ratio*, no. 76.

30. See Francis J. Beckwith, "Public Education, Religious Establishment, and the Challenge of Intelligent Design," *Notre Dame Journal of Law, Ethics, & Public Policy* 17 (2003): 461–519.

31. Richard Swinburne, *The Existence of God* (Oxford: Clarendon Press, 1979).

32. See the opinion of Judge Jones, in *Kitzmiller v. Dover Area School District*, Federal District Court, December 20, 2005.

33. Heb 13:8, cited in the last lines of John Paul II, *Centesimus annus*, no. 62.

Chapter Four

Natural Law and Divine Command: Some Thoughts on *Veritatis Splendor*

David Novak

NATURAL LAW AND PHILOSOPHY

Veritatis splendor is the treatise-length encyclical on Catholic moral theology by the late, revered Pope John Paul II. Being a magisterial statement of Catholic moral theology addressed to Catholics (through their bishops), it would be inappropriate for a non-Catholic such as myself to offer any theological comments on *Veritatis splendor*, let alone argue with it theologically. Nevertheless, *Veritatis splendor* also makes philosophical assertions, especially assertions for the idea of natural law. Since any genuine philosophical assertion is addressed to whoever is rational, it is not at all inappropriate for any such person, irrespective of his or her religion (and even nonreligion) to respond both exegetically and critically to the philosophical assertions of a treatise like *Veritatis splendor*.

That distinction notwithstanding, we now need to examine how philosophical assertions are truly integrated into the overall theological exposition of *Veritatis splendor*. Otherwise, we might fall into the error of seeing a theological text and then isolating a self-sufficient philosophical subtext therein. Regarding natural law, one sees that sort of error in the way certain modern Thomists took Thomas Aquinas's articles on natural law in the *prima secundae* of the *Summa theologiae* and dubbed them a "Treatise on Law," something Aquinas himself did not do. But, by so doing, they missed the fact that the more philosophical treatment of natural law there cannot be fully understood unless it is seen as the introduction to Aquinas's very theological treatment thereafter of the "Old Law" and the "New Law" in what is, after all, a *summa theologiae*, not a "summa philosophiae." In fact, were one to carry this approach to a further extreme, one could even ascribe a "two truths" epistemology to a thinker like Thomas Aquinas or Karol Wojtyła, though neither one of them would ever have accepted any such ascription.

In *Veritatis splendor* (or anywhere else in his vast oeuvre, as far as I know), John Paul II is not treating natural law as some sort of supplement to Catholic moral theology; rather, he seems to regard natural law as being both an essential *part of* Catholic moral theology as well as being *presupposed by* Catholic moral theology. Nevertheless, natural law is *not derived from* theological texts, whether Scripture or any other canonical document. The precepts of natural law are what have been concluded by moral philosophy or practical reason from reflection on the common human condition in the world. When that philosophy is derived from dogmatic theology—anyone's dogmatic theology—that philosophy becomes an unconvincing rationalization or "apology" (in the pejorative sense) for that theology. And, as such, it does not even serve the project of that theology at all well, precisely because it is such bad philosophy.

Theology does not provide the fully universalizable propositions one finds in genuine philosophy. That is because "theology," strictly speaking, is the reformulation of the data of a divine revelation, an event that occurred at a certain time in a certain place and whose gracious message and normative content have been accepted, recorded, interpreted, and transmitted by a certain community. I say "certain" rather than "particular" of the time, place, and recipients of revelation because the revelations affirmed by Judaism and Christianity (and perhaps Islam) are not taken by their adherents to be "parts" of some greater whole. These adherents refuse to allow their founding revelations to be particularized into some larger, more inclusive process.[1] To be sure, theologians engage in rational argument about the meaning of the singular truth that has been given them in revelation (*fides quaerens intellectum*), but that is quite different from the work of philosophers who construct various meaningful hypotheses in order to reach the universal truth they hope to discover in the world and persuade others to do likewise. The methodologies of both disciplines are quite different, and at times they only seem to share the common axioms of formal logic along with some similar rhetorical strategies.

Being certain or *singular* rather than being merely particular makes a theology, in the eyes of its faithful adherents, superior to the still more abstract universality that characterizes philosophical discourse.[2] But, unlike theological arguments, philosophical arguments are made to *whomever, whenever, wherever*. Nevertheless, what theology now lacks in universality, it gains in intensity and in ultimacy, for it speaks to a culturally richer, more concrete, and more transcendently oriented human community than the more abstract "humanity" addressed here and now by philosophy. Moreover, theology often proclaims that this richer and more concrete and more transcendently oriented community will include all humankind at the consummation of history. In other words, at that end-time (*eschaton*), the final redemption will fully integrate the universality of philosophy with the intensity, ultimacy, and cultural "thickness" of the community to whom theology now speaks. Before that end-time, however, philosophy and theology cannot claim to be one and the same human enterprise, but they cannot ignore one another except at their mutual peril (as John Paul II pointed out in that most personal of all his encyclicals, *Fides et ratio*). One might see the interrelation or correlation of theology and philosophy to be dialectical.

By its present universality, philosophy provides the necessary human background for theology. And theology, while presently addressing the elected children of Abraham (whatever their communal name), ought never forget that they have not ceased to be the created children of Adam.[3] That background, though, is still not sufficient for a human existence in this world, for sustaining a human community capable of holding out until all humankind is redeemed. As such, when philosophy is taken to be a presupposition *for* theology, theology is able to appropriate philosophical truth out of its universal background in a way that philosophy cannot appropriate the theological truth that lies on its horizon. All that should be required in this appropriation is that theologians use philosophical assertions accurately and attempt neither to deduce these philosophical arguments from specifically theological premises nor to remake theology so that its historical origins are now unrecognizable.

Philosophy should not be distorted by appeals to authority for its propositions rather than by offering rational arguments for them. Philosophy serves theology (*ancilla theologiae*), but it is not broken down and reconstructed de novo. Even when serving theology, philosophy's autonomy should be left intact.[4]

Pope John Paul II, speaking as *the* Catholic theologian of his time, has been admirably clear in respecting the logical independence of philosophy from theology without, however, granting to philosophy any substantial autonomy. Moreover, I do not think he has correlated theology and philosophy in a way that could not have been done by a Jewish theologian, mutatis mutandis. That is because one can constitute the idea of *nature*, which is central to all natural law theory, by the same philosophical methods, irrespective of the Abrahamic tradition out of which one does his or her philosophy. Yet that in no way minimizes *the* theological difference between Judaism and Christianity—*la différence même* as the French would say. In this world at least, that difference is greater than all our philosophical commonality, but it is not over the question of what constitutes nature, it is over what constitutes grace. Nevertheless, when we talk natural law theory with each other, we can

bracket the question of grace, which is, however, very different from ignor-
ing it altogether.

NATURE AND MORAL OBLIGATION

In *Veritatis splendor* John Paul II states that "natural law . . . receives this
name not because it refers to the nature of irrational beings, but because the
reason which promulgates it is proper to human nature" (no. 42). This is a key
philosophical assertion of the encyclical. One could ask three questions about
it: (1) How does human nature differ from nonhuman nature? (2) If they are
different, why are "nature" and "law" predicated of both rational and irrational beings? (3) How does "nature," human or otherwise, promulgate a law;
that is, how does nature actually *command* rational beings like humans to perform some acts and not to perform other acts?

By confining nature to rational beings, John Paul II is distinguishing natural law (*lex naturalis*) from what is usually referred to as the "laws of nature"
(*lex naturae*). In earlier theories of natural law, though, this distinction between human and nonhuman nature was not made or not made as sharply as
John Paul II makes it here.

In these earlier theories, everything that exists in the world has a specific order proper to it called "nature" (*physis*). That order is formal; that is, it is intelligible to the mind, but it is not an object of sensible experience. Thus, it is
not a part of that which it so intelligently orders; rather, what is ordered by its
own nature becomes included or participates in that nature, which orders this
"matter" for its own sake. Furthermore, the specific nature of each entity in the
world is ultimately coordinated into one worldly or cosmic order, what we
would call *Nature* (with an upper-case N) in English or *die Natur* (with the def-
inite article) in German. Thus the nature *of* each entity is ultimately coordinated *within* cosmic nature. That coordination is most coherent and intelligible when taken to be *teleological*, that is, when each entity is inclined or
striving to act in a certain way as an act for its own sake as well as pointing to
something above it on the ontological ladder, so to speak. At the apex (*telos*)
of the universe, one infers the existence of that being (*ousia*) whose action is
totally sufficient unto itself (*kath'auto*), hence totally self-referential: the God
of the philosophers, best represented by Aristotle.[5] Moreover, this God is one
or univocal simply because its existence is identical with its essence or nature,
hence nothing else participates in its being; it has no multiple instantiations. It
is what it is and nothing else. Because of that attraction to God/Being by all
intelligent beings, each one of them strives to be as much like God as possible, to the extent of its natural capacity (*dynamis*). In the case of humans our-

selves, we see that our natural tendency or orientation (*inclinatio naturalis*) is most essentially our rational tendency or orientation (*inclinatio rationalis*), which is to know that which nothing greater can be conceived.

Jewish, Christian, and Muslim philosophers, who accepted this basic metaphysical scheme and who also have had to affirm the theological doctrine of creation (especially *creatio ex nihilo*), also had to affirm that this cosmic natural order is infused into the world by God (what the Talmud called *sidrei beresheet*) simultaneously with God's creation of the matter that this natural order orders or in-forms, both specifically and generally.[6] Nevertheless, these same monotheistic theologians were hard pressed to show how it makes any difference in their cosmological philosophy whether that order is creatively infused by God or had just been there for all eternity. Since their metaphysics and the ethics they built onto it were so teleological, it made no real difference to say whether God *is* the end (*telos*) of the whole universe or that God *designated Himself to be* that cosmic end for all that is not-God.[7] Whether creationist or not, in this metaphysics, God functions in exactly the same way.[8] God is the object of all striving, the final cause of the cosmos. God is not *for* the cosmos; instead, the cosmos is *for* God. God is not inclined *toward* what is less than God; instead, what is less than God is inclined *toward* God. In this way, natural theology and notions of cosmic justice (*dikē*) are correlated.

In this metaphysical scheme, humans occupy a rather peculiar cosmic intersection. On the one hand, they are more intelligent than the animals beneath them, not only having animal consciousness but also having reason. On the other hand, though, humans are not as intelligent or rational as the heavenly bodies, which occupy a place in the cosmos just below that of God. Having the property of reason is enough to essentially distinguish humans from animals.[9] But having freedom of choice, as it were, demotes humans' stand to a cosmic position below the higher, heavenly or celestial intelligences in the great chain of being.[10] Humans have to strive to direct themselves toward their ends, both toward the ultimate or final end as well as toward penultimate or more proximate ends.[11]

By contrast, celestial beings have *always* been at their final end, hence they have never had to make any choices as regards how to get there. They have never been doing anything else except being in constant attraction to God's self-sufficient perfection. Even lower than humans are earthly beings who, like humans, are in a state of flux but do not seem to be making the type of deliberate choices humans regularly have to make. Operating by what seems to be blind necessity (what Plato and Aristotle called *anangkaion*), contrary to human beings, these animals seem to be unaware of their temporality with its possibilities. Contrary to celestial beings, animals seem to have *never* been aware of their final end.

Freedom of choice presupposes a range of possibilities—standing mid-point between "always" and "never"—from which one has to make a choice. "Possibility" is a metaphysical term; in ethical terms, we would call these possibilities "options." Only a being like man, who is aware of his essential temporality, could have the essential property of freedom of choice, that is, to be free to make moral choices from a limited range of possibilities. And, inasmuch as the human property of free choice is due to a metaphysical lack, as it were, free choice does not operate in the *natural* world, strictly speaking. The natural world is characterized by necessity at both its upper celestial level and its lower subhuman level. Humans have freedom of choice because humans are not quite part of the natural world; they can only strive to be part of it at its higher, intelligent level.[12]

However, aren't these choices what we would call *moral* choices? Isn't a moral choice to be made when one is addressed by a commandment? Aren't such choices inevitable when one person makes a claim upon another person and that claimed person is free to answer or reject the claim being made upon him or her? But, since neither Nature nor the God of Nature makes any claims on anyone, there is no real moral *law* here. A law is a command made by one person (or persons) for another person (or persons) to keep for the sake of either a third person or for the sake of the one who commanded the act. The one who uttered the command is free to do so or not, and the one to whom the command is addressed is free to keep it or not. Furthermore, just as the freedom of the one who utters the command is a positive attribute, so the freedom of the recipient of the command is a positive attribute. Indeed, despite the asymmetry between the freedom of the Creator and the freedom of even his most exalted creature, nonetheless freedom is still what they have most in common. Yet, in the classical metaphysical scheme, to attribute freedom to God would be an anthropomorphic insult to God since it would be ascribing to God the very lack in humans that makes them two degrees less than divine (and one degree less than the heavenly intelligences).

In the classical view, law is rational when the reason for its promulgation is already known or could be known.[13] But such law is not "natural" inasmuch as Nature does not manifest will nor can it even be inferred that Nature has will. Instead, moral law is patterned after Nature. In the words of Aristotle, "nothing contrary to nature [*para physin*] is right."[14] It is what the Stoics taught about natural law (*nomos physikos*) being "in harmony with nature."[15] It is what Cicero called "reason's imitation of nature" (*quam imitata ratio res*).[16] In this classical view, God is not the ultimate source of law; rather, God, like man, acts and even rules best only when subordinate to nature.[17]

In the classical view, unaffected as it was by the biblical emphasis on commandment, one might say that since Nature is teleological throughout, law is an effort by a human efficient cause to direct itself and other humans (material cause) to their final end (*telos*), which is *informed* by a vision of what that final end really is in all its attractiveness. Moreover, in the classical view, for those humans whose moral excellence (*aretē*) is deeply habitual, no law need be promulgated for them. They are considered to be beyond the agonizing choices that lesser persons constantly have to make. For them, law is a presupposition lying behind them rather than a task lying ahead of them. One sees this in Plato's exemption of the guardians of his "republic" from the rules by which lesser persons are governed; and less brazenly, one sees it in Aristotle's view that intellectual friendship is beyond any concern with the rules of justice.[18]

It would seem, then, that John Paul II's continual effort in *Veritatis splendor* to speak of natural law as divine command would have to reject this whole metaphysical-ethical scheme I have outlined above. So, for example, he writes: "man is certainly free inasmuch as he can understand and accept God's commands" (no. 35). Yet the fact is that in his more philosophical expressions of natural law, especially here in *Veritatis splendor*, John Paul II often retains what seems to me, anyway, to be too much residue from a metaphysical-ethical outlook that is not in keeping with his emphasis on the correlation of law/commandment and freedom of choice. So, far from being the metaphysical lack it is in the classical view of human nature, freedom of choice is the most positive feature of human nature for any metaphysic that regards human nature, and human nature alone, to be the *immediate* image of God. Freedom of choice is by no means a metaphysical privation; by reflecting the freedom of God's will, human free choice indicates that humans are more than even the angels because they are more proximate to God's freedom.[19] In classical philosophy, conversely, humans require constant mediation in their relationship with God.

Over and above the fact that this classical metaphysics is too beholden to a now-superseded scientific paradigm to be able to be independently employed, I also find the residue of it in the thought of John Paul II somewhat out of keeping with the philosophies formulated by Kant, Husserl, Scheler, and Levinas, which so influenced Karol Wojtyła in his more strictly philosophical writings. Indeed, these philosophies could not have been formulated if the old metaphysics were still arguable and in force.

MORALITY AND GOODNESS

The old metaphysical-ethical residue in *Veritatis splendor* is problematic because it seems to be discontinuous with the central thesis of the encyclical.

The thesis about the correlation of freedom and truth, and about natural law as divine commandment, is one I indeed applaud, both as a Jew and as a philosopher. So, even when arguing *with* some problematic concepts employed in *Veritatis splendor*, I continually confirm its central philosophical thesis. Furthermore, as mentioned at the beginning of this paper, *Veritatis splendor* does not contain a theological text and a philosophical subtext. But it does, to my mind, contain a philosophical text (fully integrated into the theological text) *and* a philosophical subtext. I think that the philosophical subtext can be separated from the main text, and that this does no violence to the main text. In fact, it might actually strengthen the encyclical's fundamental philosophical point.

We have now seen where the metaphysical problem lies. So, where does the ethical problem lie? And in locating these problems, I realize that it did not begin with John Paul II, but, rather, it comes from an older philosophy he has inherited.

The problem, as I see it, lies in the use of the term "good," taking it to be the most basic term in practical/moral philosophy or ethics. Thus John Paul II writes: "[T]he goodness that attracts and at the same time obliges man has its source in God, and indeed is God Himself . . . [who is] the final end of human activity" (no. 9). For very different reasons to be sure, G. E. Moore (who it could be said made ethics a respectable field of inquiry for analytic philosophers already at the beginning of the twentieth century) declared ethics to be concerned primarily with "What is good? And what is bad?" both of which pertain to "self-evident" truths.[20]

Differing with thinkers as disparate as John Paul II and G. E. Moore, I think it can be shown that "good" (and its obverse "bad") is not primarily a moral term, and that when "good" is predicated on morally significant acts, that predication is metaphorical. It seems that "good" is a more elementary term (in Wittgenstein's sense of an "elementary proposition") when used in an aesthetic proposition or in an instrumental or pragmatic proposition.[21]

Aesthetically speaking, to call something "good" or "beautiful" (*kalos k'a-gathos*, as Plato and Aristotle would say) means that it is attractive in and of itself. It is Plato talking about (better, alluding to) "the Good or Goodness itself" (*t'agathon kath'auto*), which is the apex of the cosmos, being identified with God by his student Aristotle.[22] This Goodness certainly may not and cannot be used by anyone less than it for anything less than it. As such, we cannot derive moral obligation or commandment from something aesthetically designated *good* since the very term is descriptive, albeit a highly evaluating description. To call something "good" is to make an aesthetic judgment; it is not telling or commanding anyone *to do* anything. The term is not essentially normative.

In fact, philosophy itself, for Plato, emerges out of aesthetic experience. Philosophical reflection is "theoretical," which means it comes from the act of "gazing" (*theōrein*) up at the heavens, admiring its ordered beauty. Socrates, however, comes closer to Hebraic notions of philosophy emerging out of moral experience inasmuch as Socrates was more concerned with justice (*to dikaion*) than he was with "theory."[23] And that is why Emmanuel Levinas was mistaken in his attempt to enlist Plato's Form of *the Good* for his Kant-like project of making ethics replace metaphysics as the discipline dealing with "first things."[24]

When "good" is predicated of something in this Platonic way, it means: "X participates in and is an instantiation of a nonphysical entity that is called Goodness/Beauty." (A Platonic Form, or *eidos*, is the hypostatization of a qualifying adjective like "good" or "beautiful" by turning that adjective into a noun.) Goodness itself does not command anyone how to relate to it; instead, one person has to command another person to treat what is good/beautiful correctly. It is like the museum guard telling a spectator: "Don't touch the *beautiful* painting!" One's admiration of the good or beautiful object is meant to be intangible. It is like the professor of art telling an art student: "Be reverent when looking at the *beautiful* painting." Often such reverent, admiring behavior resembles worship (which probably goes back to the time when all great art was religious). The modern expression *l'art pour l'art* expresses much the same notion. Conversely, calling an object of aesthetic experience "bad" means that it does not qualify for participation in Goodness/Beauty. It is not an end-in-itself. So, calling a commandment "good" means that *like* something inherently beautiful it should not be considered as a means to some other end, and it should be done without any instrumental intention. Still, the "good" commandment needs someone to command it *be done*.

On the other hand, "good" is also a pragmatic or instrumental term, such as when one says: "Dicing the vegetables is good for my salad." Here an act is judged "good" or "bad" by how it benefits or harms something else. In this example of the instrumental meaning of "good," I am saying that dicing the vegetables is good for the salad that is good for me. Here we are dealing with a good to which one relates tangibly. The short-term good here is that dicing the vegetables makes the salad taste good to me; the long-term good there is that eating a well-prepared salad is good for my overall bodily health. Moreover, along these lines, one could say that God's declaration about light in the creation narrative—"that it is good" (*tov*; Gn 1:4)—means that light's shining is *good for* all the rest of creation that follows.[25] In other words, what is good is what *benefits* whatever it operates on *well*. (Indeed, in biblical Hebrew, "good" functions much more frequently as an adverb than it does as an adjective.)

Somewhat ironically, though, "good" in this instrumental sense has more imperative force than "good" in the aesthetic sense just noted above. Persons are very likely to do something if they are convinced that it is *good for them*. That is what we call self-interest. Many people feel they *have to do good* for themselves: They usually *want* to do it. (Think of the popularity of "self-help" psychology.) But what if something is not good for me: Could I be persuaded to do that act because it is good? Good for whom? Let us say I am convinced that giving charity is not good for me. (I would rather keep all my money to myself.) Could I be persuaded to give charity anyway *because it is good for* the beggar who is asking for it? The answer here is "no" when "good" is taken in this instrumental sense. To judge an act "good" only "commands" me in the sense of persuading me or pulling me in its direction when it is in my own immediate interest. (This is what Kant called an amoral "hypothetical imperative.")[26] Yet what I do by myself is rarely the subject of ethics. The basic concern of ethics is with *transactions* between persons. And even here, one could say, for example: "I should not drink too much because drunkenness prevents me from properly fulfilling my duties, or from fulfilling my duties at all, to those who need my well-functioning body and mind—like my wife, my children, my students." Thus, when I believe that what I am doing is good or beneficial for someone else, it seems I need to be convinced that the other person has a just claim or *right* to my beneficence in order for me to do that good as my *duty*. Some of the most interesting cases calling for a particular practical action involve conflicts between my good and someone else's right.

Clearly, one cannot get any moral obligation out of the aesthetic meaning of "good," and one only gets a rather weak and self-centered "obligation" out of the instrumental meaning of "good." In both cases, we still have the problem, so famously stated by Hume, of trying to derive an "ought" from an "is."[27] So, "good" functions best for moral discourse when it functions adverbially rather than imperatively. For example: "Adam responded quite *well* to Eve's claim on his spousal affection. He fulfilled his duty of *beneficence* to her in a *good* way." Note how the good Adam did for Eve was not caused by that good itself, nor did Adam do it because it was in his immediate self-interest. Instead, Adam benefited Eve because Eve had a justifiable claim on his affection as her husband. Now Adam might very well have enjoyed fulfilling that claim, and, in fact, his enjoyment of what he is doing helps him fulfill his duty *better*. Nevertheless, that enjoyment was an accompaniment or addition to the just act, not the final cause of what he did. (This latter point against hedonism is one about which Plato, Aristotle, and Kant agreed.)[28] Along these lines, one could note John Paul II quoting St. Alphonsus Maria di'Liguori: "It is not enough to do good works; they need to be done well" (*Veritatis splendor*, no. 78).

JUSTICE, RIGHTS, AND DUTIES

The most basic moral terms are not "good" and "bad"; they are "just" and "unjust." Some would say that "right" and "wrong" more accurately function as the basic moral terms than do "just" and "unjust."[29] However, "right" and "wrong" sound too much like "correct" and "incorrect" or "true" and "false," all of which seem to be primarily epistemological terms. (Also, I take "right" to denote a just claim, hence functioning like a verb rather than as an adjective; that is why I do not use it as a synonym for "just.") Now, the fact that "just" and "unjust," like "innocent" and "guilty" (or "exonerated" and "condemned"), sound essentially legal does not detract from their moral primacy, that is, when one believes (as Aquinas and John Paul II certainly believed) that law not grounded in morality obliges no one.[30] And, it should be noted that all significant moral issues involve humans as the socially conscious, transactional beings we surely are (what Aristotle called a *politikon zō'on*).[31] These issues inevitably become the subject of what we call "landmark cases" in the courts. Such cases deal with basic issues of justice. Justice (*dikaiosyne*), Aristotle pointed out, is *the* political excellence.[32]

"True" and "evil" can also be taken to be primary moral terms, that is, when the obverse of "true" is not "false" but "deceitful," and, that is, when the obverse of "evil" is not "good" but "unjust," and when "evil" is not synonymous with "bad." The word for "evil" in biblical Hebrew—*resha*—denotes culpable guilt: what cannot be done with impunity, and what is to be judged in a court (whether human or divine).[33] On the other hand, in biblical Hebrew, the word for "bad" is *ra*, which primarily denotes what we experience as harmful to us. Part of that harmfulness is the uncanniness or unpredictability of *bad things*, which makes it very hard for us to use precaution in avoiding them. Thus *the bad* only connotes morally evil action metaphorically: like what is bad, moral evil is harmful to someone; unlike what is bad, though, we know what causes moral evil. That is, we know *who* is responsible for it, *how* he or she is responsible for it, and *why* the morally evil act was performed. In other words, for an act to be judged *evil*, we need to know its subject, its method, and its intention. Evil is only like what is bad in its harmful effects. That is why God can be called "creator of what is bad [*ra*]" (Is 45:7).[34] But God could not be called the creator of "evil" (*resha*) since evil/injustice is what is ultimately anti-God (and God is not revealed as being suicidal).

We see the problem with assigning moral primacy to "good" and "evil" most clearly when John Paul II elaborates on Aquinas (*Summa theologiae* I–II, q. 90, a. 4, ad 1), who states about natural law: "The natural law is promulgated by the very fact that God instilled it into man's mind so as to be known by him naturally." This comes from Aquinas's insistence that law must be promulgated in order to be valid.[35] That also shows the crucial distinction between *lex naturalis* and the "laws of nature" (*lex naturae*), as the latter are not commandments because commandments could only be addressed or promulgated to free subjects.[36] Hence "laws of nature" are only "laws" in a rather metaphorical sense, perhaps by analogy to the metaphorical description of God's creative action as being what "He commanded" (see Ps 33:9; 148:5). But, for the classical philosophers, to whom the Loquacious-Creator-God is unknown (or denied, as in the case of Spinoza), such a metaphor would be inept; hence for them there is only "natural order." (That is why, by the way, I think it is better the use the earlier Latin term *ius naturale* than the medieval Latin term *lex naturalis*.)

John Paul II holds that natural law is instilled in the human mind through conscience. Thus "the judgment of conscience is a practical judgment" (*Veritatis splendor*, no. 59), and it has "an imperative character" (no. 60). But how does conscience command? It would seem that in his reading of Aquinas, John Paul II sees conscience commanding by inclining humans toward "the specific moral value of certain goods toward which a person is naturally inclined" (no. 48). So, also, "the authentic good . . . is established as the eternal law by divine wisdom, which orders every being towards its end" (no. 72). But, while God is the ultimate good (*summum bonum*) to be pursued (primarily in contemplation), God is not the exclusive good. God and the lone human person do not exist in a symbiosis. There are other "goods" besides God.[37] But where is the voice of God heard within our hearts, which most people think of as "conscience"? Where is the divine commandment here?

For Aquinas, "good is to be done" (*bonum est faciendum*).[38] That is taken by some Thomists to mean: Good calls for its own instantiation in our doing good deeds and avoiding evil deeds.[39] Yet that also means the good is effectively accomplished *through* human moral subjects rather than *by* them, strictly speaking. Moreover, in this view of moral good, the good seems to come from itself. Human moral subjects, then, do not command themselves (as in liberal notions of autonomy), but they are also not commanded to do what is good, neither immediately nor ultimately, by God or anyone else, by any *other*. As John Paul II states: "Obedience to God is not . . . a heteronomy" (no. 41). Moreover, these "goods" that seem to command themselves are not particular, isolated acts; rather, they are ongoing states of activity done for their own sake.

What we have just heard above is a very Aristotelian reading of Aquinas, one that has been the subject of controversy among Thomists for centuries. Thus Suarez, for example, placed much more emphasis on God commanding that good be done. Though unlike what might be termed "theological positivists" for whom God both commands that good be done and also reveals *what* that good is, Suarez only needs God's explicit command for doing good in general.[40] The specific content of the good so commanded is something human subjects can discover for themselves (although not invent for themselves as many modern liberals would have it). And that, in fact, suggests a way of getting out of the dilemma of trying to derive an "ought" from an "is." Phenomenologically speaking, it is the opposite: We derive an "is" from an "ought" in the sense of having to learn *what something is* because we have been commanded *to do* something with it. (I think Wittgenstein's argument with Augustine about naming objects makes this same point.)[41]

The problem with the version of Aquinas's notion of good mentioned above is that it only points out how we are *attracted* to certain good or inherently *attractive* states of active being, but it does not show how we are *commanded* to do them. That is a big problem for John Paul II inasmuch as he constantly emphasizes the centrality of commandments (what the Jewish tradition calls *mitsvot*) in the moral life. In fact, in a virtual paraphrase of Maimonides' most important treatment of free choice (which I doubt whether John Paul II knew), the pope writes: "[M]an is certainly free, inasmuch as he can understand and accept God's commands."[42]

As I have argued earlier, commandments do not command themselves, and only a commanded morality gives us a strong and coherent sense of moral obligation, namely, obedience. Karl Barth made that point, with typical brilliance, in his critique of Kant's notion of autonomy.[43] At times, Kant seems to mean by "autonomy" that the law itself—*nomos autos*—commands itself to be done through those persons who perceive it and accept it.[44] The Good commanding its own instantiation sounds to me very much like Kant—that is, Kant in his most Platonic mode of thinking.[45] But doesn't this kind of moral logic elide the source, the subject, the act, and the object of the act when they should be kept separate? In other words, isn't something commanding itself to be done employing self-referential, reflexive language by becoming its own source, its own subject, its own act, and its own object? Doesn't a transitive verb like "command" denote A telling B to do C for the sake of D? Isn't it illogical to treat the verb "command" or "oblige" as if it were an intransitive verb? Isn't the object or purpose of the commanded act the person *for whom* the act is being done, not the act itself as something irreducibly good? Isn't it better to speak of the person for whom an act as moral obligation is being performed as the end of the act rather than speaking of the act as being done for *its* own sake? Yet John Paul II writes that "the object of the act of willing is in fact a freely chosen kind of behavior" (no. 78). All of these questions are perfectly appropriate to ask of the philosopher Karol Wojtyła, whose main philosophical work is called *The Acting Person*.[46]

This emphasis of commandment, however, does not lead us into a "deontological" ethics where commandments seem to be commanded because they are commanded by some authority. (Speaking more theologically, one could call this approach "fideistic," namely, one believes what one believes because one has been commanded to believe it without any interest in discovering a reason for this commandment.) The obedience involved in natural law as commandment, however, is not "blind" because we know or can know just *why* God commands them as he does. Along these lines, my revered teacher, Professor Germain Grisez, called natural law "an intellect-size bite of reality."[47] These reasons of the commandments (what the Jewish tradition calls *ta`amei ha-mitsvot*) are *ends* with which human beings can identify, but they are not ends which humans can project willy-nilly.

When dealing with the thought of John Paul II, who famously referred to much of our contemporary culture as a "culture of death," it is surely appropriate to bring as an example how the prohibition of murder might be promulgated. "Thou shalt not murder" (Ex 20:13; Dt 5:17) is promulgated *because* murder is an unjustified assault on a human person created in the image of God. The image of God deserves respect: minimally, not to be harmed; maximally, to be loved. Such an assault is an affront or contempt or disrespect committed against God; such love is a true affirmation of God.[48] Indeed, the commandment is *true* in the sense that to keep it affirms what is true about human nature, and to violate it is to *actively belie* human nature. (And actions speak louder than words.) Moreover, the image of God deserves respect and love not simply because its human bearers *are* awesome and attractive, but because like the God whom they reflect they *ask* for respect and they *ask* for love. (To ask or request some act from someone else is to command or claim a more voluntary response from a willing subject.) And when a commandment is made as a personal request, the source of the commandment and the object of the commandment are frequently identical. It is like a beggar asking us to help him, which asks us to properly respond to the truth of his existence as the image of God who needs our help here and now.

John Paul II says: "Freedom then is rooted in the truth about man" (no. 84); it is here that "the link between freedom and truth is made manifest" (no. 61). Note how something called "the good" or "goods" is not invoked in this correlation of freedom and truth, unless of course one puts truth and goodness on a par, something that Aquinas (and Maimonides) did not do when he assigned "truth" strictly speaking to the realm of theoretical reason.[49] For this reason, I think we have to separate theoretical "truth," whose obverse is "falsehood," from practical "truth," whose obverse is "deceit" or "treachery." In biblical Hebrew, *emet*, which is the word usually translated as "truth" (as in the Septuagint's translation of it as *alētheia* or in the Vulgate's translation of it as *ver-*

itas), has the primary and practical meaning of "faithfulness" or "trustworthiness."[50]

There is another problem with asserting the moral primacy of "good." If good is what is to be pursued, and evil is what is to be avoided, how do we account for sins of omission? It would seem that one has only sinned if he or she has done what is *not to be done*, that is, one has violated a negative precept, what John Paul II calls "kinds of behavior prohibited by the moral commandments expressed in negative form" (no. 52). But it would seem that one's passivity in the face of a positive commandment, following this kind of teleological ethic, could only be, at best, a missed opportunity rather than a violation of God's law every bit as serious as the violation of a negative ("thou shalt not") commandment.

John Paul II does write that "the natural law expresses the dignity of the human person and lays the foundation of his fundamental rights and duties" (no. 51). But wouldn't it be better to say that natural law *comprises* the full range of rights and duties that pertain to all humans in any human society? (In that way, couldn't we avoid having to talk about "the good" or "goods" as nouns or gerunds altogether?) In other words, there are certain fundamental claims humans have on one another. When these claims are justified, we call them *rights*. When the responses to rights qua claims are justified in proportion to them, we call these justified responses *duties*.[51] Among these rights are my justified claims *upon* others that they benefit me (that is, *do good for me*) and that they not harm me (that is, *not act badly to me*). Among these duties are my justified obligations to others to benefit them (that is, *do good for them*) and not to harm them (that is, *not act badly to them*).[52]

Maximally, we have a right to the beneficence of others, that is, as long as we are willing to respond to their claims upon our beneficence.[53] Minimally, we have a right not to be harmed by others, that is, as long as we recognize their same right or claim upon us. As the Talmud put the most basic moral command: "What is hateful to you, do not do to another."[54] That is the Jewish way of saying what the Roman jurist Ulpian said is a basic precept of justice: "Do not harm others" (*alterum non laedere*).[55]

Justice is the systematic, general coordination of all these specific rights and duties and their correlations. It is best designated by the biblical word *mishpat*, which functions very similarly to the way "nature" functions adjectivally in "natural" law.[56] This systemic justice is divine law insofar as its subject is the human person, both individually and communally, who is the image of God. It is *natural* law because the image of God is human nature. So, for example, to say that every human person has the right to life means when any human person is about to become the object of an assault, he or she (never "it") is entitled to say or have it said on his or her behalf (one way or

another): "Do not harm me, I am the image of God." And when pressed to the
farthest limit, it is as if God is saying: "Do not harm whoever is created in my
image!" That is the divine justification of the negative commandment, one
whose reason is perfectly evident, hence it is natural law (or what the Jewish
tradition calls a "rational commandment").[57] And, it is as if God is saying:
"When you harm whoever is created in my image, you will have to answer to
Me as Cain had to answer to Me when he murdered his fellow human person,
his brother Abel." And, Cain was expected to know this truth about his human brother even before the Ten Commandments were given at Mount Sinai.
He was expected to know this by his human reason and to act accordingly. It
is very likely that before Cain's murder of his brother Abel, Abel asked or
begged his brother Cain not to kill him.[58] Cain, then, ignored *whom* it was
who was making this desperate request of him.

Similarly, such statements of divine commandment, mediated by the
claims of man as the image of God, can be made in the event of would-be assaults on rightfully obtained human property (robbery), or when an inappropriate claim is made on another human body as when, for example, someone
makes sexual overtures to a married woman for intimacy with her body. In
each of these cases, there is a minimal right to be "left alone" on the part of
the object of a would-be unjust act, and there is the duty to "leave him or her
alone" on the part of the subject of this would-be unjust act.

About all such violations of human personhood prohibited by negative
commandments, John Paul II wrote that they are "universally valid. They
oblige each and every individual, always and in every circumstance. . . .
[They are] a lower limit, beneath which the commandment is broken" (no.
52). When I read that I was reminded of a famous essay, written over thirty
years ago, by the Israeli-Jewish theologian Rabbi Aharon Lichtenstein, where
he wrote about what could be considered a Jewish view of natural law as follows: "[T]he existence of natural morality is clearly assumed in much that is
central to our tradition. . . . [N]atural morality establishes a standard below
which the demands of revelation could not possibly fall."[59] Neither of these
statements requires or even suggests making "good" and "bad" basic terms
for morals or for the metaphysic of morals. Both statements can be elaborated
in the language of justice, the language of rights and duties alone.

AN AFTERWORD

In *Veritatis splendor* the pope wrote: "Certainly the Church's magisterium
does not intend to impose upon the faithful any particular theological system,
still less a philosophical one" (no. 29). I take this to be the pope's admission

to Catholics that they can question parts of the reasoning of a magisterial statement like a papal encyclical as long as they do not reject its conclusions, both in theory and especially in practice. (Thus it would seem that John Paul II's argument with the Catholic moral theologians he criticizes here is largely over the practical applications of their misguided theories made by themselves or by others influenced by them.) As a Jew I am not under the authority of the pope. And, indeed, there are many papal statements, especially in more strictly theological areas, with which I could not agree in either theory or practice. But that is not for me to do there. Here, however, with almost all the moral teaching of *Veritatis splendor*, it is appropriate for me to respectfully question its philosophical reasoning. In fact, I think such a questioning response to some of *Veritatis splendor*'s philosophy is invited by its author from whomever reads it, and that certainly includes a Jewish philosopher like myself, who is not only a fellow philosopher but, even more importantly, a member of the people whom John Paul II called his "elder brothers." Such questioning in no way challenges the pope's authority for his own community. Indeed, I actively celebrate his great wisdom for the whole world by interrogating it. Of course, John Paul II is not here to answer my questions himself. But perhaps there are those closer to his thought than I who will show me that I did not plumb the depths of his thought deeply enough and that the problems I have raised are all apparent, not real.

NOTES

1. See David Novak, *Natural Law in Judaism* (Cambridge: Cambridge University Press, 1998), 82–89.

2. See David Novak, *Jewish-Christian Dialogue* (New York: Oxford University Press, 1989), 129–38.

3. See Hermann Cohen, *Religion of Reason out of the Sources of Judaism*, trans. S. Kaplan (New York: Frederick Ungar, 1972), nos. 8.5–10 (115–19).

4. That is quite different from what Hegel did when he broke down theology and reconstructed its concepts to make it serve his philosophy. See Hegel, *Phenomenology of Spirit*, trans. A. V. Miller (Oxford: Oxford University Press, 1977), 483–86.

5. See Aristotle, *Metaphysics*, 12.9 (1074b35).

6. *Babylonian Talmud*: Shabbat 53b.

7. See Maimonides, *Guide of the Perplexed*, 2.19.

8. Maimonides, *Guide of the Perplexed*, 1.69.

9. See Aristotle, *Nicomachean Ethics*, 3.1 (111b14).

10. Aristotle, *Nicomachean Ethics*, 6.3–5 (1139b20–1140b30).

11. Aristotle, *Nicomachean Ethics*, 1.1 (1094a1–5).

12. See Aristotle, *Nicomachean Ethics*, 6.7 (1141a20–30).

13. See Thomas Aquinas, *Summa theologiae*, I, q. 2, a. 1, for the distinction between what is *ratio quoad nos* (i.e., what is already known) and what is *ratio per se* (i.e., what could be known).

14. Aristotle, *Politics*, trans. E. Barker (Oxford: Oxford University Press, 1948), 7.3 (1325b10; 338). See Aristotle, *Nicomachean Ethics*, 5.7 (1134b19–31).

15. Epictetus, *Discourses*, vol. 2, trans. W. A. Oldfather (Cambridge: Harvard University Press, 1928), 3.18.6 (110–11). See Epictetus, *Discourses*, 1.4.29 (vol. 1, 34–35).

16. Cicero, *De legibus*, trans. C. W. Keyes (Cambridge, Mass.: Harvard University Press, 1928), 1.8.26 (324–25).

17. See Cicero, *De legibus*, 1.7.23 (pp. 32–33). Cf. Plato, *Timaeus*, 29A–29C.

18. Plato, *Republic*, 389B–C; Aristotle, *Nicomachean Ethics*, 8.1 (1155a26–30).

19. See Saadiah Gaon, *Book of Beliefs and Opinions*, trans. S. Rosenblatt (New Haven: Yale University Press, 1948), 4.1–4 (181–84).

20. G. E. Moore, *Principia Ethica* (Cambridge: Cambridge University Press, 1903), 1.2 (3), pref. (viii–ix).

21. Ludwig Wittgenstein, *Tractatus Logico-Philosophicus*, 4.221.

22. See Plato, *Republic*, 505A–E; *Metaphysics*, 1.2 (982b5–10) and 12.9 (1074b35). See also Dante, *Paradiso*, 33.145.

23. See Plato, *Phaedo*, 97C–99B.

24. See Emmanuel Levinas, *Totality and Infinity*, trans. A. Lingis (Pittsburgh: Duquesne University Press, 1969), 102–3.

25. For the Bible's use of "good" (*tov*) in the sense of what benefits an other, see, for example, 1 Kgs 19:4; Ps 73:1; Est 10:3.

26. See Immannuel Kant, *Groundwork of the Metaphysic of Morals*, trans. H. J. Paton (New York: Harper, 1964), 108–9.

27. See David Hume, *A Treatise of Human Nature*, 3.1.1.

28. See Plato, *Philebus*, 63A–E; Aristotle, *Nicomachean Ethics*, 10.2 (1172b10–1173a13).

29. See David Novak, *Covenantal Rights* (Princeton, NJ: Princeton University Press, 2000), 13–22.

30. Thomas Aquinas, *ST* I-II, q. 90, a. 4.

31. See Aristotle, *Politics*, 1.1 (1253a9).

32. Aristotle, *Nicomachean Ethics*, 5.1 (1129b25–34).

33. See, for instance, Ps 5:5.

34. See *Mishnah*: Berakhot 9.5, re Deut. 6:5.

35. Thomas Aquinas, *ST* I-II, q. 90, a. 4.

36. Cf. Spinoza, *Tractatus Theologico-Politicus*, ch. 3.

37. See John Finnis, *Natural Law and Natural Rights* (Oxford: Clarendon Press, 1980), 81–99.

38. Thomas Aquinas, *ST* I-II, q. 94, a. 2.

39. See Germain Grisez, "The First Principle of Practical Reason," *Natural Law Forum* 10 (1965): 168–201.

40. See Cicero, *De legibus*, II.7.5–8.4.

41. Ludwig Wittgenstein, *Philosophical Investigations*, 1.1–7.

42. John Paul II, *Veritatis splendor*, no. 35. See *Mishneh Torah*: Repentance, 5.1–3.

43. Karl Barth, *Church Dogmatics*, 2, 2.38.2–4.

44. Thus when Kant famously (*Kritik der praktischen Vernunft*, ed. K. Vorländer [Hamburg: Felix Meiner, 1967], conclusion, 186) speaks of the moral law as what amazes him, he speaks of it being *in mir* not *von mir*. He compares it to the starry sky that is *über mir*. Neither the starry sky nor the moral law could be regarded as human inventions; rather, they are human discoveries of the human ability to will good like God.

45. For Kant as a Neoplatonist, see *Critique of Pure Reason*, B375.

46. Karol Wojtyła, *The Acting Person*, trans. A. Potocki (Boston: Reidel, 1979).

47. Grisez, "First Principle of Practical Reason," 174.

48. Thus the second-century (A.D.) sage Ben Azzai saw the commandment "You shall love your neighbor as yourself" (Lv 19:18) as being grounded in the attractiveness of human persons as the *imago Dei*. See my late revered teacher, Louis Finkelstein, *Akiba* (Philadelphia: Jewish Publication Society of America, 1936), 210.

49. Thomas Aquinas, *ST* I-II, q. 94, a. 2. Cf. Maimonides, *Guide of the Perplexed*, 1.2.

50. See Gn 47:29; Jer 42:5.

51. See D. Novak, *Covenantal Rights*, 3–12.

52. For the notion that even the punishment of a criminal is for his or her ultimate benefit, see *Babylonian Talmud*: Sanhedrin 6b re 2 Sam 8:15.

53. See Maimonides, *Commentary on the Mishnah*: Peah 1.1, for the notion that mutuality lies at the heart of all norms governing interhuman relations.

54. *Babylonian Talmud*: Shabbat 31a.

55. *Digest*, 1.1.10.1.

56. See Gn 18:25.

57. See D. Novak, *Natural Law in Judaism*, 62–76.

58. See Louis Ginzberg, *Legends of the Jews*, vol. 1 (Philadelphia: Jewish Publication Society of America, 1909), 107–9.

59. Lichtenstein, "Does Jewish Tradition Recognize an Ethic Independent of Halakha?" in *Modern Jewish Ethics*, ed. M. Fox (Columbus: Ohio State University Press, 1975), 63, 65.

Chapter Five

The Asymmetrical Relation: Novak and Novak

Michael Novak

It happens that in the various Slavic tongues the name "Novak" means new man, newcomer, stranger. Novak was a name often given to wanderers to a town, who might be of Jewish or of Christian background. Those of us whose name is Novak (or Novick or Nowak or Novakoff or Novacek, or other variants)—and there are a lot of us—cannot be sure on encountering that name whether the bearer is Christian or Jewish.

So it happens that my "cousin" David Novak is a most distinguished rabbi and learned scholar of both Judaism and Christianity, who generously admits into his friendship his "cousin" Michael Novak, the Catholic scholar-writer. Even our political leanings are in several areas quite opposite. Friendship, though, is a more powerful bond.

I thought I might seize on the happenstance of our common name to develop a theme that David has often drawn upon in his work, and I myself have elaborated (in an essay on "Jacques Maritain and the Jews"): namely, the asymmetrical relation between Jews and Christians. Playfully put, the asymmetry between Novaks. But there is more to this happenstance, symmetries and asymmetries both, than our mere sharing in a common surname. There is friendship. And as with us, so with Jews and Christians generally, the time is right for talking about the asymmetries between Christians and Jews, precisely because the bond between us has become so close.

"To everything there is a season." Some questions, which cannot be addressed for quite concrete and practical reasons at earlier times, may be addressed quite comfortably when the time is right. As Rabbi David has explained, for some centuries Jews felt that they must keep themselves safe from Christian proselytizing, not to say heavier pressures, and so must emphasize everything that separates and differentiates Jews from Christians. Thus, for many centuries, the inheritances that Jews and Christians shared in common went virtually unmentioned, if not wholly ignored.

Yet nowadays it is different, Rabbi Novak points out. In these days of an aggressive antireligious fever and a rising secularism, days in which, simultaneously, generations of amicable pluralistic experience have nourished bonds of trust and familiarity between Jews and Christians that were seldom felt before, something new is possible. It is even necessary. That is, to stress what Jews and Christians share in common. At the same time, it is also necessary for the integrity of both parties, and for the durability of the conversation between them, that they should begin for the first time to set forth and analyze the asymmetries involved in their relationship.

Judaism is not Christianity. Christianity is not Judaism. There are points at which the two religions are, or *appear* to be, in complete contradiction to one another. (That "appear" phrase pops up in order to allow for God's way of seeing the matter.) Christians must hold that, in some way which Jews cannot in honesty accept, Christianity adds to and goes beyond Judaism. And Jews must hold, in some way which Christians cannot in honesty accept, that Christ is not, alas, what he said he was—a very good, prophetic, and holy teacher, yes, but not the Messiah and certainly not "the Son of God," a term that must appear to Jews blasphemous.

To Jews, the Trinitarian God of Christianity must seem a breach of monotheism. To Christians, the God of Judaism must seem inadequately revealed in his inner dynamism and communion of life.

To repeat, Judaism and Christianity do not completely overlap. From some angles, they contradict each other. And yet they are remarkably symmetrical—or at least shaped so as to fit into one another and to join together—in many highly significant ways.

For good and honest dialogue to go forward, it is helpful for Jews and Christians both to know precisely where they cannot go forward together, but must respectfully and perhaps even affectionately separate and go different ways. These points of difference being clear, there remains a very large universe of common cherishing, mutual reinforcement, and brotherly prodding and stimulation.

But the term "points of difference" does not go far enough. Also involved is a quite different "angle of vision" or "horizon." And the effect of differences of this sort can be quite immense, indeed. Let us consider this question in more detail.

SYMMETRIES AND ASYMMETRIES

In my earlier essay, I identified one crucial asymmetry in this way: In order to understand their own faith, Christians must also accept as true nearly the whole of the Jewish faith. Pope John Paul II described it this way, speaking to the Synagogue of Rome on April 13, 1986, "The Jewish religion is not 'extrinsic' to us, but in a certain way is 'intrinsic' to our religion. With Judaism, therefore, we have a relationship which we do not have with any other religion."[1] But the reverse is not true for Jews in respect to the Christian faith. Jews can perfectly well understand themselves without accepting the truth of the Christian faith.

In fact, a self-respecting Jew may hold that in certain important respects—about which he may in courtesy choose to be silent in public intercourse with Christians and others—Christian faith must be in error. By comparison, the Christian, while accepting that Jewish faith is true as far as it goes, and while holding that it lays the premises of and prepares the way for Christ's coming, may ponder what it is that prevents Jews from seeing the truth of Christianity as he does. Why do Jews refuse to accept Christ?

I have long thought that there is a good book to be written by a Jewish author, or authors, about why the figure of Christ fails to attract Jews while it succeeds in drawing Christians. Why are Jewish ways of looking at Christ so far from Christian views? I think rejection cannot always be based upon avoidance of reading or thinking about Jesus.

By comparison, it is not so hard to imagine what it is that holds Jews back from Christianity, not only because of remembered historical wrongs, but even in the contemporary period, on account of its social unattractiveness, or even repulsiveness. A good number of persons who have become, for example, Roman Catholics, after having been raised Anglicans, Presbyterians, Lutherans, or in other Protestant communions, have written about how the human appearances and real faults of the Catholic body actually repulsed them. It was not the "beauty" or the "aesthetics" of being Catholic that drew them; not at all. Jacques Maritain, Avery Dulles, John Jay Hughes, and others have described how they had to overcome their own inward revulsion.

Lest these wider reflections cloud the main point of our investigation, however, let me return to the currently hot question of asymmetries. In the past I have tended to look at the basic asymmetry from the point of view of the affirming attitude toward Judaism that is built into Christian self-understanding in contrast to the wariness toward, not to say fairly wholesale rejection of Christianity that is built into Jewish self-understanding. For example, in fidelity to themselves, Christians begin by affirming the God of Abraham, Isaac, and Jacob; affirming the prophets; affirming the Psalms, the Proverbs, the Histories, indeed the whole of the Jewish books of the Bible; affirming the faith and the prayers and the traditional virtues of the mother of Jesus and Jesus and his apostles; and the like. In contrast, Jewish self-understanding has necessarily begun with more guarded and limited affirmations about Christian faith, specific virtues, and Christian practice. Noting that nowadays the time is right for attending more to symmetries and common interests, in speaking of asymmetries at all David Novak has concentrated on several more technically stated ones. So let us turn at this point to his quite marvelous book, *Talking with Christians*.

In a statement signed by a number of Jewish scholars in 2000, followed up by a book called *Christianity in Jewish Terms*, Rabbi Novak and his colleagues considered the narrower question of Christians living in a Jewish polity and Jews living in a Christian polity. "From a Jewish perspective, the only way that Christians could live in a Jewish polity—governed by Jewish law, that is—would be in sort of resident-alien status, a status held by one whom Scripture calls 'the sojourner in the city' (Ex 20:10)."[2] The same subordination has been experienced by Jews living under the Christian polities of early and medieval Christendom. In other words, the asymmetry between the two religions is such that neither can accept in good faith living under subordination to the other. Jews cannot in good faith accept Christian theories that their own religion has been "superseded" by Christianity, whether in the radical sense of vacating the covenant of Moses with God or in the less severe sense of "a branch grafted onto the tree" (Rom 11:17–24)—but one of those branches grafted so close to the base of the trunk that it virtually takes over, becoming in later years the main part of the tree.

Thus, the asymmetrical relation requires the abandonment of metaphors that suggest one genus to which both religions belong; Rabbi David here mentions "Israel," and I wonder whether even "one people of God" might receive the same stricture. Rather, he and his colleagues propose looking to certain "overlapping commonalities" to carry the conceptual load for the new experiences of amity and the new experiments in cooperation. These overlapping commonalities do not require "prior agreement on principles or agreement on final conclusions."[3] Law and commandments occupy just this territory, intermediate between first principles and the endpoint, or telos. Since first principles in this matter will become clear only at the endpoint, and since the endpoint is shrouded "behind an eschatological horizon," our best present prospects for mutual progress lie in any case in this intermediate territory. And since the three most basic normative categories of the Noahide law and/or the natural-law traditions of some Christians consist of prohibitions against idolatry, bloodshed, and sexual immorality, there will be much common work for Jews and Christians in precisely this territory.

For example, the idolatry of totalitarian power claimed by communism and Nazism in the twentieth century, that is, the absolutizing of the state, leaving no room for the Lord God the Creator of heaven and earth, obliged Jews and Christians to discern in a fresh way the liberating power of religious liberty as the first of all human rights in a secular society, "and to recognize that the denial or the belittling of the human quest for God entails an assault on human dignity and destiny."[4] Simultaneously, though, this struggle against one form of idolatry helped unmask another: the absolutizing of the untrammeled, unconnected, deracinated individual under the "doctrinaire liberal secularism" of the West. Although not by way of atrocities such as those of related forms of secularism, liberal secularism has also been hostile to communal, traditional, and public religions such as Judaism and Christianity. Liberal secularism tries to lock Judaism and Christianity out of the light of public life, in the dark and private recesses of the basement. Here, too, work for religious liberty is demanded of both communities.

In obedience to prohibitions against wanton bloodshed, Jews and Christians also have much to do together, Rabbi David and his colleagues tell us, to achieve in the public square "the broadest possible definition of human personhood in order to include everyone genetically human" within the prohibition against homicide.[5] John Paul II taught that the "common heritage [of Jews and Catholics] drawn from the Law and the Prophets" required a "collaboration in favor of man."[6] They must fight together for an inclusive definition of human rights, expanding rather than contracting the circle of those born of human parents, in the image of God. This battle is especially acute in an age when too many groups claim superiority over other classes of humans in order to terminate them. The strong seek justifications for terminating the weak, the powerful for terminating the powerless.

In days of publicly lauded and highly promoted sexual immorality, it is also necessary for Jews and Christians to come to the defense of family life, the core of all authentic human community, by steadfastly opposing all those degradations of the human body that "Judaism and Christianity teach to be universally prohibited (incest, adultery, homosexuality, and bestiality)."

> All of the prohibited sexual acts contradict the claims of the heterosexually constituted human family to be the exclusive arena for sexuality, with the purpose of conception, birth, and rearing of children (including the lifelong identification of children with their parents' union, even when they themselves are adults).[7]

It is no accident, our authors go on, that "for Jews, Jewish identity is primarily familial; and it is no accident that, for Christians, Jesus was raised in a traditional family."

There is one last point that Rabbi David Novak and his colleagues add that goes beyond a narrow sense of the ethical, although it is an important part of the law and the commandments, namely, the worship of God and the conduct of a lifelong conversation with God.

> Worshiping the same God as we do, and reading the same book [*biblos*] as we do, it is inescapable that our religious ways of life are often parallel. Indeed,

throughout our historical interaction, Christians have learned significant things
from Jewish piety, and Jews have learned significant things from Christian piety.
That is because we have been commanded by the same God. Thus it is the centrality of the same *mitzvah* to us both that offers the greatest content and the
greatest hope for our relationship in this world and the next.[8]

The Jewish scholars rightly qualify this point. We learn from each other in
prayer by analogy, not by identity. Analogy emphasizes essential differences,
even while also emphasizing some significant similarities. If Jews and Christians adopted a common religious life together, one side or the other would
have to capitulate, perhaps only slowly and subtly, but inexorably. This is no
place for syncretism.

Still, both honesty and good faith with each other allow for plenty of room
to learn from each other and to deepen one's own faith by studying deeply in
another's. John Paul noted that "our two religious communities are connected
and closely related at the very level of their respective religious identities."[9]
There are, for certain, many profound lessons for Christians to learn by drinking deeply of the Torah and the other books of the Hebrew Bible, and by
plumbing the original roots, usages, and meanings of key Hebrew words such
as compassion, faith, *shekinah*, contrition, love, penance, and the like. Some
Jews have learned much by studying Christian monastic classics on contemplation, abandonment, and the love of God. There is much to learn about the
Christian Eucharist by celebrating the Passover with Jewish friends, as there
are usually some surprises in store for Jews who discover the Jewish elements
in their first Catholic Mass. In 2000, speaking to the chief rabbis at Hechal
Shlomo in Jerusalem, John Paul gave this exhortation and benediction:
"There is much that we have in common. There is so much that we can do together for peace, for justice, for a more human and fraternal world. May the
Lord of heaven and earth lead us to a new and fruitful era of mutual respect
and cooperation, for the benefit of all!"[10]

ASYMMETRY IN CONVERSION: EDITH STEIN

The tide of feelings and understandings between Christians and Jews, therefore, sometimes flows inward, centripetally, to stress what we can learn from
each other and what we have in common; but at other times that tide flows in
the other direction, outward, centrifugally. There are moments when, in order
to be honest and faithful to ourselves, our judgments and our sympathies dare
not coincide. Our two faiths cannot both be embraced by the same person,
holding to the same communal identity before and after. It may be possible—

it sometimes happens in concrete human experience—that a Christian becomes a Jew, or a Jew a Christian. But this conversion normally means a severe rupture with the earlier community of belonging. For the two communities do not stand upon identical ground, nor do they even face in the same direction. The Jew who becomes a Christian may well have come to believe that Judaism does point beyond itself and into Christianity, and so follow conscience where it leads. Put another way, a Jew who comes to believe that Judaism, no matter how much or how little she used to love and cherish it as the first home of her soul, is by the will of God superceded by Christianity, must become a Christian. Conversely, a Christian who does not believe that Christianity has anything to add to, or that goes beyond, Judaism, is likely sooner or later to ask why he does not become a Jew.

In one vision, Judaism is aimed beyond itself. In the other vision, Judaism is not only a sufficient but a more truthful and morally saner alternative. These two visions are asymmetrical. At some vital and salient points, they do not cover identical spiritual realms but, on the contrary, realms that are mutually contradictory. To be seen embracing one of them is to be seen turning away from the other. But this is to view the conversion from outside.

In real life, people do have conversions, often turbulent conversions, sometimes quiet ones. Among our own families and friends, most of us can probably think of examples in both directions, from Christian to Jew, and from Jew to Christian. We can probably also testify that the experience for the one undergoing the conversion—the *interior* experience—is quite different from what the two external communities, the Jews and the Christians most closely involved with the convert, experience. For example, it may well happen that the Jew who in good conscience becomes a Christian, precisely by believing that Jewishness finds its intended completion in union with Christ, experiences a rush of gratitude for every aspect of his or her Jewish experience as a marvelous preparation for the new experience of living as a Christian. Such a person may feel no insuperable contradiction at all between the earlier and the later belonging, but only a certain preparatory "fit" between the two, as though both belonged in the nature of things to one another. This interior experience is only what one would expect of a genuine conversion, led by the deepest stirrings of personal conscience. The soul would be at rest in its new state, peaceful in its internal pilgrimage.

This internal peace, however, is often the opposite of the pain, confusion, sense of betrayal, noncomprehension, and even anger experienced by that person's parents, siblings, other relatives, and childhood friends, in his or her community of birth and rearing. In these two different experiences of the same act of conversion we encounter yet another, and painful, meaning of "asymmetry."

Rabbi David Novak treats this painful asymmetry profoundly and beauti-fully in a delicate and painstaking essay on the conversion of Edith Stein. Edith Stein, he discerns, "considered herself not a runaway from Judaism (however rudimentary her own Judaism was) but, rather, a Jew whose Ju-daism brought her into the Church. Her logic was clearly supersessionist. How could it have been otherwise?"[11]

Since "supersessionist" is a fighting word to many on both the Jewish and Christian sides today—infuriating some of the former, and embarrassing some of the latter—Novak quickly points out that supersessionism need not lead Christians to denigrate Jews. On the contrary, Christians may believe they ought to learn from Jews, their "elder brothers," as Pope John Paul II liked to call them.[12] Further, they can affirm that just as God made a new covenant with Christians, He did *not* annul his first covenant with the Jews. On the contrary, it is precisely because God, on his side, is everlastingly faith-ful to his covenants, that Christians may have utter trust in Him. Their trust in Him depends on his fidelity to his first love, his firstborn, his first people, his first covenant with the Jews. For if God can break his covenant with the Jews, why should Christians trust that He will be faithful to them, especially in the light of their own falls and betrayals?

Besides all this, there is immense and beautiful continuity between the old law and the new, which repays much close, attentive, and inexhaustible study down the ages. All this and more Rabbi Novak concedes in his long and pen-etrating book. Yet the stubborn asymmetry stares us in the face. We cannot in-voke Edith Stein as patron saint of our dialogue, a bridge between us, "be-cause in this world one cannot be both a faithful Jew and a faithful Catholic in tandem. These necessarily communal identities are mutually exclusive here and now."[13] If we meet under the sign of Edith Stein as we engage in Christ-ian-Jewish dialogue, how will Jewish participants not be placed in a dishon-est position? They cannot pretend to hold to supersessionism without betray-ing their own community, whose communion is based upon an opposite conviction. They cannot take Edith Stein as a model for Jewishness, except insofar as she was a holy and learned person, faithful to conscience.

Thus it happens that the road of converts is very often a lonely road. They "cannot expect the approval of the covenanted community" they have just left. They must go off like Abraham, far from home. They often go without even a peaceful farewell; in fact, quite often the reverse

Rabbi Novak points out that devout Jews may well *em-pathize* with the Catholic community for the entrance into its daily life of a holy, intelligent, and devoted person such as Edith Stein, even as they sorrow that their com-munity has lost so holy a life. But they cannot *sym-pathize* with Catholics.

Jews can *feel for* Catholics in this happy event, but they cannot *feel with* Catholics. They can imagine how Catholics feel, and be glad for them, but in their own hearts they cannot feel the same way as Catholics feel about the action of Edith Stein.

This account captures the existential pain of our asymmetries at a point of high feelings on both sides—high feelings, but different feelings.

In this world of our real existence, Rabbi Novak concludes, "we are still strangers to each other." But, of course, even here we live in the presence of the great Lord and Creator of all things, who sees into our souls. And so he concludes: "It seems that we shall have to remain strangers to each other until God judges us all in the end in a world where we all hope to be the lasting friends of God and thus lasting friends of each other. May that day come speedily, even in our own lifetime on earth!"[14]

THE FEARFUL SYMMETRY

This last sentiment of Rabbi Novak actually limns a beautiful symmetry, a fearful symmetry, which lies behind and gives ground to the asymmetries that have been the focus of these brief reflections. The great Jewish lay philosopher Milton Himmelfarb, who passed into the presence of Yahweh just at New Year, once announced at an agitated meeting and with tremulous voice: "One thing Judaism opposes is paganism." He went on to speak of the difference it makes to a life, and to a civilization, when it is lived in the presence of, and under the undeceivable eye of, the Lord God Jehovah, Creator of all things above and below, within and without. And what a difference it makes to know, really know, that no idol may ever be set in the place of the One True God, before whom no false gods shall be tendered. What a difference the reality of that God made to the idea of limited government and even divided government under watchful checks and balances. And even to private conduct, in the secrecy of one's room, with no other eyes upon oneself.

Judaism taught the world the *mysterium* and *tremendum*. The beginning of wisdom is fear, fear of the Lord. That is also the beginning of tenderness. For one must learn to see all others, even the most humble and vulnerable, as friends of God to be cared for. This perception lies at the heart of the law and the prophets.

In our secular world, most educated people seem to have lost the sense of mystery and all sense of the *tremendum*. (The Latin here suggests "tremendous," yes, but far more profoundly: *Be afraid; be very attentive.*) If there is a replica of the Ten Commandments in a courtroom or in a public park, many educated persons think nothing of it. They accept such things as pagans accept them. Perhaps even they want them banned, because something about such symbols vaguely disturbs them and yet no longer means anything to them—so ban them. But God gave Moses *physical* stones, to be seen and touched and weighed, so that the people would have a visible sign, a sign that told them to be aware of *mysterium*, the all-seeing presence of the Lord God, and *to be afraid*: *tremendum* lest any false gods be placed in the sacred souls of individual citizens. For since these individuals are made in the image of the Lord God Jehovah, the value of each individual exceeds the value of the state, and even of civil society.

Such individuals, for their protection, need limited government. And they need their immortal, inalienable rights protected under the eyes of eternal Justice. These replicas of Moses's commandments, then, are not mere wood, or plaster, or stone. They are physical reminders that are, in effect, the voice of the living God. In the fire of that voice have our liberties been forged.

"One thing Judaism is opposed to is paganism." And so also, its daughter, Christianity. For both of them, the reason for that resistance is the love of the living God, whom paganism would deny, ignore, and disdain. Love and resistance—in that fearful symmetry is inextricably rooted communion between Jews and Christians in this world and the next.

NOTES

1. John Paul II, "The Roots of Anti-Judaism in the Christian Environment," discourse during his visit to the Rome Synagogue (April 13, 1986), http://www.vatican.va/jubilee_2000/magazine/documents/ju_mag_01111997_p-42x_en.html.

2. David Novak, *Talking with Christians: Musings of a Jewish Theologian* (Grand Rapids: Wm. B. Eerdmans, 2005), 40.

3. D. Novak, *Talking with Christians*, 42.

4. D. Novak, *Talking with Christians*, 43.

5. D. Novak, *Talking with Christians*, 43.

6. John Paul II, "To the Synagogue in Rome" (April 13, 1986), in George Weigel, *Witness to Hope* (New York: HarperCollins, 1999), 485.

7. D. Novak, *Talking with Christians*, 44.

8. D. Novak, *Talking with Christians*, 45.

9. John Paul II, meeting with representatives of Roman Jewish organizations (March 12, 1979), in Weigel, *Witness to Hope*, 485.

10. John Paul II, "Visit to the Chief Rabbis at Hechal Shlomo" (March 23, 2000), http://www.vatican.va/holy_father/john_paul_ii/travels/documents/hf_jp-ii_spe_20000323_chief-rabbis_en.html.

11. D. Novak, *Talking with Christians*, 164.

12. "You are our dearly beloved brothers and, in a certain way, it could be said that you are our elder brothers." John Paul II, discourse to the Rome Synagogue (April 13, 1986), http://www.vatican.va/jubilee_2000/magazine/documents/ju_mag_01111997_p-42x_en.html.

13. D. Novak, *Talking with Christians*, 165.

14. D. Novak, *Talking with Christians*, 166.

Part III

BIBLICAL-SYSTEMATIC REFLECTIONS

Chapter Six

Reclaiming God's Providence: John Paul II, Maimonides, and Aquinas

Matthew Levering

To my knowledge, little poetry has been written by Christians about the Holy Land. Karol Wojtyła / John Paul II, here as elsewhere, is an exception. In poems published by Wojtyła / John Paul in his forties and his eighties, the Holy Land plays a significant role. In these poems he envisages the Holy Land as a sign of the need to trust in God's Providence. The Holy Land thus receives a theological interpretation—but one which at first glance might sound rather dull. After all the historical crises connected with the Holy Land, including most recently the *Shoah*, the formation of the state of Israel, and the ongoing violence in the region, why does Wojtyła / John Paul II approach the Holy Land through the lens of divine providence?

His theological interpretation of the Holy Land reflects, I think, his concern about the ramifications of the loss of an understanding of God's Providence in post-Enlightenment cultures. In his last book, *Memory and Identity*, John Paul observes, regarding communism, Nazism, and the culture of death:

> What is the root of these post-Enlightenment ideologies? The answer is simple: it happens because of the rejection of God *qua* Creator, and consequently *qua* source determining what is good and what is evil. It happens because of the rejection of what ultimately constitutes us as human beings, that is, the notion of human nature as a "given reality"; its place has been taken by a "product of thought" freely formed and freely changeable according to circumstances.[1]

Russell Hittinger has similarly contrasted the pre-Enlightenment view of the human creature as "located in an order of divine providence" with modern Enlightenment accounts of human nature in which "natural law came to mean the position of the human mind just insofar as it is left to itself, prior

to authority and law."[2] Thus, trust in divine providence may be more relevant to reflection on the Holy Land than might at first appear.

   This essay will seek to probe this possibility by means of three steps: first,
exploration of John Paul's poetry regarding the Holy Land; second, exploration of Maimonides' understanding of Providence; and third, consideration
of Thomas Aquinas's reflections on Providence and the natural law. This approach no doubt will still seem odd to those accustomed to thinking of the
Holy Land primarily in geopolitical and interreligious terms. As our first section will show, for Wojtyła / John Paul, the poet and pastor, the Holy Land is
first and foremost a reminder—even if at times a difficult and puzzling one—
of God's Providence, which provides the crucial context for understanding
geopolitical and interreligious issues. The meaning of "Providence," for Jews
and Christians, will then be unpacked in the second and third sections through
attention to the great medieval thinkers Moses Maimonides and Thomas
Aquinas. These latter two sections seek to uncover the theological and philosophical underpinnings of John Paul's pastoral account of the kind of place
that the Holy Land is.

KAROL WOJTYŁA / JOHN PAUL II
ON THE HOLY LAND

In his cycle of poems "Journey to the Holy Places," published in 1965 under
the pen name Andrzej Jawien, Karol Wojtyła connects the Holy Land not simply with Jesus Christ, but first of all with the person of Abraham. As a wan-
derer, Abraham embodies the journey of each person toward God: "A whole
people must repeat and repeat again the wanderings of Abraham."[3] Abraham
is "a man of the great encounter."[4] This great encounter with God requires
that human beings learn to journey in complete trust of God's plan. It requires
also that, by their outward wanderings, human beings steel themselves for the
journey inward to God in their soul. Yet Wojtyła fears that modern conven-
iences have left human beings unprepared for such difficult journeys, for the
wandering that is trusting in God. He asks, "Have we distanced ourselves
from the hardship of wanderings, transferring the barrenness of old earth to
the wide open spaces?"[5] Abraham's wandering, his trust in God, contrasts
with modern cities, which have few spiritual roots. Even though it seems we
are more settled, we are less so. We who live in cities must return again and
again to Abraham's wandering, so as to apprehend how our lives together
have meaning. This meaning is found only in journeying in the presence of
God—and ultimately, Wojtyła suggests, in the Cross as the ultimate self-
abandoning to God's Providence.

The same theme of divine providence marks Wojtyła's poetic reflections on why this particular land is "holy." The Holy Land, for Wojtyła the pilgrim, *draws* human beings into its providential meaning. Pilgrimage to the Holy Land indicates one's desire to share more deeply in how God has known and loved human beings in the earthly place of the Holy Land. The earthly place thereby becomes also an interior place: God's providential plan, enacted in the Holy Land, is now enacted in the heart of the believing pilgrim. Wojtyła writes,

> Oh, corner of the earth, place in the holy land—what kind of place are you in me? My steps cannot tread on you; I must kneel. Thus I confirm today you were indeed a place of meeting. Kneeling down I imprint a seal on you. You will re-main here with my seal—you will remain—and I will take you and transform you within me into the place of new testimony. I walk away as a witness who testifies across the millennia.[6]

Wojtyła thus can rejoice at seeing a well in the Holy Land both because it reminds him of the wells built by the patriarchs and the meeting of Jesus with the Samaritan woman at the well, and because he himself encounters God at the well. By seeing the visible Holy Land around him, he finds himself more attentive to the reality that he, too, is an actor in God's providential plan. He explains, "I am on a pilgrimage to identity. . . . This is the identity of finding one's own self in landscape. Here I come on a pilgrimage. And this place is holy."[7] The landscape is the view from Mount Tabor, the sights of Galilee, Lake Genezareth, and so forth; but it is also the inner landscape in which one's pilgrimage to the Holy Land becomes a more conscious entering into God's providential plan as realized in these very places. In turn, the pilgrim becomes increasingly able to share the Holy Land with others. As Wojtyła puts it, "Oh, place, you have to be carried to many, so many places."[8] He knows well that "since those times the sand has run interminably through over and over again. Not a grain is left."[9] Nonetheless carrying stones from the Holy Land is, he recognizes, a way to share his faith in God: He tells that he carried some stones from the shore of Lake Genezareth back to Poland and put them "in the hardworking hand of a fisherman by the Notec River."[10]

A connection with the earthly place of the Holy Land enables us to recog-nize more deeply that God gives us, too, a place in his providential plan. In Wojtyła's words, "A place, the place is important, the place is holy." He ex-plains that pilgrims do not fill the Holy Land with their own personalities, but rather pilgrims are marked and filled by the identity of the Holy Land as the earthly expression of God's plan. As Wojtyła says in another poem about the desert of Judea: "Land of meeting, the one and only land, through which all earth became this land, as everything became that which it is through Him

Who Is."[11] All comes into being through the Creator; all receives its full identity in and through the deeds accomplished in the Holy Land. The Holy Land is the place where God fulfills his plan for union with humankind. It follows that the Holy Land is not solely an earthly place but a place that expresses God's active wisdom and love for human beings. Speaking to God, Wojtyła remarks, "You chose this place centuries ago—the place in which You give Yourself and accept me."[12] Or as he says in the same vein in the first poem of this cycle: "And today, why do I come? Don't be surprised. Here for nineteen hundred years each gaze passes into that one gaze which never alters."[13]

In 2003 Wojtyła, as Pope John Paul II, published a last set of poems, titled *Roman Triptych: Meditations*. The first poem of the triptych places John Paul in his beloved mountains wondering how the created order both discloses and hides God. The second poem places him in the Sistine Chapel meditating upon the Book of Genesis, upon the human being as the image of God capable of self-giving love, and upon his own death and the selection of the successor to the Apostle Peter. Finally, the third poem places him on pilgrimage in the land of Abraham. In these three poems John Paul moves from the wonder of the philosopher, to the revelation that human life is in the divine image of God the Creator, to the original revelation of God's redemptive plan.

The third poem, therefore, carries forward his earlier poetic meditations on the Holy Land and on his own experience of pilgrimage. He writes, "If today we go to these places whence, long ago, Abraham set out, where he heard the Voice, where the promise was fulfilled, we do so in order to stand at the threshold—to go back to the beginning of the Covenant."[14] The threshold, for John Paul, is the place of hope for the fulfillment of the promise, of trust that God will accomplish his plan. Each human being must stand at this place. As a place on earth, the Holy Land inspires each human being to trust God. John Paul focuses our attention upon the land of Moriah where God commanded Abraham to sacrifice Isaac, his beloved son and the son of the promise. It would appear that the Holy Land is a place of terrifying renunciation. Yet in the land of Moriah, Abraham finds the meaning of the Holy Land: a complete reliance on God to accomplish his plan for us. Abraham's hopes center upon the continuance of his line in Isaac, and yet Abraham finds fulfillment by his willingness to let these hopes go and to trust God. Abraham learns in the land of Moriah "what it means for a father to sacrifice his own son—a sacrificial death."[15] The beloved Son's free and loving sacrificial offering of himself stands at the heart of God's providential plan in which human beings are transformed from self-centered to self-giving.

For Karol Wojtyła / John Paul II, therefore, the fact that a particular land on earth is called "holy" indicates that human beings, in our brief sojourns on Earth, have a "place" where our lives are measured and valued not by time but by the eternity of divine wisdom. In order to find this "place," each human being must learn, like Abraham, to entrust his or her "wanderings" to God, to enter upon a life that is sacrificial. To meditate upon and make pilgrimage to the Holy Land is to allow oneself to be filled by the guidance of God's wisdom and to find a "place" within God's plan, rather than vainly seeking to establish a permanent place in the world on one's own. The Holy Land provides a sign that human beings receive their path from God's wisdom, rather than constructing autonomously their own paths.

Wojtyła / John Paul's insistence, in his poetic reflections on the Holy Land, on the necessity of a God-centered life—a life by which we enter more and more deeply into our "place" (the land of encounter with God and union with him) in God's providential plan—invites further investigation of the understanding of Providence in the Jewish and Christian tradition. For Wojtyła / John Paul, recovering a God-centered account of human life is crucial to the renewal of both Jewish and Christian belief and practice, and thus also to the renewal of a theological understanding of the "Holy Land" as more than a place of geopolitical conflict. What theological and philosophical resources for this recovery, intimated poetically by Wojtyła / John Paul as a pastor, are found in the writings of Maimonides and Aquinas?[16]

MAIMONIDES ON DIVINE PROVIDENCE

Maimonides approaches the reality of God's Providence in light of the problem of the suffering of the just. Following Alexander Aphrodisiensis's summary in his treatise *On Providence*, Maimonides recounts some ancient philosophers' denial of an omniscient God. He observes, "The principal reason that first induced the philosophers to adopt their theory is this: at first thought we notice an absence of system in human affairs. Some pious men live a miserable and painful life, whilst some wicked people enjoy a happy and pleasant life."[17] If the good suffer and the wicked flourish, the ancient philosophers reasoned that either God is ignorant, or else he knows; and if the latter, either he knows and arranges matters perfectly, or he knows but is powerless, or he knows but despite sufficient power does not care to help. Of these three alternatives, says Maimonides, the last two are clearly unworthy of God, and so it comes down to either God knows and arranges matters perfectly, or else God is ignorant. The ancient philosophers who pondered this problem, in finding that human affairs do not seem (by and large) to be well arranged, concluded that God is ignorant of them.

Maimonides, naturally, is rather scandalized by this conclusion. He points out, first, that such philosophers "have fallen into a greater evil than that from which they sought to escape, because they refuse to say that God neglects or forgets a thing, and yet they maintain that his knowledge is imperfect, that he is ignorant of what is going on here on earth, that he does not perceive it."[18] Second, they ignore their own principle that human suffering originates either in human beings' material principle or in the human will. Maimonides grants that they base their judgment about God's lack of knowledge on philosophically sophisticated claims: They argue that God, since his knowledge does not depend upon the senses, can know only the species, not individuals (differentiated by matter); and similarly they argue that since God's knowledge, like his being, is one, he can know only himself rather than many things. Yet for Maimonides they err not only philosophically, by implying imperfection in God, but also by differing with the teaching of Scripture.

Having identified, and registered preliminary disagreement with, the key problem with the doctrine of Providence—namely the apparent disorder in the world—Maimonides (still following Alexander) proceeds to set forth briefly four ancient philosophical theories of Providence. The first, credited to Epicurus, is that there is no Providence, but rather there is solely chance; Maimonides relies upon Aristotle in rejecting this view. The second Maimonides attributes to Aristotle: The unchanging spheres, the unchanging species, and individuals insofar as they possess natural inclinations are governed by divine providence, but other movements of individuals belong strictly to chance and are not governed by Providence. Maimonides applies to Aristotle's view a text from Ezekiel: "It is the belief of those who turned away from our Law, and said: 'God hath forsaken the earth' (Ez 9:9)."[19]

The third and fourth theories belong to distinct groups of Muslim thinkers, the Ashariyah and the Mu'tazila respectively. In the third theory, God causes everything, including all natural processes and all sufferings. Everything that happens is ultimately necessary, even if it appears, from the human perspective, that there are multiple possibilities. Maimonides holds that this view not only takes away the truth of free will but also thereby leaves God fully responsible for all injustice. This aspect makes the theory intolerable for Maimonides:

> When we see a person born blind or leprous, who could not have merited a punishment for previous sins, they say, It is the will of God; when a pious worshipper is tortured and slain, it is likewise the will of God; and no injustice can be asserted to Him for that, for according to their opinion it is proper that God should afflict the innocent and do good to the sinner.[20]

Such a God would be arbitrary and unjust. The fourth theory affirms human free will, God's supreme justice, and God's Providence over all things. Maimonides again finds "contradictions and absurdities" in this theory. He won-

ders, for instance, whether it can really succeed in accounting for human suffering as truly good for the sufferer. In particular, however, he focuses upon
questioning God's Providence over nonhuman creatures:

> We ask them why is God only just to man and not to other beings, and how has
> the irrational animal sinned, that it is condemned to be slaughtered? and they re-
> ply it is good for the animal, for it will receive reward for it in the world to
> come; also the flea and the louse will there receive compensation for their un-
> timely death: the same reasoning they apply to the mouse torn by a cat or vul-
> ture; the wisdom of God decreed for the mouse, in order to reward it after death
> for the mishap.[21]

For Maimonides, it seems absurd to suggest that God has indeed cared for the
irrational animal in allowing its violent and painful destruction.

Maimonides admires elements of each of the last three theories. From Aristotle he takes respect for common-sense observation of the world around us;
from the Ashariyah, God's omniscience; and from the Mu'tazilites, God's justice. To these elements, Maimonides, in proposing his own theory, adds the
view that

> in the lower or sublunary portion of the universe, divine providence does not ex-
> tend to the individual members of species except in the case of mankind. It is
> only in this species that the incidents in the existence of the individual beings,
> their good and evil fortunes, are the result of justice, in accordance with the
> words, "For all his ways are judgment" [Dt 32:4].[22]

Maimonides thinks that God's universal Providence over human beings as
well as God's perfect justice in this regard are confirmed beyond doubt by
Scripture. For God's universal Providence over human beings he adduces
Psalm 33:15: "He fashioneth their hearts alike, he considereth all their
works"; Jeremiah 32:19: "For thine eyes are open upon all the ways of the
sons of men, to give every one according to his ways"; and Job 32:21: "For
his eyes are upon the ways of man, and he seeth all his goings."[23] Similarly,
he argues that the entire histories of Abraham, Isaac, and Jacob confirm God's
perfect Providence over human beings. Regarding the perfect justice of God's
Providence over human beings, he appeals to texts from the Torah that describe God's promise to judge human sins; see Exodus 32:33–34 and Leviti-
cus 20:6, 23:30, and 26:16. To this degree, then, the Ashariyah and the Mu'-
tazilites are correct.

By means of Aristotle and Scripture, however, Maimonides seeks to avoid
the difficulties found in the Muslim accounts, which, as we have seen, Maimonides fears leave insufficient room for free will or for the confused state
of the world. The key scriptural passages, Maimonides holds, come from the

Psalms: "What is man, that thou takest knowledge of him?" (Ps 144:3) and "What is man, that thou art mindful of him" (Ps 8:8). These psalms suggest that while human beings are (however undeservedly) fully known by God, other less important things need not be fully known. Maimonides agrees with Aristotle, in other words, that some things happen by chance. As Maimonides puts it with delightful verve, "nor do I hold that when a certain spider catches a certain fly, that this is the direct result of a special decree and will of God in that moment; it is not by a particular divine decree that the spittle of a certain person moved, fell on a certain gnat in a certain place, and killed it."[24] This view absolves God from particular providential care for animals and thereby makes morally intelligible the slaughtering of animals by human beings.

Moreover, this view corresponds with the words of the prophet Habakkuk. Habakkuk, as Maimonides notes, observes that it might appear that God, by allowing the idolatrous Chaldeans to destroy the righteous among the people of God, is making "men like the fish of the sea, like crawling things that have no ruler" (Hab 1:14) and are indiscriminately killed by the fisherman. Habakkuk goes on to state that in fact God is using the Chaldeans as instruments of punishing justly the sins of his people. In the context of Maimonides' argument, the point is that while fish do not have a (providential) ruler, human beings do. As in the Psalms, Maimonides finds here a scriptural referent for limiting the doctrine of divine providence to human beings. It follows that although many events necessarily occur by chance, the involvement of human beings in these events always introduces the aspect of divine providence. Thus a shipwreck, Maimonides says, may be the product of a chance weather pattern, but the deaths of particular human beings on that ship belong firmly to the governance of divine providence.[25]

Why does Maimonides give human beings this special prerogative? Certainly the warrant of Scripture would suffice, but Maimonides also offers a reason.[26] "Divine providence," he states, "is connected with divine intellectual influence, and the same beings which are benefited by the latter so as to become intellectual, and to comprehend things comprehensible to rational beings, are also under the control of divine providence, which examines all their deeds in order to reward or punish them."[27] Because human beings are intellectual creatures, they have received the benefits of God's wisdom, a certain receptive sharing in God's wisdom. Therefore they are answerable to the divine wisdom in all their acts. Their acts are free: By God's will human beings have free will, and so human acts are their responsibility. Precisely as the rational acts of free creatures who have been gifted by God's wisdom and will, then, human actions must accord with God's wisdom and will. For Maimonides, God judges human acts with "strict justice," albeit inscrutable;

every pain is a freely merited punishment, and every pleasure a freely merited reward.

While Maimonides finds this affirmed by the law and by the rabbinic tradition, he makes clear that human responsibility and God's justice apply to everyone, not merely to those who have received the law: "He [God] will reward the most pious for all their pure and upright actions, although no direct commandment was given them through a prophet; and . . . he will punish all the evil deeds of men, although they have not been prohibited by a prophet, if common sense warns against them, as for example, injustice and violence."[28] The reason that God's absolute Providence (or governance) and justice apply to all human beings, not solely to those who have received the Mosaic law, is that in receiving intellect and free will human beings have received an ability to understand and freely will actions that befit God's wisdom and will. Human beings, and human beings alone, are therefore properly disposed to be governed by divine providence. God's Providence strictly governs each human being, while leaving other created things to chance, because human beings bear the influence of divine wisdom and have freedom, and so can do good or evil.

Some scriptural passages, Maimonides admits, seem to suggest that divine providence extends even to irrational creatures. He gives examples of such texts from three psalms: "He giveth to the beast his food" (Ps 147:9); "The young lions roar after their prey, and seek their meat from God" (Ps 104:21); and "Thou openest thine hand, and satisfiest the desire of every living thing" (Ps 145:16). Maimonides grants that God has complete providential knowledge of all species; each species is governed by God toward its end. Since God knows all species, he knows everything; Maimonides frequently insists that he accepts the doctrine of God's omniscience as flowing from God's intelligence as the Creator. Only as regards human beings, however, does God have knowledge of particular individuals in the species, so that he might govern each human being toward its end.

Such governance is necessary for human beings, who by rationally and freely choosing good and avoiding evil attain their end and thereby participate in their own governance. But the governance of individual animals, who lack this rationality, is not necessary for their attainment of their end; it suffices for God to govern the species. For the cow, in other words, it suffices to be a cow and to receive what pertains to the species. Individual human beings, in contrast, merit reward and punishment by their intelligent and free choices. Maimonides seems to be sensitive to concerns that excluding individuals of other species from God's providential care might seem to deprive them of their proper dignity as living and sensate creatures. He therefore emphasizes that his position does not mean that human beings can rightly be cruel to individuals of other species.

Maimonides also elaborates in an important manner upon the reason for the privilege of human beings. Observing that only individuals, not species, truly exist, he holds that "the result of the existing divine influence, that reaches mankind through the human intellect, is identical with individual intellects really in existence, with which, for example, Zeid, Amr, Kaled, and Bekr are endowed."[29] The "divine influence" thus in this case governs the end of individuals, rather than solely the end of the species, because the divine influence "is identical with individual intellects really in existence." Divine providence governs human beings toward the good to the degree that human beings come to share intellectually in the "divine influence." Maimonides states that "the greater the share is which a person has obtained of this divine influence, on account of both his physical predisposition and his training, the greater must also be the effect of divine Providence upon him, for the action of divine Providence is proportional to the endowment of intellect."[30]

Maimonides explains prophecy, and indeed all intellectual and moral virtue, in this way. Prophets share profoundly in divine providence because their minds are profoundly receptive to the divine wisdom, so that they can apprehend the good that God wills for human beings; and all wise and good human beings possess in varying degrees this greater share in divine providence. As Maimonides puts it,

> The relation of divine providence is therefore not the same to all men; the greater the human perfection a person has attained, the greater the benefit he derives from divine providence. . . . For it is the intensity of the divine intellectual influence that has inspired the prophets, guided the good in their actions, and perfected the wisdom of the pious.[31]

The more one's intellect is perfected, the more one apprehends and participates in divine providence's governance of human beings toward the good. The human intellect is a real participation in God's providential governance:

> I hold that divine providence is related and closely connected with the intellect, because Providence can only proceed from an intelligent being, from a being that is itself the most perfect Intellect. Those creatures, therefore, which receive part of that intellectual influence, will become subject to the action of Providence in the same proportion as they are acted upon by the Intellect.[32]

Divine Intellect, in acting upon and being participated by individual human intellects, communicates divine providence to human beings who are thereby enabled to know the good and to attain their end. Were one to lack such an account of divine providence as participated intellectually by human beings, Maimonides warns, one would undermine the foundations of human moral and intellectual virtues.

Good human beings receive and nourish the divine intellectual influence; bad human beings ignore and neglect it. The latter degenerate to the level of animals, and, in their wickedness, can be justifiably killed. Maimonides remarks, "In the same proportion as ignorant and disobedient persons are deficient in that divine influence, their condition is inferior, and their rank equal to that of irrational beings; and they are 'like unto the beasts' (Ps 49:21)."[33] In contrast to the wicked, the good are blessed by the guiding influence of divine providence, and their minds are uplifted so that they know what is good. To exemplify those who live according to reason and thereby conform to the wisdom of divine Providence, Maimonides turns both to the lives of the patriarchs and to the insights of the ancient Greek philosophers. Regarding the latter, he notes, "Abu-nasr, in the introduction to his *Commentary on Aristotle's Nicomachean Ethics*, says as follows: — Those who possess the faculty of raising their souls from virtue to virtue obtain, according to Plato, divine protection to a higher degree."[34] Regarding the former, he observes God's special promises of protection to Abraham (Gn 15:1), Isaac (Gn 26:3), and Jacob (Gn 28:15). The same holds for the highest prophet, Moses (Ex 3:12), and for Joshua (Jos 1:5). God's Providence is, in this view, the influence of the divine intellect upon human intellects; some persons receive and appropriate this influence more than other persons, and thereby merit a greater reward — divine protection from suffering — in this life. For Maimonides, then, suffering in this life manifests a lack of conformity to divine providence; he argues that "Providence protects good and pious men, and abandons fools; 'He will keep the feet of his saints, and the wicked shall be silent in darkness; for by strength shall no man prevail' (1 Sam 2:9)."[35] He cites also Psalm 34:16, 21, and Psalm 91:15.

It should be clear that by the end of his discussion of divine providence Maimonides has arrived at a doctrine of natural law, although he does not use the phrase. Throughout his discussion, Maimonides is concerned with the twin problems of God's governance (and knowledge) and creaturely disorder. The key point for our purposes is that Maimonides refuses to attempt to solve the problem strictly on the side of the creature. Rather, he affirms:

> I do not ascribe to God ignorance of anything or any kind of weakness; I hold that divine providence is related and closely connected with the intellect, because Providence can only proceed from an intelligent being, from a being that is itself the most perfect Intellect. Those creatures, therefore, which receive part of that intellectual influence, will become subject to the action of Providence in the same proportion as they are acted upon by the Intellect.[36]

The rational creature's passive reception of "part of that [divine] intellectual influence" comes about by the action of divine wisdom upon the creature.

This action of divine wisdom in granting the creature "part of that intellectual influence" is, Maimonides says, "the action of Providence" in the creature.

God's action, then, is primary throughout in enabling human (participatory) action. Human beings, on this view, do not constitute the natural law, nor can the natural law be understood abstracted from God's action. On the contrary, God's action in bestowing a share in the divine intellect, upon which depends the "action of divine providence," enables the rational creature increasingly to attain perfection in wisdom and thus to manifest "the effect of divine providence," namely an ability to act in accord with reason, to do the good and to avoid evil. As Maimonides remarks, "For it is the intensity of the divine intellectual influence that has inspired the prophets, guided the good in their actions, and perfected the wisdom of the pious."[37] The "effect of divine providence"—what one might call the natural law—is thus the passive participation in divine action. It is fundamentally received, not constructed. In other words, Maimonides' account of Providence and its effect—an account shaped by philosophical, Islamic, and biblical sources—provides a God-centered account of human participatory action.

AQUINAS ON PROVIDENCE IN LIGHT OF MAIMONIDES

For Maimonides, God providentially governs human beings in all aspects of their lives, and God does so particularly by acting upon human beings so that some participate more in the divine intellect (and thus in divine providential governance) and others less, to the degree that some persons no longer participate in the divine intellect. Maimonides also argues that God's Providence does not extend to nonrational creatures. While both Maimonides and Aquinas recognize the centrality of God's action in enabling human beings to participate in the divine wisdom, two points merit at least brief exploration here: Aquinas holds that the natural law can be obscured but not expunged in human beings, and he affirms, somewhat like the Muslim thinkers with whom Maimonides is arguing, that God's Providence extends to everything.

Regarding whether the natural law can be expunged in particular human beings, Aquinas begins with the gloss on Romans 2:14, a key New Testament locus for reflection on natural law. Romans 2:14 states, "When Gentiles who have not the law do by nature what the law requires, they are a law to themselves, even though they do not have the law." The gloss on this passage, according to Aquinas, comments that "the law of righteousness, which sin had blotted out, is graven on the heart of man when he is restored by grace."[38] It seems from this gloss that the natural law can be expunged from human beings on account of sin, just as mortal sin entirely cuts human beings off from the relationship of grace. Certainly this is Maimonides' position: Human beings can behave so irrationally and idolatrously as to be entirely removed from the divine intellectual influence. Aquinas's response is based upon an appeal to human nature as a created gift: "Although grace is more efficacious than nature, yet nature is more essential to man, and therefore more enduring."[39] Since integral human nature is a body-soul unity, to remove human practical rationality would be to obliterate human nature.

Without question, God can obliterate his gift of human nature. Aquinas's point is that human beings cannot do it. God alone can obliterate what he has given; human beings cannot change their own natures into something radically different, even by the most atrocious and bestial sins. The general principles of natural law—for example, self-preservation, to know the truth, and so forth—cannot be expunged from the person because practical reason, in apprehending (as applied to action) the teleological ordering of the person to the common good, discerns certain basic truths regarding action that bear the character of law, of a "rule or measure of acts." These principles can, however, be ignored and effaced in particular actions, "in so far as reason is hindered from applying the general principle to a particular point of practice, on account of concupiscence or some other passion."[40] Moreover, the secondary precepts of the natural law, which practical reason attains by way of reasoning to conclusions, can be entirely expunged by sin or by bad instruction, since these precepts are not immediately apprehended but rather require a process of reasoning.[41]

Regarding the extent of divine providence, Aquinas engages Maimonides' position directly.[42] In favor of Maimonides' position, he cites a text from none other than St. Paul: "Is it for oxen that God is concerned?" (1 Cor 9:9; in Aquinas's Latin version, "God does not care for oxen").[43] Thus Aquinas indicates that he will agree with a significant portion of Maimonides' claim, even while disagreeing with Maimonides that the issue necessitates removing God's Providence from nonrational creatures. As Aquinas notes, "Since a rational creature has, through its free will, control over its actions . . . it is subject to divine providence in an especial manner, so that something is imputed to it as a fault, or as a merit; and there is given it accordingly something by way of punishment and reward."[44] Because of human participation (as instrumental causes) in divine providence, it is correct to distinguish, as Maimonides does, between God's providential care for rational and nonrational creatures. Furthermore, Aquinas thinks that Maimonides also rightly emphasizes that holy and wise persons participate more deeply in God's Providence than do sinful and ignorant persons. As Aquinas puts it, again citing St. Paul: "God . . . extends his Providence over the just in a certain more excellent way than over the wicked; inasmuch as he prevents anything happening which would impede their final salvation. For *to them that love God, all things work together unto good* (Rom 8:28)."[45]

Like St. Paul, Aquinas accounts for God's special providential care for holy and wise persons not in terms of the divine gift of natural wisdom, as Maimonides does, but in terms of the gratuitous gift of grace; and yet both Aquinas and Maimonides arrive at the conclusion of special providential care. Similarly, Aquinas can agree up to a certain point with Maimonides' claim that God leaves some persons bereft of a connection with his providential influence: "[F]rom the fact that he does not restrain the wicked from the evil of sin, he is said to abandon them: not that he altogether withdraws his providence from them; otherwise they would return to nothing, if they were not preserved in existence by his Providence."[46] The wicked do indeed fail, foolishly, to participate in God's providence as they should. For Maimonides and Aquinas, the wicked are brought within the order of God's Providence by means of the justice of punishment, which the wicked freely merit. To deny that God's Providence governs the wicked through punishment, in Maimonides' view, would be to deny the justice of God and thereby deny (when carried to its conclusions) the existence of real justice at all, with devastating consequences.

Maimonides, however, does not see how "justice" can apply to, for instance, the drowned gnat. God can be said to care for and govern providentially human beings because human beings clearly merit reward or punishment, and so God's justice makes sense of what happens to human beings. But in the case of the gnat, why, Maimonides asks, should its early demise embody any aspect of just governance? Numerous evils simply seem outside the order of justice and thus outside the order of governance. Aquinas argues in response to this problem: "It is otherwise with one who has care of a particular thing, and one whose providence is universal, because a particular provider excludes all defects from what is subject to his care as far as he can; whereas, one who provides universally allows some little defect to remain, lest the good of the whole would be hindered."[47] As examples of God's permission of defect in service of the common good, Aquinas mentions the lion, whose good requires the slaying of other animals, and also the death of the martyrs, by whose witness the saving gospel of Christ spreads. Such permitted defects, whether the lions are eating other animals or eating human martyrs, belong within the justice of the common good that God, through the missions of the Son and Holy Spirit, is accomplishing by bringing the rebellious and suffering world to its ultimate end in God. Until the eschaton, only God fully knows this common good, and God's permission does not justify evil actions, which in themselves are ordered to the common good through punishment. God in Christ has taken upon himself this punishment, through the satisfaction accomplished by his Cross; and by Christ's resurrection God has made manifest the first fruits of the common good for which he created the universe.

Ultimately God possesses universal Providence because he is the Creator: Since creatures are finite participations in God's own being, God must from eternity know and will every created reality. The gnat, and its death, has its place in the justice of the common good. As Aquinas observes,

> A thing can escape the order of a particular cause; but not the order of a universal cause. For nothing escapes the order of a particular cause, except through the intervention and hindrance of some other particular cause. . . . Since then, all particular causes are included under the universal cause, it could not be that any effect should take place outside the range of that universal cause.[48]

God's universal causality governs both particular nonrational (and thus "necessary") causes and particular rational, free causes.[49]

Does this mean that God does everything directly, thereby making a mockery of human free will, as Maimonides fears? Certainly, Aquinas holds that God "governs all the acts and movements that are to be found in each single creature"; otherwise, God would not truly be the intelligent Creator, the giver and sustainer of all finite being, which is a participation in him and which he directs to its goal, the goal that moved him to create.[50] As Aquinas explains: "[I]n every governor there must pre-exist the type of the order of those things that are to be done by those who are subject to his government."[51] This means that God, from eternity, knows all that he creates, not only as regards their being, but also as regards their action (which flows from being). It is this that makes God a lawgiver: "Wherefore as the type of divine Wisdom, inasmuch as by It all things are created, has the character of art, exemplar, or idea; so the type of divine Wisdom, as moving all things to their due end, bears the character of law."[52] Yet there is no reason that this action, on the part of rational creatures, cannot be free. Indeed, natural law is precisely this participation of free creatures in God's eternal law. God's providential governance enables him both to know all things as ordered to their end, and to bestow upon creatures the dignity of causality, which in rational creatures is a free causality—although as created, sustained in being, and teleologically governed, not an autonomous causality.[53]

CONCLUSION

Has anything been gained by placing Karol Wojtyła / John Paul II's poetic and pastoral understanding of the Holy Land in the context of the philosophical and theological accounts of divine providence and natural law offered by Maimonides and Aquinas? Recall Karol Wojtyła / John Paul's words: "I come across these places which You [God] have filled with Yourself once and for all. I do not come to fill them with my own self, but to be filled. Oh, place, you have to be carried to many, so many places."[54] The Holy Land is the "place" where God manifests and accomplishes his teleological governance of the world, his ordering of our lives to the end of union with him—what Wojtyła / John Paul calls "meeting": "Land of meeting, the one and only land, through which all earth became this land, as everything became that which it is through Him Who Is."[55] Reflecting on the meaning of the Holy Land today recalls us to the reality that our lives, in order to find their true "place," must be God-centered. Like Abraham, human beings become receptive to God's guidance so as to attain this "meeting." The Holy Land signals to all believers that despite human violence, God is accomplishing in human history this teleological "meeting."

In their reflections upon God's providence and natural law, Maimonides and Aquinas teach us, with John Paul, how to understand the world as the locus of "meeting" and thus to understand how we, as creatures, may enter more and more deeply into God's providential plan by obeying his life-giving law.

NOTES

1. John Paul II, *Memory and Identity: Conversations at the Dawn of a Millennium* (New York: Rizzoli, 2005), 12. John Paul continues, "I believe that a more careful study of this question could lead us beyond the Cartesian watershed. If we wish to speak rationally about good and evil, we have to return to Saint Thomas Aquinas, that is, to the philosophy of being. With the phenomenological method, for example, we can study experiences of morality, religion, or simply what it is to be human, and draw from them a significant enrichment of our knowledge. Yet we must not forget that all these analyses implicitly presuppose the reality of the Absolute Being and also the reality of being human, that is, being a creature. If we do not set out from such 'realist' presuppositions, we end up in a vacuum" (12). Cf. his remarks at the Yad Vashem Holocaust Memorial in Jerusalem on March 23, 2000: "How could man have such utter contempt for man? Because he had reached the point of contempt for God. Only a godless ideology could plan and carry out the extermination of a whole people." *John Paul II in the Holy Land: In His Own Words*, eds. Lawrence Boadt, C.S.P., and Kevin di Camillo (New York: Paulist Press, 2005), 99–100.

2. Russell Hittinger, *The First Grace: Rediscovering the Natural Law in a Post-Christian World* (Wilmington, DE: ISI Books, 2003), xi–xii.

3. Karol Wojtyła, "One Tree," in *The Place Within: The Poetry of Pope John Paul II*, by Karol Wojtyła, trans. Jerzy Peterkiewicz (New York: Random House, 1982), 116.

I wish to thank Piotr Lichacz, O.P., for checking the English translations of Wojtyla/ John Paul's poetry.

4. Wojtyła, "One Tree."

5. Wojtyła, "One Tree."

6. Wojtyła, "Identities," in *The Place Within*, 114–15.

7. Wojtyła, "Identities," 115.

8. Wojtyła, "Identities," 114.

9. Wojtyła, "Identities," 114.

10. Wojtyła, "Identities," 115.

11. Wojtyła, "The Desert of Judea," in *The Place Within*, 113.

12. Wojtyła, "The Place Within," in *The Place Within*, 118.

13. Wojtyła, "Mount of Olives," in *The Place Within*, 111.

14. John Paul II, "A Hill in the Land of Moriah," in *The Poetry of John Paul II. Roman Triptych: Meditations*, by John Paul II, trans. Jerzy Peterkiewicz (Washington, DC: United States Conference of Catholic Bishops, 2003), 35.

15. John Paul II, "A Hill in the Land of Moriah."

16. David Novak observes that while many modern commentators emphasize Maimonides' influence on Aquinas's metaphysical thought, nonetheless "one could well argue that the influence of Maimonides on Aquinas was far more extensive in the area of practical reason, which covers the joint area of ethics and politics" (Novak, "Maimonides and Aquinas on Natural Law," in *Talking with Christians: Musings of a Jewish Theologian*, by David Novak [Grand Rapids, MI: Eerdmans, 2005], 68). Novak goes on to expose the profound influence of Maimonides' *Guide for the Perplexed* on Aquinas's treatise on law in the *Summa theologiae*, although he wishes that Aquinas had also been able to read Maimonides' *Mishneh Torah*.

17. Moses Maimonides, *The Guide for the Perplexed*, trans. M. Friedländer, 2nd ed. (1904; New York: Dover, 1956), 280 (pt. 3, ch. 16).

18. Maimonides, *The Guide for the Perplexed*, 281. David Novak has argued that "the relationship [between God and human beings] Maimonides constitutes is more than anything else a relation *to* a God who seems to closely resemble the God of Aristotle. It is a relation where only God and not man is the object of love. All concern is in one direction: from man to God. Maimonides in no way ever attempts to constitute a truly responsive role for God. There is no real reciprocity here. But the covenant is surely characterized by constant transaction between God and Israel, with that activity being mutual" (D. Novak, *Natural Law in Judaism* [Cambridge: Cambridge University Press, 1998], 135). At least as regards God's knowledge, Maimonides' God is not the God of Aristotle.

19. Maimonides, *The Guide for the Perplexed*, 283.

20. Maimonides, *The Guide for the Perplexed*, 284.

21. Maimonides, *The Guide for the Perplexed*, 284.

22. Maimonides, *The Guide for the Perplexed*, 286.

23. Maimonides, *The Guide for the Perplexed*, 287.

24. Maimonides, *The Guide for the Perplexed*, 286.

25. Maimonides, *The Guide for the Perplexed*, 287.

26. On Maimonides' use of reason and revelation, see David Novak, "Maimonides' Teleology of the Law," ch. 4 of his *Natural Law in Judaism*.

27. Maimonides, *The Guide for the Perplexed*, 287.

28. Maimonides, *The Guide for the Perplexed*, 286.

29. Maimonides, *The Guide for the Perplexed*, 289 (ch. 18).

30. Maimonides, *The Guide for the Perplexed*, 289.

31. Maimonides, *The Guide for the Perplexed*, 289. Again this point seems to me to provide for the covenantal mutual relation that Novak rightly requires but finds lacking in Maimonides.

32. Maimonides, *The Guide for the Perplexed*, 288.

33. Maimonides, *The Guide for the Perplexed*, 289.

34. Maimonides, *The Guide for the Perplexed*, 290.

35. Maimonides, *The Guide for the Perplexed*, 289.

36. Maimonides, *The Guide for the Perplexed*, 288.

37. Maimonides, *The Guide for the Perplexed*, 289 (ch. 18).

38. Thomas Aquinas, *Summa theologiae* I-II, q. 94, a. 6, obj. 1.

39. Thomas Aquinas, *ST* I-II, q. 94, a. 6, ad 2.

40. Thomas Aquinas, *ST* I-II, q. 94, a. 6.

41. Thomas Aquinas, *ST* I-II, q. 94, a. 6.

42. Thomas Aquinas, *ST* I, q. 22, a. 2, c., and ad 5.

43. Thomas Aquinas, *ST* I, q. 22, a. 2, obj. 5.

44. Thomas Aquinas, *ST* I, q. 22, a. 2, ad 5.

45. Thomas Aquinas, *ST* I, q. 22, a. 2, ad 4.

46. Thomas Aquinas, *ST* I, q. 22, a. 2, ad 4.

47. Thomas Aquinas, *ST* I, q. 22, a. 2, ad 2.

48. Thomas Aquinas, *ST* I, q. 22, a. 2, ad 1.

49. Thomas Aquinas, *ST* I, q. 22, a. 4.

50. Thomas Aquinas, *ST* I-II, q. 93, a. 1.

51. Thomas Aquinas, *ST* I-II, q. 93, a. 1.

52. Thomas Aquinas, *ST* I-II, q. 93, a. 1.

53. Thomas Aquinas, *ST* I, q. 22, a. 3.

54. Wojtyła, "Identities," 114.

55. Wojtyła, "The Desert of Judea," 113

Chapter Seven

Elder Brothers: John Paul II's Teaching on the Jewish People as a Question to the Church

Bruce D. Marshall

I

Pope John Paul II articulated his teaching on the Jewish people and the Jewish religion in a continuous series of statements over more than twenty-five years. These statements took a variety of forms, including homilies and parts of encyclicals, but most were addresses to audiences of Jews and Christians in Rome and around the world. Equally, though, John Paul II embodied this teaching by his actions. Nowhere did word and gesture strengthen one another more than in his visit to the Chief Synagogue of Rome in April 1986 and in his pilgrimage to the Holy Land in March 2000. John Paul's statements on the Jewish people and Judaism return again and again to the same basic themes, gathering depth and detail as they go along. His address to the Jews and Christians gathered in the Rome synagogue epitomizes his teaching as perhaps no other statement does. So I would like to look at what the Holy Father said there, and reflect a bit on the challenge his words continue to pose to the Church, as she seeks to understand, and to live out, her relationship with the Jewish people and Jewish faith.

Early in his address at the Rome synagogue, the pope underscores the Church's rejection of all forms of anti-Semitism, "'directed against the Jews at any time and by anyone.' I repeat, 'by anyone'" (no. 3).[1] Here John Paul cites *Nostra aetate* (no. 4), the Vatican II declaration which consistently serves as his point of departure in statements about the Church and the Jewish people. Some years later, first in Rome in the spring of 2000 and then at the Western Wall in Jerusalem, Pope John Paul went further and publicly prayed to God for the forgiveness of the sins of centuries, including those of the Church's members, against the children of Abraham.[2]

The complete rejection of anti-Semitism is surely a continuous moral imperative for the Church, as, in John Paul's vision, is the Church's confession of the past and present sins of the baptized, which remain temptations for them.[3] By themselves, however, neither the Church's repudiation of anti-Semitism nor her confession of sins against the Jewish people implies any special relationship between the Church and the Jews. According to *Nostra aetate*, no. 4, the fundamental motive for the Church's rejection of anti-Semitism is simply Christian charity, which of course extends to all human beings, and not only to the Jews. The Church unequivocally rejects, moreover, not only anti-Semitism and anti-Judaism, but all forms of racism and religious discrimination (see *Dignitatis humanae*, Vatican II's Declaration on Religious Liberty). John Paul II reiterated this point many times. It would therefore be conceivable, at least in the abstract, for the Church to reject anti-Semitism on the most basic moral grounds yet see no distinctive relationship between herself and the Jewish people, no abiding significance of Jewish election and Jewish faith for the life and faith of the Christian community. For this reason it seems to me that John Paul's condemnation of anti-Semitism—while it probably had the greatest public impact, and perhaps also the greatest historical significance, of the things he said in the synagogue in Rome—was less telling theologically and doctrinally than the remarks which then followed.

II

Having reaffirmed the Church's rejection of anti-Semitism, the pope turns to the hope that his visit to the Jewish community in Rome will prove decisive in securing a "fuller recognition" on both sides of the "bond" and "common spiritual patrimony" which unite Jews and Christians.[4] He does this by drawing out three points he finds "especially relevant" in *Nostra aetate*, no. 4. The Jewish people are, first of all, the spiritual "elder brothers" of Christians. Second, since there can be no "ancestral or collective" blame imputed to the Jewish people for the death of Christ, there is no theological basis for any kind of discrimination or retribution against the Jews. Third, Christians have no basis for claiming that the Jews are "repudiated or cursed," but must rather follow Scripture in affirming that God has "called them with an irrevocable calling."

I want to pause over the first point. It actually comes as the conclusion of a short paragraph, in which each of the four sentences makes a distinct and fundamental theological statement about the Church's understanding of her bond with the Jewish people and with Judaism. That paragraph runs as follows:

The Church of Christ discovers her "bond" with Judaism by "searching into her own mystery." The Jewish religion is not "extrinsic" to us, but in a certain way is "intrinsic" to our own religion. With Judaism, therefore, we have a relationship which we do not have with any other religion. You are our dearly beloved brothers and, in a certain way, it could be said that you are our elder brothers.[5]

In these four sentences, it seems to me, John Paul II actually presents us with all the most basic elements, the distilled essence, of his theological teaching on the Jewish people. By reflecting on this one paragraph we can get at the heart of what John Paul wanted to say about this matter, which he held to be of such great importance, and we can also come to see the considerable theological challenge his words now pose for us.

To begin with, John Paul picks up a statement from the beginning of *Nostra aetate*, no. 4. "The Church of Christ discovers her 'bond' with Judaism by 'searching into her own mystery.'" This, I think, has both a negative and a positive import. Negatively, it means that Christians cannot regard the central mysteries of the faith—the Trinity, the Incarnation, the unique and universal saving significance of Jesus's Passion and Resurrection, the Catholic Church and her sacraments as the divinely willed means by which Christ communicates his salvation to the world—as obstacles to their spiritual bond with the Jewish people and Jewish faith. A fair amount of recent reflection on the relationship between Christians and Jews urges Christians to tone down such doctrines, or perhaps repudiate them entirely, in order to establish their needed bond with the Jewish people. Some have even proposed that these uniquely Christian doctrines, especially the claim that Jesus alone is the savior of all people, are ultimately responsible for the historic persecution of the Jews by Christians. At the very least, Pope John Paul seems to say, it is paradoxical to suppose that the relationship between Jews and Christians can be furthered by having Christians give up Christianity.

Positively, the Holy Father's initial statement means that the perception by Christians of their bond with Judaism can and must grow out of the very heart of the Church's faith. The Christian doctrines which might seem to be obstacles to a proper appreciation of Judaism should in fact be seen as the basis for recognizing how much we have in common. Differently put, it is precisely those doctrines which are distinctively Christian, doctrines which Jews naturally cannot share, which enable Christians to see how deep is their bond with the faith of the Jewish people. This is perhaps the reverse of the usual picture of how Christianity is related to Judaism or to any other religion. But only so, the pope seems to say, when it arises from the heart of Christian conviction, will a new and better sense of our common "spiritual patrimony" with the Jewish people take hold in the Church.

What the Church discovers about Judaism when she "searches her own mystery," when she looks to the heart of her faith, is that "the Jewish religion is not 'extrinsic' to us, but in a certain way is 'intrinsic' to our own religion." This is the second theological point in this crucial paragraph. Or as John Paul put the point very early in his papacy, and subsequently repeated, "our two religious communities are connected and closely related at the very level of their respective religious identities."[6] I will leave it to our Jewish brothers and sisters to say whether John Paul is right to suggest that this relationship is really mutual, that is, whether Christianity is "in a certain way 'intrinsic'" to Judaism. By saying that Judaism is intrinsic to Christian identity, though, the pope is making a strong claim about Christian self-understanding. Our beliefs, like those of any religious community, are basic to our identity, even if they are not the whole of it. If another religion is intrinsic to our own identity, then we can only understand the import of our own beliefs—we can only grasp whom we ourselves are—by coming to know and appreciate the beliefs, the religion, of another community. When we say this about the relationship of the Church to Judaism, we are pinning our own identity, in some irreducible way, on a community which is, as the pope goes on to say, clearly distinct from our own, and one whose beliefs are in some very important ways opposed to our own.[7]

The pope's third theological point is that the Church has this intimate relationship *only* with Judaism. Only to Jewish faith is there a relationship intrinsic to Christianity and, at least in part, constitutive of Christian identity. All other religions are, by comparison, extrinsic to Christianity. However much respect the Church may have for other religious communities and their distinctive gifts, our bond with the faith of the Jews is in a class of its own. Thus John Paul's own words: "With Judaism therefore we have a relationship which we do not have with any other religion."

In his first three points the pope had been concentrating on the relationship of the Church and the Church's faith with the Jewish religion, with Judaism. In the fourth and final sentence of this freighted paragraph he links everything he has said on this score to the Jewish people themselves. "You," he says to the Jews gathered in the Rome synagogue, "are our dearly beloved brothers, and in a certain way it could be said that you are our elder brothers."[8] The relationship of the Church to the Jewish people is not merely one of shared conviction, a partial overlap of concept and judgment between two religions, two claims to revealed truth. A relationship to the Jewish *people*, and not only to their religion and their beliefs, is intrinsic to the Church and at least partly constitutive of Christian identity. The Church, searching her own heart and the mysteries of her own faith, is closer to the Jewish people than to any other. They are, in the original Italian of John Paul's synagogue address, "our especially beloved brothers" (*nostri fratelli prediletti*). Though it emanates from the Vatican, the English translation of John Paul's address seems inadequate to capture the force of his words at this point. The Jews are our "dearly beloved" brothers, to be sure, but more than that: The Church, when she knows her own heart, has a predilection for the Jews, a special affinity and delight, a preferential option, if you like, for the Jews. Taken literally, what the pope says means that the Jewish people are—or should be—the first love of Christians.

John Paul II's celebrated statement that the Jewish people are the "elder brothers" of those who belong to the Church of Christ might be taken in a rather modest sense. Jews and Christians both profess faith in the God of Abraham, Isaac, and Jacob, and these patriarchs and their descendants according to the flesh did so before the largely gentile Church. But there are indications that the Holy Father had something stronger in view. Having linked that faith in the God of Israel which Christians share with Jews to a unique fraternal relationship of the Church to the Jewish people, it would be odd to cap the whole thing off with a historical triviality: Your ancestors believed in the one true God before mine did. Here the setting of John Paul's utterance is surely crucial to fixing its meaning. He is not making a written statement in the third person, a statement *about* the Jews: *They* are our elder brothers in faith. He is making an oral statement in the second person, a statement *to* a living congregation of Jewish worshippers: *You* are our elder brothers in faith, the faith we share, for all our differences. You are our elder brothers in a shared faith, at this very moment. It is not just that your people had the faith of Abraham before mine did. Your present adherence to the faith of Abraham in some way enables us, here and now, to believe. The Church's faith in the God of Israel, here and now, somehow depends on the faith of the synagogue, however differently we may understand the saving actions, and indeed the very being, of Israel's God.

John Paul's last address to the Chief Synagogue of Rome reinforces this strong interpretation of his first one. On May 22, 2004, too beset with illness to attend in person, John Paul sent a message to Chief Rabbi Riccardo Di Segni on the occasion of the synagogue's centenary. There he observes that "in writing to the Romans (cf. Rom 11:16–18), St. Paul was already speaking of the holy root of Israel on which pagans are grafted onto Christ, 'for the gifts and the call of God are irrevocable' (Rom 11:29), and you continue to be the first-born people of the Covenant."[9]

This statement underlines John Paul's high view, often repeated, of Jewish election. In his interpretation of Romans 11:29, he apparently goes further than does *Nostra aetate*, no. 4 (and *Lumen gentium*, no. 16). The Jews remain "most dear to God," indeed, but they are more than that. The electing love of God which made Abraham, Isaac, Jacob, and their descendants according to the flesh "the first-born of the Covenant" continues to make their descendants today, the Jews of Rome, the covenant's firstborn. God's original covenant with the Jewish people remains in force; "the Old Covenant," as John Paul puts it elsewhere, is "never revoked by God."[10] And being the firstborn of the covenant is just what makes the Jewish people the "root" onto which the gentiles, as Paul sees it, are grafted in Christ, so as to receive life and salvation. Not only is faithful Israel before Christ the root from which the gentiles live in Christ, but faithful Israel now, the Jews gathered with their chief rabbi in the Great Synagogue of Rome, are the root from which the gentile Church now lives in Christ. This is a very strong reading of Roman 11, and a very strong sense in which the Jewish people are "elder brothers" to us Christians.

To summarize: With regard to the importance of the Jews and Judaism for the Catholic Church's faith and life, John Paul II teaches (1) that the Church's appreciation for the religion of the Jews flows from the heart of the Church's own faith, (2) establishing a relationship which is intrinsic to and partially constitutive of Christian faith and identity, (3) a relationship which is, for Christians, unique to Judaism, and (4) calls forth a special love of Christians for the Jewish people, who are chosen by God to be the firstborn of the covenant and, as such, those upon whom the Church's own faith in the God of Israel in some way still depends.

III

In order to clarify this teaching, it may be useful to contrast it briefly with some alternative possibilities. Pope John Paul II combines a high theological estimate of Judaism as a religion with a high theological view of the Jews themselves, both as God's irrevocably elect people and those with whom Christians should naturally—or perhaps better, supernaturally—have a unique intimacy. While to some of us these claims may seem mutually necessary, a package that demands to be accepted as a whole, the matter is often seen differently.

First of all, we might recall the theology of the Jews and Judaism put forward by Catholic thinkers like Jacques Maritain and Charles Journet. Both wrote extensively on the Jewish people and the Church's relationship with the Jews, beginning in Maritain's case in the 1920s and continuing throughout the long career of each. Maritain, writing on these matters as a Christian philosopher, was deeply affected by the novelist Léon Bloy, and in turn clearly influenced Journet, writing as a dogmatic theologian. Long before *Nostra aetate*, both of these Catholic thinkers passionately reject anti-Semitism, Maritain tracking and denouncing the Nazi persecution of the Jews from the mid-1930s on. Both have a high theological view of Jewish election and of God's everlasting fidelity to the Jewish people, a view stemming, as they see it, from Scripture and from Christian faith itself. Both also make much of the unique and ongoing role of the Jewish people in the history of salvation and of the unique relationship of the Church with the Jewish people, likewise ongoing. So Maritain writes in 1937: "It is no small thing for a Christian to hate or despise, or to wish to treat in a debasing way, the race whence issued his God and the immaculate Mother of his God."[11] He is equally firm on the permanence of Jewish election.

> To see nothing more in the destinies of the people of Israel than in the destinies of some social aggregation or other; to pretend that the election of Israel to the title of God's people was purely and simply revoked by the coming of Christ—this is to simplify things to the point of substituting an altogether *natural* kind of thought for Saint Paul's *supernatural* thought, and it is utterly to extenuate his teaching. "Hath God cast off his people? God forbid." [Rom 11:1].[12]

These two thinkers do not, however, have a similarly high estimate of Judaism, that is, of the religion of the Jewish people since the time of Christ. Borrowing a phrase from Maritain, Journet asks rhetorically, "From that time [the time of Christ], will Judaism be anything else than 'the spiritual form in which Israel has cut herself off from her Messiah'?" "St. Paul's word," Journet goes on to observe, "is stringent: 'With regard to the gospel, they are adversaries' (Rom 11:28)."[13] To be sure, God's electing love, his undying mercy and tenderness toward Israel, will heal this "sacred wound." Here too, Journet argues, "the word of St. Paul is clear: 'They are beloved because of their fathers, for the gifts and the call of God are without repentance' (Rom 11:28–9)."[14] So Journet, again following Maritain, foresees the full reintegration of Israel into the Church, in which Jewish identity will be preserved and the Jews will have their own distinctive and indispensable eschatological task.

It seems, then, that these thinkers affirm the Church's ongoing and uniquely intimate relationship with the Jewish people, and indeed God's electing love for the Jews, in spite of their religion—their Judaism—not because of it. For Pope John Paul II, by contrast, the Church professes a unique intimacy with the Jewish people in good part precisely because of their religion. And this means, it would seem, that Christians need to see Jewish faith, the practice of the Jewish religion after Christ, not as a humanly imposed obstacle to God's electing love, but as in some deep way the very fruit of that love.

Just as it is possible to combine a high view of Jewish election with a relatively low view of Judaism, so, conversely, it is possible to combine a low view of Jewish election with a high view of Judaism, especially where the practice of Judaism is viewed as the chief way to maintain Jewish identity. Indeed, some Jewish thinkers, such as Mordecai Kaplan, if I understand him correctly, seem to do this.[15] A view of this kind is also preferred by Christian theologians who are influenced by pluralist accounts of religious diversity, like that of John Hick. In the ambit of English-speaking Catholicism Paul Knitter is perhaps the best-known representative of this approach.[16] Here the idea is that Judaism and Christianity, along with all the other enduring religious traditions of the world, are equally valuable and effective paths to the transcendent. A view of this kind naturally requires that each religious community play down, if not renounce altogether, any doctrine which suggests that it enjoys privileged access to ultimate things. The election of Israel is surely such a doctrine. So on this view it will be perfectly in order to cultivate Jewish identity through the practice of Judaism or, mutatis mutandis, Christian identity through the practice of Christianity. But it will not be in order for this practice to include the belief that God has a special and permanent relationship with the Jewish people, or they with him. The same goes, a fortiori, for Christian belief in the election of the Church.

A view of this kind poses a number of problems from the standpoint of Catholic doctrine and theology.[17] With regard to our current concern, it clearly runs counter to John Paul II's insistence that the Jewish people alone are, and remain, "the first-born people of the Covenant." By the grace of God the Jewish people have a uniquely intimate relationship with God. To them belongs from its inception the only saving covenant God makes with human beings. In this covenant with the God of Israel, the Church, to be sure, believes that she shares to the fullest possible degree—but not to the exclusion of the covenant's firstborn, the Jewish people. From this shared blessing of God's covenantal love arises, John Paul also suggests, the unique intimacy of the Church with the Jewish people.

IV

For John Paul II, then, Christians need to have a high view not only of the Jewish religion but also of the election of the Jews, and with that of the unique bond of faith and love which ties the Church forever to the Jewish people. As he sees it, these convictions and affections are bound up with the central mysteries of the Catholic faith itself. Therein lies the question, and the challenge, posed to the Church by John Paul's teaching on the Jews and Judaism. Quite simply, how shall we understand this teaching? How shall we take it in, in all of its boldness? John Paul calls us to understand the Catholic faith in such a way that it embraces the high claims he makes about the religion of the Jews and the election of the Jewish people. *That* we must do so is surely the fundamental theological imperative of John Paul's teaching on the Jews and Judaism. *How* we are to do so is far from clear, at least to me. I have no answer ready to offer here, but will conclude simply by indicating where I think the basic issue lies.

The basic question posed by the Holy Father's teaching, it seems to me, is how to square the irrevocable election of the Jewish people with the universal saving work of Christ, and thereby with the universal mission of Christ's Church. This considerably simplifies a complex problem, so I will try to explain why I think this way of putting the issue gets to the heart of the matter.

The problem is not soteriological in the usual sense. Catholic teaching insists on the real possibility of salvation for every human being, and thus for all non-Christians. The question, rather, has to do with the nature or character of the salvation won for all by Christ, with what belongs constitutively to Christ's saving work.

According to the New Testament, the eternal Father has reconciled to himself all things in heaven and earth through the cross of Christ (Col 1:20; cf. Eph 1:10). By raising and exalting the Crucified to his own right hand, the Father has made Christ "the head over all things for the Church, which is his body" (Eph 1:20–23). Not every human being is a member of the Church. But Christ is nonetheless the head over every human being, which is to say that he aims to unite each human being in the most intimate possible way with himself. In this intimate union with Christ the salvation of each human being consists. To be intimately united with Christ, though, is to be a member of his body. Now the Church is his body. So to say that Christ is head of all human beings is to say that Christ aims to bring all human beings into the Church. In just this sense Christ is head of all "*for* the Church," as Ephesians 1:22 puts it. Christ is the head of all just in order to call all into the Church, and in that way give them the full reality of himself. The being of all in the Church is the telos of Christ's headship.

Guided by this biblical teaching, Catholic doctrine holds that the Catholic Church and her sacraments are the means, the instrument, by which Christ daily offers his salvation to all human beings.[18] In the well-known phrase of Vatican II, the Church, because it is Christ's own body, is "the universal sacrament of salvation."[19] The Church is not merely a conventional sign of the salvation accomplished by the cross of Christ, which might be replaced by another which served the same purpose as well or better. It is a genuine *sacramentum*, a sign uniquely suited to make present the reality it signifies, which is saving union with Christ.

God's call to salvation in Christ is therefore a call to enter and remain within the Catholic Church. Given the very nature of salvation in Christ, the call to life in the Catholic Church can be no less universal than the call to salvation.

"The Father," as the *Catechism of the Catholic Church* puts the point, "willed to call the whole of humanity together into his Son's Church" (no. 845; cf. no. 1). Or more bluntly, in the language of Vatican II's decree on missions: "Everyone, therefore, ought to be converted to Christ" and incorporated "into the Church which is his body" (*Ad gentes*, no. 7). For various reasons beyond their own control some will not be able to heed this call, and will not thereby forfeit eternal salvation. But *that* the call to life in the Catholic Church is universal is basic to Catholic teaching.

Why should this teaching on the Church's universal mission, about which John Paul II is as clear as one could wish, conflict with the irrevocable election of Israel? Because, in a word, the Jewish people cannot continue to exist in the long run without Judaism. John Paul has a clear eye for this point as well. The irrevocable election of the Jewish people evidently requires the permanence of their religion. There is more, no doubt, to Jewish identity than the practice of Judaism. It is possible to be recognizable as a Jew even if one refuses to practice Judaism, or practices it badly. But without a substantial core of faithful Jews, who practice Judaism well and teach their children to do the same, it seems impossible that the Jewish people could endure in the long run. Without Judaism, the Jewish people would surely, if slowly, disappear from the earth, as other ancient people have done.[20] They would cease to be as a distinct people, and vanish into *gentilitas*, as medieval Christian theologians called the mass of us not descended from Abraham, Isaac, and Jacob.

If God has never revoked his covenant with the Jewish people, if his choice of this people as his treasured possession (Dt 7:6) is in fact irrevocable, then it seems as though God must also never have revoked the law he gave them, or, with that, the religion by which he taught them to worship him and draw close to him. In permanently electing Israel, it seems that God has also permanently willed the practice of Judaism. The existence of faithful Jews is not simply an empirical likelihood or a devout hope, let alone an evil God puts up with, but belongs to God's own good and unalterable purposes. Or so we must conclude, if, as it seems, the practice of Judaism is a necessary condition for the very existence of God's elect people, those descended according to the flesh from Abraham, Isaac, and Israel.[21]

Thus the question posed for Christian faith seeking understanding by the teaching of Pope John Paul II on the Jews and Judaism. If God in Christ wills the salvation of all by calling every human being into the Catholic Church, then it seems as though God cannot will that the practice of Judaism continue permanently. If God calls every human being into the Church, therefore, it seems that God does not will the permanent election of Israel. If, conversely, God wills the permanent election of Israel, then it seems as though God does will that the practice of Judaism continue permanently. In that case, God must will that there always be human beings who remain outside the Catholic Church. If God wills (positively desires, and does not simply permit) that there always be those who remain outside the Church, then God does not call every human being into the Church, or will the salvation of all in that way. The Church's mission is not, therefore, genuinely universal.

Most writers on this issue sense the problem I have been trying to bring out, even if they do not articulate it explicitly. There are, I think, basically three strategies for dealing with the issue. I cannot do justice to any of them here, but will try to indicate briefly what each is, and ask whether any is entirely successful.

1. The Jews, or at least some of them, are not really called to life in the Church, or at least not in the same way, or to the same life, that the gentiles are. In its stronger form, this is the "two covenants" view of the relationship between Israel and the Church. The God of Israel has, on this view, established two different saving arrangements in the world, one through carnal election and Torah for Jews, the other through faith in Jesus Christ for gentiles.

   This view essentially denies that Christ, and even more his Church, have a universal saving mission, as the conceptual cost of upholding the permanence of Judaism and (thereby) of Jewish election. As such the "two covenants" view does not so much understand the faith as undercut it. To be sure, Christians (including John Paul II) naturally talk about old and new "covenants" as a basic feature of the faith. But there cannot, at bottom, be two numerically distinct saving relationships of God to humanity. There can only be one—in Christ—which has two different phases or aspects. To think that there really are two (numerically) distinct covenants puts "two covenant" theology in ironic league with liberal supersessionism of the sort represented by Schleiermacher. He thought that Christianity had no inherent relationship with Judaism or the Jews, but merely a transient historical connection, long severed. By treating Christianity as a wholly gentile religion, the "two covenants" approach comes to basically the same conclusion, though of course for different ends.

   In its weaker or more qualified versions this view allows that there is only a single saving relationship of God with humanity. Ultimately all who attain salvation are saved by Christ. In that sense Christ's saving mission is universal; it extends eschatologically to Jews as well as gentiles. But the Jewish people are not presently called by God to faith in Christ and life in the Church. They are called, rather, to the faithful practice of Judaism, and so to continuing existence outside the Church and faith in Christ. On this view salvation is finally through Christ alone, but for now, and perhaps until the end of time, God intends no saving mission of Christ, let alone of the Church, to the Jewish people. Christ's saving purpose for the Jews is dormant, as it were, until the eschaton. It seems questionable, though, whether we can suppose that God genuinely intends for the Jews, or for anyone else, an ultimate good already available in the world (life in Christ), which at the same he actively wills them not to reach, or prevents them from reaching—quite apart from Paul's insistence that the gospel of Christ is for the Jew first (Rom 1:16).[22]

2. Linking the old covenant to the new as "figure" to "reality" or "shadow" to "truth" is, by contrast especially with the stronger versions of (1), a way of insisting that the Church and her faith do have an inherent connection to the Jewish people and theirs. This approach goes quite deep in the Christian tradition, and admits of many variations. Its advocates are characteristically committed to the unity of God's saving purpose in Christ, enacted "figurally" under the old law, then with temporally unsurpassable clarity by the incarnation of the Word, who brings forth in his Passion and Resurrection the saving sacraments of the new law. Those who follow this approach are also typically committed, often deeply so, to God's love for Abraham's fleshly descendents as an irrevocable element of his saving design in Christ.

   The examples of Maritain and Journet suggest, however, that this position makes it difficult to find room for the thought that God wills the permanent practice of Judaism. What God wills is the call of all into the Catholic Church, which for those who take this approach tends to mean (or at least imply) that God does not will the permanent practice of Judaism. He may allow it, grant space to it as an indifferent or even evil practice he permits for his own purpose, namely to preserve the Jewish people for the eschatological reconciliation of all things in Christ. But while God surely brings good *out of* evil, God does not permit (still less will) evil *in order* to realize his own good purposes, purposes he could have even if the permitted evil did not obtain. To the extent that Jewish election depends on the practice of Judaism, this second approach seems incompatible with the permanent election of Israel. If so, it raises disturbing questions (sometimes against the express intentions of those who follow it) about God's fidelity to the one covenant he has made with Jews and gentiles, a saving arrangement which takes its start from God's promise to Abraham, Isaac, and Jacob that their fleshly descendents will be God's "treasured possession" forever.

3. A third possibility has recently emerged. The Jews *are* called to faith in Christ and to Christian communal life, but in such a way that they retain enough Judaism to be recognizable as Jews, including, among other things, their own worship and the continued observance of Jewish dietary

laws. This is basically the approach of Messianic Judaism, as represented by a theologian like Mark Kinzer, but it also overlaps in part with the view of the Orthodox Jewish theologian Michael Wyschogrod (who holds that Jews should not be Christians, but if they are going to be, they should remain recognizable as Jews, for reasons postsupersessionist Christians should be able to appreciate).[23]

This third approach recognizes both the necessity of distinctively Jewish practice and identity for Jewish election, and the universality of Christ's saving mission. It thereby deliberately aims to avoid the implicit or explicit denial of the latter in (1), and of the former in (2). This view has so far been relatively little discussed in Christian theological reflection on the Jewish people, but as an effort to come to grips with the problems in established approaches it surely deserves more attention than it has yet received.

A preliminary worry does emerge, however. Is this the best of both worlds—the needed way of upholding both Jewish election and the universal saving mission of Christ and his Church—or is it the worst, a way of upholding neither? John Paul II identifies the concern in his synagogue address. "Each of our religions, in the full awareness of the many bonds which unite them to each other . . . wishes to be recognized and respected in its own identity, beyond any syncretism and any ambiguous appropriation."[24] It is not clear, for example, how this approach (which is not just an idea, but a reality embodied in a number of Messianic Jewish congregations) can hold that, by his Cross, Christ has united Jews and gentiles in one body (cf. Eph 2:11–22). It sometimes seems as though Christ has two bodies—two churches—neither of which has a universal saving mission. With that, the sense in which Christ himself has a single saving purpose for all ceases to be apparent.

Yet if we follow the teaching of John Paul II, there can be no real antinomy between the universal mission of Christ's Church and God's irrevocable election of Israel. If none of these strategies quite succeeds in showing how the two fit together, there must be something, perhaps several things, we have missed. As with other difficult problems of faith seeking understanding, the question is not whether the genuine commitments of Christian faith cohere, but rather how they do. Or, to return to John Paul II's address in the Chief Synagogue of Rome, the question is just how the Church's conviction of God's undying fidelity to the Jewish people grows, as it must, from the heart of her own faith.

We may be tempted to give up on what is surely a very difficult question and invoke St. Paul's appeal, on just this matter, to the unsearchable will and ways of God (Rom 11:33). There is of course a mystery here, but we should resist the temptation to invoke it prematurely. The mystery of God's will and ways is not a substitute for the *intellectus fidei*, but precisely what faith seeks to understand. Here, as elsewhere, we will only begin to appreciate the unfathomable mystery of God's ways when we have searched them out to the fullest extent we can.

NOTES

1. Pope John Paul II, *Spiritual Pilgrimage: Texts on the Jews and Judaism 1979–1995*, ed. Eugene J. Fisher and Leon Klenicki (New York: Crossroad, 1995), 62.

2. See John Paul II, *In the Holy Land: In His Own Words*, ed. Lawrence Boadt, C.S.P., and Kevin di Camillo (New York: Paulist, 2005). The text of the prayer for forgiveness placed in the Wailing Wall is on 121. See also the pope's homily for the "Day of Pardon" (*Acta Apostolica Sedis* 92 [2000]: 621–24), which reflects on the confession of sins undertaken by John Paul II at the Mass for the First Sunday of Lent (March 12) in the Jubilee Year 2000.

3. For a more detailed analysis of John Paul II's public statements against anti-Semitism (through 1997, when the article was written), including the pope's suggestions, even before the Day of Pardon in Lent of 2000, that Christians are continually called to repent of their sins against the Jewish people, see Jean Stern, M.S., "Jean Paul II face à l'antijudaïsme," in *Radici dell'antigiudaismo in ambiente cristiano* (Vatican City: Libreria editrice Vaticana, 2000), 54–78. Stern takes the pope's sharp words in the 1986 synagogue address ("I repeat, 'by anyone'") to be a clear reference to anti-Semitic acts of previous popes; cf. 59.

4. John Paul II, "Address in the Synagogue of Rome," no. 4. The quotations which follow are all taken from this section of the pope's speech, in John Paul II, *Spiritual Pilgrimage*, 62–63. For more on the idea of a "bond" between the church and the Jews and the importance of this idea for John Paul, see Jean Stern, "Le lien «sacré» entre l'église et le peuple juif selon Jean-Paul II," in *Virgo Liber Verbi: Miscellanea di studi in onore di P. Giuseppe M. Besutti, O.S.M.*, ed. Ignazio M. Calabuig, O.S.M. (Rome: Edizioni «Marianum», 1991), 629–48.

5. In the pope's original Italian: "Il primo è che la Chiesa di Cristo scopre il suo 'legame' con l'Ebraismo 'scrutando il suo proprio mistero'. La religione ebraica non ci è 'estrinseca', ma in un certo qual modo, è 'intrinseca' alla nostra religione. Abbiamo quindi verso di essa dei rapporti che non abbiamo con nessun'altra religione. Siete i nostri fratelli prediletti e, in un certo modo, si potrebbe dire i nostri fratelli maggiori." *AAS* 78 (1986): 1120.

6. "Address to Representatives of Jewish Organizations" (March 12, 1979), in John Paul II, *Spiritual Pilgrimage*, 4; cf. 10, 18.

7. On this opposition see no. 5 of the synagogue "Address," in John Paul II, *Spiritual Pilgrimage*, 63–64.

8. On the Jews as "elder brothers" to Christians, see also *Catechism of the Catholic Church*, no. 63.

9. John Paul II, "Message for the centenary of the Great Synagogue of Rome" (May 22, 2004), no. 2, http://www.vatican.va/holy_father/john_paul_ii/speeches/2004/may/documents/hf_jp-ii_spe_20040523_rabbino-segni_en.html.

10. John Paul II, "Address to Representatives of Jewish Organizations," in John Paul II, *Spiritual Pilgrimage*, 15. See also *Catechism of the Catholic Church*, no. 121.

11. Jacques Maritain, "The Mystery of Israel," in *Ransoming the Time*, by Jacques Maritain, trans. Harry Lorin Binsse (New York: Charles Scribner's Sons, 1941), 175. Maritain continues, quoting Léon Bloy from 1910: "We forget, or rather we do not wish to know, that our God made man is a Jew, by nature the Jew *par excellence*, the Lion of Judah; that his Mother is a Jewess, the flower of the Jewish race; that the apostles were Jews, just as much as all the prophets; and finally that our sacred liturgy is altogether drawn from Jewish books. How, then, can we express the enormity of the outrage and blasphemy which lie in vilifying the Jewish race?" (175, translation altered).

Maritain published versions of this essay several times in French and English between 1937 and 1941, originally under the title "L'impossible antisémitesme." He issued it for the last time as the title essay of his collection *Le mystère d'Israël et autres essais* (Paris: Desclée de Brouwer, 1965), 19–62; the passages just quoted are on 61–62. The various versions of this essay differ not only in title but in content, and the differences are not always trivial; cf. note 13 below.

12. Jacques Maritain, "Answer to One Unnamed," in *Ransoming the Time*, 190 (in the original French, *Le mystère d'Israël et autres essais*, 130–31). Biblical faith in the election of Israel demands the deliberate rejection of anti-Semitism, just as anti-Semitism inevitably looks for ways to deny the scriptural teaching on divine election: "The first one responsible for the concept of an elect race, that concept being taken at its pure source, is the God of Abraham, of Isaac and of Jacob, the God of Israel— *your God*, dear Christians who turn yourselves against the chosen olive tree into which you were grafted" ("Answer to One Unnamed," 183; *Le mystère d'Israël et autres essais*, 124).

13. Charles Journet, "L'économie de la loi mosaïque," *Revue Thomiste* 63 (1963): 526–27 (also in Journet, *L'église du Verbe incarné*, vol. 4: *Essai de théologie de l'histoire du salut*. Oeuvres completes de Charles Journet [Éditions Saint-Augustin, 2004], 777); see also Charles Journet, *Destinées d'Israël: A propos du salut par les Juifs* (Paris: Egloff, 1945), 151. The phrase quoted by Journet is from Maritain's "The Mystery of Israel"; cf. Maritain, *Ransoming the Time*, 155. Journet cites from the version which appeared as "L'impossible antisémitisme," in Maritain, *Questions de conscience: essais et allocutions* (Paris: Desclée de Brouwer, 1938), 64–65: "L'aversion de la croix est essentielle au judaïsme, en tant que ce mot désigne la forme spirituelle selon laquelle Israël s'est retranché de son Messie." In the later English version of this essay, Maritain is clearly talking about Judaism of the diaspora following the rejection of the crucified Messiah and the destruction of the Second Temple ("Judaism of the Exile"), not what "Judaism is by essence," namely "Christianity's first outline and imperfect beginning." The English essay, moreover, characterizes Israel's "severance" from her Messiah as "typical" of postbiblical Judaism, not "essential" to it (*Ransoming the Time*,

155). However, the final version of the essay in French retains the language of 1938 without comment, at least at this point. Cf. *Le mystère d'Israël et autres essais*, 41.

14. Journet, "L'économie," 527 (also in *L'église du Verbe incarné*, vol. 4, 777). In its basic outlines, Journet's Christian theology of Israel seems similar to that of Karl Barth, which has been much discussed in recent theological dialogue between Christians and Jews. See Michael Wyschogrod, *Abraham's Promise: Judaism and Jewish-Christian Relations*, ed. R. Kendall Soulen (Grand Rapids: Eerdmans, 2004), especially Wyschogrod's essay, "Why Was and Is the Theology of Karl Barth of Interest to a Jewish Theologian?" (211–24).

15. See David Novak, "Mordecai Kaplan's Rejection of Election," *Modern Judaism* 15 (1995): 1–19.

16. See John Hick, *An Interpretation of Religion: Human Responses to the Transcendent*, 2nd ed. (Basingstoke: Palgrave Macmillan, 2004); Paul F. Knitter, *No Other Name? A Critical Survey of Christian Attitudes toward the World Religions* (Maryknoll, NY: Orbis Books, 1985).

17. For a carefully argued rejoinder to this sort of approach from a Catholic point of view, see Paul J. Griffiths, *Problems of Religious Diversity* (Oxford: Blackwell, 2001), esp. chs. 2.4 and 5.1.

18. Thus *Lumen gentium*, no. 9: "Established by Christ as a communion of life, love, and truth, [the Church] is taken up by him also as the instrument for the salvation of all"; cf. *Catechism of the Catholic Church*, nos. 776 and 846: "All salvation comes through Christ the Head through the Church which is his body."

19. *Lumen gentium*, no. 48; cf. no. 9.

20. On this see Gary A. Anderson, "How to Think about Zionism," *First Things* 152 (2005): 30–36.

21. To put the point in a slightly more technical way: If God wills the existence of the Jewish people until the end of time, and the practice of Judaism is necessary for the existence of the Jewish people, then God wills the practice of Judaism until the end of time. In willing the permanent existence of the Jewish people, as in willing any good, God also wills the means necessary for that good, in this case the practice of Judaism. Since the means necessary for an end God wills must be as good as the end itself, the practice of Judaism can no more fall under the heading of evils God permits than can the existence of the Jewish people itself.

This argument raises, to be sure, difficult (and painful) questions about how Israel's rejection of Christ, which according to St. Paul is "transgression" (Rom 11:11–12) and calls down God's own "rejection" (Rom 11:15) and "severity" (Rom 11:22), is related to the postbiblical religion of the Jewish people. And it raises large questions about God's relation to evil, especially in light of Paul's statements that God not only permits Israel's transgression, but "hardens" part of Israel (Rom 11:7, 25).

Here let me only observe that it is, I take it, quite fundamental that God does not will (moral) evil. Talk of God's "hardening," let alone of God's permitting evil, cannot, therefore, be allowed to slide into the suggestion that God does evil so that good may come. Israel's rejection of Christ is "transgression" only if it is not willed by God. And if it is not willed by God, then, while God may turn it to a good end, it naturally cannot be a means God Himself wills for the good end of Israel's election.

Therefore to whatever extent Judaism is necessary for Israel's election, Judaism cannot count as "transgression."

22. It might be thought that (1), especially in its weaker versions, presents a problem only for Catholic theology, since it refuses to separate the call to faith in Christ from a call to life in the Church. But regardless of how one understands the ecclesial mediation of faith in Christ, the underlying question is the same for Catholics and Protestants: Is Christ's own saving mission, from Pentecost to the end of time, universal, or not?

23. Mark Kinzer, *Postmissionary Messianic Judaism: Redefining Christian Engagement with the Jewish People* (Grand Rapids: Brazos Press, 2005); for Wyschogrod's views and a lively discussion by Jewish and Christian theologians, see *Modern Theology* 11 (1995): 165–241.

24. John Paul II, *Spiritual Pilgrimage*, 64 (no. 5 of the "Address").

Chapter Eight

"Man Is the Land": The Sacramentality of the Land of Israel

Gregory Vall

JOHN PAUL II'S THEOLOGY OF THE HOLY LAND

In a January 1992 address, Pope John Paul II expressed his profound hope that the Holy Land, which has seen so much violence down the centuries and in recent decades, might soon become "a special place of encounter and prayer for peoples," and that Jerusalem, which has become a veritable symbol of religious division, might soon serve as "a sign and instrument of peace and reconciliation." Eugene Fisher suggests that the pontiff's choice of words here may reflect a "sacramental" understanding of the Holy Land.[1] The phrase "sign and instrument of peace and reconciliation" does seem to contain a faint echo of the classic definition of a sacrament as *signum efficax gratie*, but the similarity should not be pressed, as it seems unlikely that John Paul wished to compare the land of Israel directly to the seven sacraments.[2] A more striking and potentially significant parallel to the pope's words is found in the description of the Church as "like a sacrament—a sign and instrument, that is, of communion with God and of unity among all men" in *Lumen gentium*, a document that also refers to the Church as "the universal sacrament of salvation."[3] It may be, then, that John Paul's choice of words is aimed at directing our attention to one facet of the relationship between Israel and the Church.

At the heart of John Paul's understanding of the Holy Land lies the conviction that the Land of Israel, and Jerusalem in particular, is a "meeting place" and the locus of historical revelation. In the 1984 apostolic letter *Redemptionis anno*, John Paul refers these terms not only to Christ's incarnate presence in the land but also to the Old Testament revelation to Israel. "Before it was the city of Jesus the Redeemer, Jerusalem was the historic site of the biblical revelation of God, the meeting place, as it were, of heaven and earth, in which more than in any other place the word of God was brought to men."[4] Because it is "the place where, according to faith, the created things of earth encounter the infinite transcendence of God," the Holy Land—and Jerusalem especially—can function as "a symbol of coming together, of union, and of universal peace for the human family."[5] The logic here is important. Because the Holy Land is a meeting place along the vertical axis— that is, between Creator and creation—it can serve as a symbol of union along the horizontal axis—that is, among human beings. The seriousness with which John Paul takes the Judeo-Christian belief in divine revelation also suggests that by "symbol" he does not mean something that is merely cultural or literary.

In connection with his 1965 pilgrimage to Israel, then cardinal Karol Wojtyła composed a series of poems dealing with the Holy Land. Not surprisingly, in these very personal meditations Wojtyła allows his spiritual insight and poetic imagination to roam free and expresses himself rather more daringly than he does later in his official statements as pope. In this "pilgrimage to identity . . . the identity of finding one's own self in landscape," he pursues a series of mystical connections—for example, between the land of Israel and the whole earth, between Christ's presence in the land and Wojtyła's own presence there two thousand years later, between Mary's womb as Christ's "inner place" and the land as his "outer place," and between Christ's body as the "outward place" he had on earth and the Eucharist as his "place" within us.[6] Most hauntingly and elusively, Wojtyła searches for the true relation between man and land, at one point baldly asserting that "Man is the land," but elsewhere developing the biblical images of the cross as the tree of life and of man himself as a plant. "Man is born to blossom like a flower," and the Holy Land is the "place of the blossoming of man."[7] Several of these connections converge in one particularly luminous composition titled, "Space which Remains in You," in which the poet adopts the persona of John the Beloved Disciple (many years after the Resurrection) and imagines what the latter might have thought and felt when he confected the Eucharist and gave it to the Mother of God.[8] These poems suggest that years of prayer and profound reflection lie beneath the surface of John Paul's comparatively straightforward official statements concerning the Holy Land. Moreover, since the notion of the Holy Land as a "meeting place" is a leitmotif running through the poems, the mystical connections explored in the poems give us some idea of what John Paul means by this phrase in his official statements.

My immediate purpose in the following pages is neither to exegete the poems of Cardinal Wojtyła nor to attempt an in-depth analysis of Pope John Paul II's statements about the people and land of Israel, nor yet again to discuss the implications of these texts for Jewish-Christian relations. Instead, I wish to offer a biblical essay on the Holy Land as "sacrament" of God's covenant with Israel and on the organic manner by which this Old Testament reality spiritually signifies a New Testament reality, namely, the sacred humanity of Christ, which he received from the Blessed Virgin Mary. My reflection thus to some extent runs parallel to, and contains points of contact with, the poems of Wojtyła and the teaching of John Paul, but I do not claim that it is an exposition of either.

At the same time, I do wish to place my theological exegesis at the service of Jewish-Catholic relations and to situate it within the context of that vitally important endeavor. During his famous 1986 visit to the Synagogue of Rome, Pope John Paul II, drawing on Vatican Council II's document *Nostra aetate*, no. 4, noted that the relationship between the Jewish and Christian religions is an "intrinsic" rather than an "extrinsic" one, and that the Church thus "discovers her 'bond' with Judaism by 'searching into her own mystery.'"[9] Four years later, in another address in Rome, he noted that the converse is also true—to understand her own mission and nature, the Church must reflect on the "mystery" of the people of Israel, especially as that mystery is disclosed in Sacred Scripture—and that biblical scholars thus play a particular role in this continued reflection.[10] The way in which the pontiff in this address repeatedly applies the theologically charged word "mystery" to both biblical and contemporary Israel is quite striking and suggests that a reflection on the land of Israel under the closely related category of "sacrament" may prove a fruitful avenue of approach.[11]

The teaching of *Nostra aetate* also informs John Paul's articulation of the biblical hermeneutic that should guide Catholic reflection on the mystery of Israel and its land. In an address in West Germany in 1980, the pope made the fascinating observation that Jewish-Christian dialogue is "at the same time a dialogue within our Church, that is to say, between the first and the second parts of her Bible." He then proceeded to quote from official Church directives for the implementation of *Nostra aetate*: "The effort must be made to understand better everything in the Old Testament that has its own permanent value . . . since this value is not wiped out by the later interpretation of the New Testament, which, on the contrary, gave the Old Testament its full meaning, so that it is a question rather of reciprocal enlightenment and explanation."[12] The effort to listen more attentively and empathetically to our Jewish brethren calls for and is in turn enhanced by a correlative effort to listen afresh to the first part of the Christian canon of Scripture and to allow it to speak in its *vox Israelitica*, as it were. At the same time, it would be foreign to the Christian spirit to attempt to read Israel's Scriptures in complete isolation from the New Testament. Therefore, in the following pages, I attempt, as a Catholic biblical scholar, to approach the theological question of the land of Israel in the manner of a dialogue between the testaments, aiming at "reciprocal enlightenment and explanation."

SPIRITUALIZATION AND SACRAMENTALIZATION

Much valuable exegetical and historical work has been devoted to the "theology of the land" in Judaism and Christianity.[13] W. D. Davies, Waldemar Janzen, and Robert L. Wilken have focused in large measure on the important issue of spiritualization, and these three scholars are in broad agreement on two points. First, they hold that the Hebrew Bible is marked by a sense of "territorial realism." However much the Torah, Prophets, and Psalms ascribe holiness and theological significance to the land of Israel and the city of Jerusalem, these texts, properly understood, refer to geographical, this-worldly realities. As Wilken puts it, "For the ancient Israelites *land* always referred to an actual land. Eretz Israel was not a symbol of a higher reality."[14] Second, Davies, Janzen, and Wilken agree that this theology of geographic realism is spiritualized in Christianity and in some forms of postbiblical Judaism. Prophecies of Israel's restoration to the land and of the glorification of Jerusalem come to be interpreted as references to a transcendent or heavenly order.

There is, however, some disagreement with regard to when exactly this occurred in Christianity. For Davies and Janzen, the process is already well under way in the New Testament (especially in the Epistle to the Hebrews), but Wilken offers a very different view of the matter. According to him, the second-century chiliasts, including Justin Martyr, Tertullian, and Irenaeus, had interpreted the New Testament correctly when they understood it to promise that "God would establish a future kingdom *on earth* centered in Jerusalem."[15] Wilken even suggests that the references to a heavenly Jerusalem in Galatians (4:26) and Hebrews (12:22) can be understood in this way. As he sees it, there is a fundamental continuity of eschatological outlook between the two testaments of the Christian Bible, and this continuity extends through the first two centuries of orthodox Christianity. According to Wilken, then, the culprit responsible for spiritualizing the territorial realism of the Bible and for "[laying] to rest the dreams of an earthly kingdom" is Origen.[16]

This hypothesis (in either form) cries out for a clarification of what is meant by "spiritualization," and it is just this that I wish to supply by viewing the land of Israel as a "sacrament." By spiritualization Davies and Wilken seem to mean that biblical words and images that originally referred to geophysical and political realities were later taken to refer to something that exists only in the realm of ideas.[17] Davies finds a pervasive "danger of unrealism" in Christian history,[18] and both he and Janzen (but not Wilken) find portions of the New Testament itself to represent a complete "abrogation" of the Old Testament's realistic promise of land. The Epistle to the Hebrews, they allege, replaces Israel's territorial realism with a heavenly homeland and sanctuary that is entirely "nonphysical."[19]

This view is mistaken, in my opinion, insofar as it overlooks the decisive element in New Testament eschatology. At the heart of the New Testament is the belief that the humanity of Christ has been glorified and is now in the presence of the Father. To speak of Christ's resurrected humanity as a "spiritual body," as Paul does (1 Cor 15:44–45), is to indicate a transformation and glorification of the physical.[20] It most certainly does not mean that the physical has been left behind. This fundamental conviction is found throughout the New Testament, not least in the Epistle to the Hebrews.

At the same time, Davies, Janzen, and Wilken tend to overlook important elements of spiritualization already present in the Old Testament. It is true that the ancient Israelites never ceased to be concerned with questions of literal possession of the land, that is, with matters of real estate and politics. At the same time, the land was never *merely* a matter of these things. It had from the beginning a profoundly spiritual meaning for Israel, inasmuch as it was a tangible sign and instrument of their covenant with God. That this meaning was not divorced from mundane realities such as agriculture or politics is quite to the point. In its historical concreteness the land mediated spiritual realities. In a word, it was sacramental.

Scripture does indeed reflect a process by which the land is spiritualized, but it is not a question of replacing physical realities with mere ideas. The process of spiritualization begins with creation itself and continues throughout Israel's existence. Properly understood, the spiritualization of the land of Israel is a matter of sacramentalization, and it is based on the sacramental role that the material universe plays in God's plan from the beginning. In other words, there is an incarnational or sacramental principle at work throughout the drama of creation and salvation.

Since it does no good to clarify one concept while introducing another that is unclear, I shall at this point indicate more precisely how I am using the term "sacrament." For this I turn to the general audience of February 20, 1980, in which Pope John Paul II discussed the "sacramentality of creation." He describes a "sacrament"—in the broadest sense—as "a sign that transmits effectively in the visible world the invisible mystery hidden in God from time immemorial," or more simply, as that which "[makes] visible what is invisible," namely, "the spiritual and the divine." According to John Paul, the body is a "primordial sacrament," and the world itself and "man in the world" are "sacraments," insofar as they are "instituted for holiness."[21] His point in using such language is not to blur the distinction between nature and grace but to point to the way in which nature is the substratum for grace and in which the order of creation is "instituted for" and taken up into the order of salvation.[22] Ultimately, to call something a "sacrament" is to specify its relation to Christ, the Incarnate Logos, who is the definitive sacrament of God's presence to the world.

THE ECONOMY OF CREATION AND SALVATION

In light of this teaching, the "dust of the earth" as presented in Genesis 2:7 can be viewed as a primordial sacramental. It represents physical matter as that which makes visible what is invisible. It is "fashioned" by God into a creature who is apt to receive the "breath of life" directly from God and thus become a body-soul unity. Man's body makes visible his own spiritual interiority, and as created in the image of God, man is designed to make visible the mystery of God himself. Drawing on the richness of this text from Genesis, the Book of Wisdom indicates that because the first man was "earth-born" (γηγενής), the earth remains "sympathetic" (ὁμοιπαθής) to man through all generations (Ws 7:1–3). Man's affinity to the earth is hinted at already in the famous Hebrew wordplay of Genesis 2:7—man (אדם) is formed from the earth (אדמה)—and the earth's sympathy with man is suggested in Genesis 3:17–19, where the ground bears a curse "on account of" man and brings forth the thorns and thistles that symbolize the multidimensional rupture caused by sin. This understanding of the earth as a primordial sacrament in the order of creation is foundational for appreciating how the particular land of Israel might have a sacramental role in the economy of Israel's covenant with YHWH, and how the close affinity between man and earth in the order of creation is taken up into the peculiar bond that is established between the people of Israel and the land of Israel within the dynamics of the covenant.

It should be noted in passing that if I speak of the symbols of Israel's covenant with God—the land, the temple, the Davidic dynasty, circumcision, and so on—as "sacraments," I view them from a Christian perspective as mediating between the primordial sacrament of creation and the definitive sacrament of Christ. These interrelations are perhaps best viewed in terms of participation. The land of Israel, as a "sacrament" of the old covenant, participates in the order of creation insofar as it is a created reality that serves as a visible sign of this covenant, while it also participates in the mystery of Christ by anticipation and preparation, insofar as the Spirit of the preincarnate Christ is present to Israel and educates Israel precisely through such "sacraments."

It is both curious and significant that the Bible's first instance of the phrase "holy land" (אדמת קדש) refers not to the land of Canaan but to the "mountain of God," called Horeb or Sinai, specifically as the site of the theophany of the burning bush (Ex 3:5). Sinai is holy because it is the primordial locus of revelation (3:2) and worship (3:12). There Moses will hear God's Name (3:14–15; 34:5–7), receive the Torah (31:18), and view the heavenly pattern of the sanctuary (25:8–9, 40; 26:30; 27:8). By means of the wilderness tabernacle, the glory of YHWH and the primordial holiness of Sinai is transported, as it were, to the land of Canaan, where YHWH's command to Moses— "Remove your sandals from your feet, for the place where you stand is holy ground" (3:5)—is repeated nearly verbatim to Joshua upon Israel's arrival in the land (Jos 5:15). The land of Canaan, then, becomes "YHWH's land" (Hos 9:3; cf. Lv 25:23; Ps 85:2 [RSV 85:1]) by a sort of adoption and is then given to Israel as their inheritance.[23] In other words, holiness is conferred upon the land of Israel through the act of salvation. From his home base at Sinai YHWH delivers Israel from Egypt and draws them to his holy mountain; from there He travels with them through the wilderness and leads them to Canaan. As the goal or telos of this act of salvation and the place of "rest" (מנוחה; Dt 12:9–10; Ps 95:11; cf. Ex 33:14; Dt 26:19), the land of Israel is from the start an eschatological symbol of sorts. Its particular holiness and sacramentality cannot be understood in abstraction from the drama of salvation history.

To stress that the land becomes holy through an act of salvation is not, however, to deny that it possesses already in the order of creation a certain aptness to receive this status. On the contrary, to adopt John Paul II's phrase, the land of Canaan was "instituted for holiness."[24] The Book of Deuteronomy extols the natural bounty of the "good land" (Dt 8:7–9) and in a particularly beautiful passage explains that whereas the flat and rainless land of Egypt is irrigated from the Nile, Canaan is "a land of hills and valleys, which drinks water by the rain from heaven, a land which the LORD your God cares for; the eyes of the LORD your God are always upon it, from the beginning of the year to the end of the year" (Dt 11:10–12 RSV). Therefore, one who would practice agriculture in Canaan is directly dependent on the rain, and since in any given year, the "early" and "latter" rains may or may not come according to the predominant pattern, there is a constant need to trust—and to please—the deity responsible for the rain. Put another way, the precipitation patterns of Canaan are regular enough to indicate God's special providence for the land and its people but just irregular enough also to indicate his pleasure or displeasure on a given occasion.[25]

The land's distinctive topography and climate had a decisive influence both on the myths and rituals of Canaanite fertility religion and on the tenets and symbols of biblical monotheism. In a sense, these two religions represent two conflicting interpretations of the land. The Canaanites served a pantheon of deities who gave mythological personification to the immanent forces of nature and to the cyclic meteorological phenomena characteristic of their land. As such, these deities were incapable of historical agency or self-revelation and thus could not enter into a moral covenant with their devotees. The "worship" they did require amounted to little more than a self-serving human attempt to manipulate the mysterious and powerful forces of nature, in part through the sympathetic magic of sexual rites.

The prophet Hosea recognized the moral degradation that this involved and observed that those who ascribed the land's bounty to Baal received it from him as "a prostitute's wages" (cf. Hos 2:7, 14 [RSV 2:5, 12]; 9:1). Moreover, he discerned clearly that both the worship of Canaanite deities and the syncretistic rites by which many Israelites attempted to worship YHWH reflected a lack of "knowledge of God" (4:1, 6; 5:4; 6:6). In truth, YHWH is "the living God" (2:1 [RSV 1:10]), who has acted in sovereign freedom—though not arbitrarily—within the course of history to claim Israel for himself and who holds them accountable to his moral will. As transcendent Creator he bestows "the grain, the wine, and the oil" on his people, not as compensation for services rendered, but in freedom and as a sign of his gracious love for them (2:10, 23–25 [RSV 2:8, 21–23]). The Israelite worshipper who understood this was able to offer back to YHWH a "first portion of the fruit of the soil," not only as an acknowledgment that the land is a gift from YHWH (Dt 26:10) but also as a way of confessing the whole series of saving historical acts by which YHWH had kept his promises to the patriarchs by delivering their descendents from bondage and bringing them to "this place" (Dt 26:3–9). As Janzen phrases it, the land is "the tangible token of God's faithfulness" and "the concrete expression of the covenant relationship."[26] Or, as John Paul II might say, the land "makes visible what is invisible."

John Paul II's strong assertion that already before the time of Christ Jerusalem was the "historic site" of revelation and the place "in which more than in any other place the word of God was brought to man"[27] would seem to fly in the face of the fact that the Torah was given to Israel not at Jerusalem, but at Mount Sinai. Indeed, our Jewish friends are probably not mistaken if they detect here a typically Christian tendency to privilege the Prophets and Psalms over the Torah. Nevertheless, it is important to note that even in the case of the Pentateuch, Scripture indicates an extremely close relationship between the gift of revelation and the gift of the land. The Book of Deuteronomy depicts Moses, on the last day of his life, giving the commandments to Israel, as it were a second time, just across the Jordan from Jericho, and it relentlessly drives home the point that these statutes and ordinances are given precisely to be observed "in the midst of the land" which Israel is crossing the

Jordan to inherit (4:5 *et passim*). In fact, the vast majority of the laws found in Deuteronomy have some more or less direct pertinence to Israel's life in the Holy Land.

The blessings that accompany obedience to God's commands are blessings of the land, and the curses that follow upon disobedience are curses of the land (26:15; 28:1–69). "Life" means to prolong one's days "on the land" (4:40; 5:30; 11:9; 25:15), and "death" means to be "uprooted from the land" (28:63; 29:27). To do what is abominable to YHWH in the land is to "bring guilt upon the land" (literally, to "cause the land to sin"; 24:4), and after Israel goes into exile the land itself will bear the scars of YHWH's wrath for all to see (29:21–26). Loving obedience to YHWH will enable Israel to "rejoice in all the goodness" of the land (26:11) and to find rest from one's enemies in the safety of the land (12:9–10), but in exile among the nations Israel will experience perpetual restlessness, anxiety, sickness, blindness, and even madness (28:27–29, 65–67).

AGRICULTURAL SYMBOLISM

We have been considering certain basic features of the Old Testament's "theology of the land" that are pertinent to our topic, drawing especially on the books of Deuteronomy and Hosea. At this point I would like to turn from what the Old Testament says more or less discursively about the land to a consideration of how the sacramentality of the land of Israel is also disclosed through symbolization.

Above I alluded to the very close bond that is established between the people of Israel and the land of Israel through the covenant. Note, for example, how people and land together constitute the twofold object of God's heavenly regard and blessing in the following prayer.

> Look down from heaven, your holy habitation,
> and bless your *people* Israel and the *land* you have given to us,
> just as you swore to our fathers: a land flowing with milk and honey. (Dt 26:15)

In similar fashion, the psalmist links land and people via poetic parallelism.

> YHWH, you have shown favor to your *land*;
> you have brought *Jacob* back from captivity. (Ps 85:2 [RSV 85:1])

But a still more powerful way of disclosing the relationship between Israel and its land is through agricultural symbolism. According to the ancient Song of the Sea, after the exodus YHWH "planted" Israel in the Holy Land (Ex

15:17). The same metaphor, with the same referent, is found in several others texts (Ps 44:3 [RSV 44:2]; Jer 2:21; 2 Sam 7:10 [= 1 Chr 17:9]) and is extended into parables about YHWH's vine or vineyard, as a way of recounting Israel's story from exodus to exile (Ps 80:9–17; Is 5:1–7; Ez 19:10–14), and sometimes beyond (Is 27:2–6). As we have already seen, the Book of Deuteronomy speaks of the punishment of exile as an "uprooting" from the land (28:63; 29:27), and several prophecies of restoration speak of YHWH's "sowing" or "replanting" Israel in the land after the exile (Hos 2:25; Am 9:15; Is 60:21; 61:3; Jer 24:6; 32:41; 42:10; 2 Mc 1:29). While the dominant image is that of vine or vineyard, Israel can also be represented as an olive tree (Jer 11:16; Hos 14:6) or fig tree.[28] Indeed, the imagery of Israel as YHWH's special agricultural project—whether vine, vineyard, olive tree, or fig tree—becomes a conventional way of telling and prophetically interpreting Israel's story, and it shows up in all of these varieties in the New Testament as well (for example, Jn 15:1–10 [vine]; Mk 12:1–12; Mt 20:1–16; 21:28–46 [vineyard]; Rom 11:16–24 [olive tree]; and Lk 13:6–9 [fig tree]).[29]

Agricultural imagery is remarkably versatile and rich in significance. It can suggest the great care and patience God shows in his dealings with his people, the moral and spiritual "fruit" he expects to receive from them, and so forth. It is also worth noting that the specific application of agricultural imagery to Israel belongs to a broader domain of metaphors by which human beings generally may be compared to various types of vegetation. "All flesh is grass, and its glory is like the blossoms of the field" (Is 40:6).[30] The proud exalt themselves like cedars of Lebanon and oaks of Bashan (2:13). The wife of the man who fears YHWH will be like "a fruitful vine" in his house, his children like "olive shoots" around his table (Ps 128:3). The degree to which such images had penetrated Hebrew thought and language is suggested by the lexicalized metaphors by which human offspring are spoken of as one's "seed" or as "the fruit of the womb" (for example, Gn 30:2).[31] Especially important for our topic, as will become clear further on, is the way the metaphor of vegetation can be joined to the symbolism by which water represents divine revelation. For example, the man who meditates on Torah is "like a tree planted by streams of water, that yields its fruit in season," but the wicked are "like chaff which the wind drives away" (Ps 1).

At the most basic level, the domain of agricultural images and symbols reflects and expresses the close existential bond to the soil experienced by peoples in nonindustrialized societies. Put simply, agriculture is one of the principal ways in which a people becomes, quite literally, one with its land. In the industrialized West, we eat mostly processed foods, and even much of the nonprocessed food we buy is shipped in from other agricultural regions. We wear clothing produced in far-off lands, much of which is made of synthetic fabrics in any case. And many household items that even fifty years ago were made of wood, metal, or glass are now made of plastics. Combined with the fact that we spend most of our lives in air-conditioned buildings and vehicles, all of this contributes to our axiomatic loss of contact with the land. By contrast, most members of a traditional society such as ancient Israel were directly involved in some capacity in raising or processing goods. And while some goods (mostly luxury items) were imported, the Israelites depended in the main on the produce of their own land. They wore clothing made from sheep wool and locally grown flax. They burned olive oil in their lamps, and local timber was used in the production of furniture, tools, window frames, and roof beams. It is hardly surprising, then, that some of the agricultural staples of ancient Canaan—grain, wine, olive oil, figs, and sheep—should serve as literary and theological symbols in Sacred Scripture. Moreover, the earth was literally taken up into the daily life of the people in even more direct ways. In ancient Israel houses were made largely of stone and adobe, and most household vessels were made of clay. Metals were used in the production of weapons, tools, and jewelry, though in many cases they were imported.[32]

The use and manipulation of the earth's resources are essential to human culture and represent a spiritualization of the material world. This is not merely a matter of using metaphorical language to represent ideas. Rather, it is a question of transforming material blessings so that, even while they remain material, they serve as bearers of spiritual realities. Instances of this include the writing of texts on stone monuments, clay tablets, or animal skins; the production of musical instruments out of a ram's horn, beaten metal, wood, reeds, or animal gut; and, of course, the offering of grain, wine, and livestock in cultic acts of worship. In each of these cases invisible realities are made visible through the mediation of the bounty of the land. In this sense, too, the land is sacramental.

But eating and drinking the produce of the land remain the most striking ways in which the earth is taken up into man. The land is literally spiritualized when its fruits are assumed into the body-soul unity of the human person. Through man the earth contributes to a new sort of fruitfulness—intellectual, artistic, and spiritual. Israel understood and expressed this through poetic symbols, such as speaking of a human person as a fruit tree or of the whole people as a vine. John Paul II's jarring metaphor—"Man is the land"—might have been more readily intelligible to them than it is to us.

The spiritualization of the land through eating and drinking its produce is probably also related to the traditional symbolism by which food and drink can represent wisdom. Thus Ben Sira speaks of "the bread of understanding" and "the water of wisdom" (Sir 15:3), and elsewhere Lady Wisdom invites those who lack understanding to come to the banquet of meat, bread, and wine that she has prepared (Pv 9:1–5; cf. Sir 24:19–21). In the Hebrew Scriptures this symbolism is applied to divine revelation, especially to the prophetic word as that which is to be internalized. Thus Jeremiah confesses, "Your words were found, and I ate them" (Jer 15:16); and Ezekiel is instructed to eat a scroll on which the prophetic word is written (Ez 3:1–3). Amos announces that there will be "a famine in the land—not a hunger for [literal] bread or a thirst for [literal] water, but rather for hearing the word of YHWH" (Am 8:11).

An important modulation of this symbolism occurs in a series of passages in which the manna provided in the wilderness is closely associated with the Torah given at Mount Sinai. Since manna was not ordinary bread and appeared in a wondrous manner, it is a particularly apt symbol for divine revelation (cf. Ws 16:26). It was given to Israel that they might "know that man does not live on bread alone, but on every [word] that issues from the mouth of YHWH" (Dt 8:3). No less than four Old Testament passages refer to the manna as "bread from heaven" (Neh 9:15; Ps 78:24–25; 105:40; Ws 16:20). The point is that true wisdom—the wisdom given uniquely to Israel—does not have its origins in the earth or in man but comes through divine revelation.

The same truth is expressed under a slightly different figure in Isaiah 55, where God's word is symbolized by "the rain and snow [that] come down from heaven" (v. 10). This passage has a particular importance for our topic since it employs the metaphor of agriculture to stress that while God's word comes from heaven, it has a real effect on earth. It is like the rain that (according to the literal meaning of the Hebrew) "causes [the land] to give birth and makes it sprout, providing seed for the sower and bread for the eater" (v. 11).[33] True wisdom does not originate in man; but when he accepts it, it transforms him and makes him fruitful.

ISRAEL'S IDENTITY AND VOCATION

The land of Canaan also plays a sacramental role in Israel's history by serving as an efficacious sign of Israel's identity as a people. A group's geographical continuity over many generations contributes to the establishment and maintaining of ethnicity by facilitating marriage within the group and the development of a distinctive culture. In Israel's case, God calls Abram and Sarai to leave Mesopotamia, so that their descendents will become a new people, distinct from the clan of Abram's father Terah. In the Promised Land they live on the fringes of Canaanite society, avoiding assimilation. When it comes time for Isaac to be married, Abraham insists on two things: first, that he not marry any of the Canaanite women; and second, that he not return to Mesopotamia.

Abraham's steward is thus instructed to fetch a wife for Isaac from Abraham's homeland and to bring her back to Canaan (Gn 24:1–9). In this way both assimilation with the Canaanites and reassimilation with the Mesopotamians are avoided, and the family of Abraham can emerge as a distinct people in the world.

Although Abraham's descendents will move away from and back into the land more than once in their history, the promise of the land as the goal of their covenant with YHWH provides a point of reference and a principle of historical continuity. The Deuteronomistic History (Joshua to 2 Kings) recounts a crucial period of six centuries in the land, from entry to exile (roughly 1200 to 600 B.C.), in which Israel is given a concrete opportunity to love YHWH and obey his commandments "in the midst of the land" (Dt 4:5). The history of Israel in this period, with its successes and failures, virtues and vices, is written not only in the books of Joshua to 2 Kings but in the land itself. From the fortified cities built by Solomon to the water tunnel dug by Hezekiah, from the "high place" discovered on a ridge in northern Samaria to the siege ramp thrown up by the Assyrians at Lachish in Judah, the story of Iron Age Israel can be "read" in the archeological record. Israel's art and architecture, religion and literacy, urban planning and agriculture, pottery styles and burial practices—all these left traces in the sacred dust.

Much as the human body gives an individual a "place" in the world, a basis for meaningful action, and thus a personal history, so the land of Canaan gave Israel the opportunity to develop a distinctive culture and identity among the nations of the ancient Near East and to play a role in the history of the world. By way of example, consider how settlement in the land made possible Israel's literary development. Had the descendents of Abraham remained seminomads or slaves in Egypt, literacy would hardly have developed to any significant degree among them. But over the centuries, and especially during the period of the monarchy, they developed a diversified society consisting of agriculturalists, artisans, merchants, professional soldiers, and bureaucrats, a society that needed and could sustain a literate class. Ben Sira observes that "the wisdom of the scribe depends on the opportunity for leisure," and he goes on to explain that whereas agriculture and crafts are necessary to an advanced society, the sage himself must be free of such occupations in order to "devote himself to the study of the law of the Most High" and to "seek out the wisdom of all the ancients" (Sir 38:24–39:11). Although the ancient Israelites could not compare to the Babylonians in astronomy or to the Egyptians in art and architecture, their literary accomplishment is astounding. Had they produced only the books of Genesis, Job, and Psalms, we should have to rank them among the most literarily gifted peoples of all time.[34]

Of course, Israel achieved this not because they aspired to literary merit but because they responded to divine revelation. And this is the heart of the matter. Living in the land of Canaan and developing a fairly advanced culture enabled Israel to assist in the "incarnation" of God's word in the "flesh" of human words. Under the impulse and guidance of the Holy Spirit, Israel drew upon the ancient Near East's already very rich cultural heritage—its politics, religion, jurisprudence, wisdom, poetry, mythology, and folklore—and transformed all of these into vectors of divine revelation. On one level the Hebrew Scriptures frequently testify to Israel's stubborn refusal to heed God's word, but these same texts, by their very existence, bear witness to a fruitful reception of revelation among faithful Israelites. To a significant degree Israel lived out its vocation to be a "light to the nations" (Is 42:6; 49:6) by composing and preserving the sacred texts. The Book of Wisdom refers to Israel as God's "sons, through whom the imperishable light of the Law [was] given to the world" (Ws 18:4).

Already in the preexilic kingdom of Judah, and especially during and after the exile, the sacramental significance of the Holy Land came to be focused upon Jerusalem and its temple. Ezekiel, Deutero-Isaiah, Haggai, Zechariah, Ezra, and Nehemiah all realized how crucial it was for at least some of the exiles to return to the land, to rebuild and repopulate the holy city, and to reinstitute the worship of the God of Israel there. Although a vibrant and important Jewish community would remain in Babylon for a millennium after the time of Cyrus the Great—and large Jewish communities were established before the time of Christ in major cities such as Alexandria, Antioch, Damascus, and Rome—Judaism could never have become a world religion apart from the postexilic restoration of Jerusalem. The Diaspora itself derived its identity and enduring significance in the world from Zion as a common focal point and symbolic center. In the postexilic period Jerusalem became, more than ever, a sacrament of unity and identity for Israel.

At the same time, Jerusalem came to symbolize Israel's unique vocation to mediate knowledge of the true God to the gentiles. Micah envisions the nations streaming *to* Jerusalem to be instructed in YHWH's ways, while he conversely speaks of divine revelation "going forth" *from* Zion (Mi 4:1–15; cf. Is 2:1–5). Trito-Isaiah speaks of foreigners "joining themselves to YHWH" and worshipping at his "holy mountain" and famously refers to the temple as "a house of prayer for all peoples" (Is 56:6–8). Another early postexilic prophet, Zechariah, speaks in similar terms of "many nations join[ing] themselves to YHWH" and becoming his "people" and links this closely with Israel's return from Babylon and YHWH's own coming to dwell in Zion (Zec 2:10–17 [RSV 2:6–13]). Significantly, it is precisely in this context that Zechariah becomes the first to refer explicitly to the land of Israel as "the holy land" (אדמת הקדש [v. 16]).

It is true, of course, that not all postexilic texts have quite so congenial a regard for the gentiles (for example, Ps 137; Is 34; Obadiah), and one might even suppose that the walls of Jerusalem rebuilt by Nehemiah symbolized isolationism, if not xenophobia. The matter is complex, but our attempt to understand it is not well served by positing a simplistic thematic opposition between inclusivity and separatism, or still less between universalism and particularism.[35] Indeed, the crux of the matter lies in the recognition that the Bible's version of universalism is not only *not* in conflict with its particularism but depends upon it and is mediated by it. Put simply, God's plan of salvation for the whole world is to come about in and through his election of Israel. This principle applies, I suggest, not only to the people of Israel but to the land as well.

The point can be illuminated by a brief look at 2 Kings 5, where the Aramean general Naaman is healed of "leprosy" by the prophet Elisha. This skillfully crafted narrative presents physical healing as a sign and symbol of spiritual conversion: The ignorant and somewhat arrogant gentile protagonist must humble himself in order to receive not only the physical cure he seeks but knowledge of the true God as well. Most commentators find a theme of theological universalism in this story, which reaches its climax with Naaman's unqualified confession that the God of Israel is the only true God (v. 15). On the other hand, the narrative's equally striking accent on particularism is generally overlooked or misconstrued. Naaman is led to healing and conversion by a humble but knowledgeable Israelite slave girl and by the prophet Elisha. But it is not only the *people* of Israel that mediate healing and knowledge of God to this gentile. Mysteriously, the *land* of Israel itself seems to play a sacramental role.

The narrative presents the land of Israel as the locus of prophetic knowledge, healing power, and true worship. The slave girl is twice said to be "from the land of Israel" (vv. 2, 4), and Naaman's healing hinges on his coming to realize that "there is a [true] prophet *in Israel*" (v. 8). Moreover, to obtain his healing, Naaman must dip himself into "the waters of Israel"—that is, the River Jordan—for which the more beautiful rivers of Damascus are no substitute (v. 12). After confessing that "there is no God in all the earth, except *in Israel*" (v. 15), Naaman asks to take home two mule loads of Israelite earth (אדמה), that he might offer sacrifice to yhwh in Syria (v. 17). Commentators who lack a sacramental view of reality are puzzled by this request. For example, John Gray finds it "naively inconsistent" with Naaman's monotheistic confession.[36] In doing so, he overlooks the fact that the confession itself contains the very same particularism, insisting as it does that the true God is "in Israel" (v. 15). Properly interpreted, Naaman's request reflects his new understanding that, by choosing to reveal Himself in a particular place, God has

consecrated the very soil of Israel to his worship. Far from being a supersti-
tious vestige of Naaman's former belief system, this conviction about the particular holiness and sacramentality of the land is *that to which* he is converted.

EARTHLY AND HEAVENLY REALITIES

Returning now to the specific symbolism of Jerusalem and its temple, I would
like to consider whether and in what way the Old Testament might prepare for
the New Testament proclamation of a heavenly Jerusalem and heavenly temple. I have already cited Robert Wilken's opinion: "For the ancient Israelites
land always referred to an actual land. Eretz Israel was not a symbol of a
higher reality."[37] Clearly, however, Wilken does not mean to exclude all symbolism from the Old Testament's presentation of the land. He readily grants
that "the land was never simply territory" or "a piece of real estate,"[38] and he
explains that after the exile the traditions concerning the promise of the land
were "reinterpreted" and "taken to refer to the restoration of Jerusalem."[39] In
this way, "Jerusalem came to symbolize the hope of redemption."[40] But
Wilken's overriding concern is to stress that throughout this process of symbolization the prophets continued "to refer to restoration of the actual city."[41]
Jerusalem never ceased to be Jerusalem, even when it symbolized something
more. On this point, I agree. In fact, that is close to what I have in mind by
speaking of land and city as "sacramental."

Ultimately, however, I find that neither Wilken's categories nor the scope
of his discussion does justice to Old Testament thought. When he insists that
the prophets spoke of "a real city, not a celestial haven," he seems to imply a
semantic opposition between "real" and "celestial."[42] Does "celestial" then
mean *unreal*? Is talk of a heavenly Jerusalem necessarily pie-in-the-sky? The
authors of the Hebrew Bible certainly distinguish between YHWH's earthly
dwelling place in Jerusalem and his abode in heaven, but they view these two
as intimately linked entities and by no means oppose them as real to unreal.
Both are real, but the earthly temple derives its reality from the heavenly
dwelling.

Let us consider a few examples. The Priestly authors of Exodus stress that
Moses must build the wilderness tabernacle according to the "pattern" shown
him on the mountain of God, so that YHWH can "dwell" in Israel's midst (Ex
25:8–9, 40; 26:30; 27:8; 29:45–46). The Book of Deuteronomy uses more
cautious language, avoiding the notion that God himself "dwells" with Israel
and speaking instead of his plan to "make his Name dwell" in the place he
will choose for an earthly sanctuary (Dt 12:11, etc.). In the Deuteronomistic
History, Solomon explicitly denies that YHWH could dwell in an earthly tem-

ple and speaks of God's "dwelling place" in "heaven" (1 Kgs 8:30). Psalm 48 speaks of Jerusalem in more daring terms, nearly assimilating Mount Zion to God's heavenly dwelling through the mediating symbolism of Zaphon, the erstwhile mountain of the gods in Canaanite mythology. For over three centuries, the city of David, graced by Solomon's temple, stood firm as a tangible sign of YHWH's commitment to Israel and his presence among them, but when this "sacrament" was destroyed in 586 B.C., at least some Israelites instinctively turned their gaze heavenward to the unchangeable reality to which the temple had always pointed. One exilic author laments the burning of "our *holy and beautiful* temple, where our ancestors praised you" (Is 64:10 [RSV 63:11]) but calls upon God to "look down from heaven and see, from your *holy and beautiful* throne" (63:15), and he even prays that God would "rend the heavens and come down" (63:19 [RSV 64:1]). After the exile, Zechariah encourages the returnees to rebuild the earthly temple by proclaiming that YHWH "has roused Himself from his holy habitation" in heaven and will "dwell in [Israel's] midst" once again (Zec 2:15–17 [RSV 2:11–13]). Finally, the Hellenistic Book of Wisdom sums up the whole tradition by portraying Solomon as praying in the following manner.

> You have said to build a temple on your holy mountain,
> and an altar in the city where You dwell,
> a copy of the holy tent which You prepared from the beginning. (Ws 9:8)

As so many variations on a theme, all of these texts view the temple as an earthly counterpart to God's heavenly dwelling. The Old Testament is shot through with this sort of thinking, and it is remarkable that Wilken ignores it almost entirely.[43]

But this hardly scratches the surface of the Old Testament's spiritualization of land and temple. Before moving on, I shall touch on just a few more aspects of this vast topic, beginning with Ezekiel's restoration oracles. Ezekiel associates Israel's return from exile with a whole series of glorious promises, at least some of which must be termed spiritual, including the forgiveness of Israel's sins and the gift of the Spirit that will transform Israel's heart of stone into a "new heart" and a "new spirit" (Ez 36:26–27). Clearly, Ezekiel envisioned a real restoration of Israel to the land, but equally clearly the reality of which he speaks cannot be reduced to its geopolitical dimension. Just as his way of speaking of God's "servant David" shepherding Israel "forever" (37:24–25) suggests something that will far transcend the glory of the tenth-century B.C. Davidic Empire, so the emphatic promise that YHWH will place his own "sanctuary" or "dwelling" in Israel's midst forever (37:26–28) points to something far more glorious than a mere rebuilding of Solomon's temple. The impression of transcendence is only strengthened by the highly symbolic vision of the temple that occupies the book's final nine chapters, throughout which Jerusalem is never mentioned by name.

Nowhere is the restoration of Zion spoken of in more glorious terms than in the final chapters of the Book of Isaiah, and nowhere else is the destiny of Jerusalem so closely linked to that of its people. Here the glorification of Zion is virtually identified with the temporal and spiritual blessings to be bestowed upon her repentant children, and this all amounts to a renewal of creation. The promise of YHWH to "create new heavens and a new earth" is identified as a plan to "create Jerusalem a rejoicing and her people a joy" (Is 65:17–18), and the returned exiles' efforts to rebuild the Jerusalem temple must be viewed from this transcendent perspective.

> Thus says YHWH:
> Heaven is my throne, and the earth is my footstool.
> What is this house that you will build for me, and where is my place of rest?
> All these my hand has made, and all these have come to be—oracle of YHWH.
> But to this one I look: to the humble one,
> to the one who is contrite of spirit and trembles at my word. (Is 66:1–2a)

The implication of this oracle is tolerably clear: YHWH will dwell on earth through the spiritual transformation of humble and repentant Israel. God's dwelling will truly be with man, for man himself will be that dwelling.

It is quite true that in the prophets' understanding none of this is divorced from geopolitical reality, but neither can it be reduced to that. The sacred authors are not concerned with what exists merely in the realm of ideas, but they are concerned with realities that are properly called spiritual and heavenly. These realities will come about only by God's power, and they will bring Israel into real communion with God. In this process the created realm is not left behind but is transformed. For the prophets the Holy Land is "the place where . . . the created things of earth encounter the infinite transcendence of God" (to use John Paul II's phrase). Finally, we must bear in mind that this encounter takes place within time and specifically within the drama of salvation history. The glorification of Zion, the restoration of Israel, and the conversion of "many nations" are eschatological in the sense that they represent the culmination of this drama, which from the perspective of Israel's prophets was still to come and not yet fully revealed.

This last consideration leads us to the decisive difference between the two testaments of the Christian canon with regard to their respective views of the Holy Land. The common premise behind all twenty-seven books of the New Testament is their authors' unanimous conviction that the eschatological and heavenly realities foretold by Israel's prophets have arrived and are truly present in Jesus Christ, who has been raised from the dead. But lest we fail to appreciate the continuity within which that decisive difference exists, we must recall that hope for the resurrection of the dead had emerged among some Israelites already toward the end of the pre-Christian period. I can hardly do justice to this topic in the present essay but would like to offer a few suggestive comments about one of the pertinent texts.[44]

The so-called Isaian Apocalypse (Is 24–27) is concerned from beginning to end with land. On the one hand, there is the earth and its inhabitants and the "city of chaos" (24:10) that they have built for themselves. On the other hand, there is the Holy Land, the people of Israel, and the "holy mountain" of Jerusalem. Not surprisingly, much of the imagery in these chapters is agricultural, and especially viticultural. The apocalyptic vision begins with the devastation of the whole earth, which "languishes and withers" because it "lies polluted" under its sinful inhabitants (24:4–6 RSV). As was the case before the Flood, the earth is under a curse, and because "the vine languishes" there is no wine to bring men joy (24:6–11; cf. Gn 5:29, 9:20). But in the next scene YHWH himself promises to provide "on this mountain" (that is, Jerusalem) a banquet of "wine on the lees," and immediately we are told that this banquet will mark YHWH's definitive victory over death (25:6–8).

This promise is emphatically universal. The banquet is prepared "for all the peoples" (25:6), and death is described as "the web that has been woven over all nations" (25:7). In accord with earlier prophecies, it is the revelation of YHWH's righteous ways that will make all the difference for mankind: "When your judgments are in the earth, the world's inhabitants learn righteousness" (26:9). A little further on, the promise of God's victory over death is expressed in terms of bodily resurrection. The "residents of the dust" will "wake up and sing for joy" (26:17–19). Toward the end of the Isaian Apocalypse, Israel comes back into view, as the prophet breaks into a new "song of the vineyard" and promises that in days to come "Jacob will take root, Israel will blossom and sprout; and they will fill the face of the earth with fruit" (27:2–6). And in the final scene, YHWH himself harvests the Holy Land, beating out the grain and gathering up the people of Israel "one by one" like so many grapes fallen from the vine (27:12).

What are we to make of all this? Using traditional imagery, the Isaian Apocalypse provides a comprehensive view of YHWH's plan for Israel and for the world. God's wrath has come upon the physical world because of man's sin, and the universal curse of biological death is symbolized by worldwide agricultural devastation. But YHWH has chosen a special piece of real estate—"from the River Euphrates to the Wadi of Egypt" (27:12)—and there he has undertaken his special agricultural project. By means of Israel—his "desirable vineyard" (27:2)—he will provide a banquet of revelation on his holy mountain and thereby "destroy death forever" (25:8). The rebirth and renewal of creation will culminate with bodily resurrection. If we bear in mind that this late Old Testament passage locates the telos of the people and land of Israel, and indeed of the whole created order, in the resurrection of the dead, we will avoid the mistake of viewing the New Testament's handling of the Old Testament's theology of the land as an abrupt and arbitrary reinterpretation.

INCARNATION AND GLORIFICATION

Turning now to the New Testament, I shall begin by summarizing the view of Davies. Near the end of his impeccably researched volume, *The Gospel and the Land*, Davies concludes that the New Testament contains two "apparently contradictory attitudes": (1) a transcendence of land, Jerusalem, and Temple; and (2) a residual concern with these same realia.[45] Although he finds a "reconciling principle" in the way the New Testament "personalizes 'holy space' in Christ, who, as a figure of History, is rooted in the land,"[46] Davies nonetheless continues to speak here, as he has throughout his treatment, in terms of replacement or substitution: "In sum, for the holiness of place, Christianity has fundamentally, though not consistently, substituted the holiness of the Person: it has Christified holy space."[47]

While Davies is careful to note lines of continuity between the testaments and anticipations of the New within the Old, the language of replacement suggests that the Christian "deterritorialization" of the promise of the land contains a significant measure of arbitrariness. According to Davies, the apostle Paul, for example, does not simply downplay or ignore the territorial aspect of the promise to Abraham; rather, he deliberately rejects it.[48] A gap opens between the testaments, and Davies does not seem especially concerned to close it. Ultimately, the problem here is hermeneutical. Davies treats the meanings that the New Testament authors assign to the traditional symbols of Judaism as extrinsic to those symbols and thus arbitrary. When he notes how Paul "replaces" the Jerusalem temple with the "living community in Christ" or with the body of the individual Christian, Davies refuses to be "detained" by the question of how "the body" came to be symbolically related to the Temple in the first place.[49] Similarly, Davies contrasts the natural symbolism by which the vine in the Old Testament is "the symbol of what attaches a man to the land"—and thus an apt figure for Israel as a people with an indissoluble connection to the land—to the Johannine parable of Jesus as the "true vine," which "takes up this metaphor" and "personalizes it completely," so that "geographical considerations are simply otiose."[50]

At times Davies comes tantalizingly close to identifying the true organic connection between the Old Testament symbols and the interpretation they receive in the New Testament. He observes that in John's Gospel "the idea of the humanity of Christ as the dwelling place of God with men and as the new temple" is rooted in "the concept of the Logos becoming flesh," and that the authors of John and Hebrews "believed in a sacramental process," such that "physical phenomena for them are the means whereby the infinite God and spiritual realities are made imaginable."[51] This is close to the mark, except that it is debatable whether the word "imaginable" does justice to the sacramentalism of John and Hebrews. Does it not reflect rather a typically modern incapacity to come to terms with sacramental thinking? In any case, Davies does not care to pursue this line of inquiry much further. Similarly, he chooses to "pass by" the "transference of Christian hope from the earthly Jerusalem, the quintessence of the land in Judaism, to the heavenly."[52] And when he does touch on this issue later in the volume, he makes a fatal error. According to Davies, in certain "strata" of the New Testament (implicitly including the Epistle to the Hebrews) "physical entities," such as the land, Jerusalem, and the Temple, have been "taken up into a non-geographic, spiritual, transcendent dimension" so that they "cease to be significant, except as types of realities which are not in essence physical." In such cases at least, it is "justifiable to speak of the *realia* of Judaism as being 'spiritualized' in the Christian dispensation."[53] Presently I shall attempt to show that this interpretation—which understands the New Testament to speak of a completely "nonphysical" realm whenever it refers to something "heavenly"—is fundamentally mistaken because it overlooks the decisive element in Christian eschatology: the glorified humanity of Jesus Christ.

Janzen, while recognizing that the Letter to the Hebrews cannot be passed over so easily, makes the same mistake in its interpretation. In Hebrews, as Janzen reads it, the "land realism" of the Old Testament is "totally dissolved" and its realia are "bracketed out as ephemeral shadows of nongeographical, nonphysical eternal realities."[54] Janzen is more positive about Paul's theology in this regard. He correctly notes that "the incarnate Christ himself represents a certain realism of geographical presence associated with the places of his ministry and the memories that attach to them. This realism of the incarnation then continues in the presence of the resurrected Christ in his body, the Church, and its members, repeatedly referred to as 'temple' by Paul."[55] This statement would be even more helpful if it spelled out clearly *how* the Resurrection extends the realism of the Incarnation to the Church. Paul's images of the Church as body of Christ and temple of God are empty metaphors unless a real connection has been established between heaven and earth. The resurrected Christ can be present to his body on earth only because he is present in his glorified humanity at God's right hand and has poured out the Holy Spirit. This is the conviction that unites Paul, Luke, John, the author of Hebrews, and every other New Testament writer (cf. Acts 2:33; Jn 16:7; etc.).

First Corinthians 15 is especially instructive in this regard. According to Paul, the difference between an earthly body and a heavenly body is a matter of "glory"—not that one is material and the other immaterial (v. 40). The resurrected body is a "spiritual body," and this is no oxymoron, for "spiritual" (πνευματικός) here is not the semantic opposite of "physical," or even of "carnal," but of "natural" or "soulish" (ψυχικός) (v. 44). Similarly, to say that through the Resurrection "the last Adam became a life-giving spirit [πνεῦμα]" is not to say that he dematerialized. Rather it is to differentiate him from the first man, who "became a living soul [ψυχή]" (v. 45), and to indicate that through his glorified humanity Christ has become the source of imperishable life. The semantic opposition between ψυχή or ψυχικός on the one hand and πνεῦμα or πνευματικός on the other hand corresponds to the very basic biblical distinction between creation and *new creation*, not to a static dichotomy between the material and the ideal. According to Paul, the corruptible body is "sown" in the earth in weakness and dishonor, but *it* (the same body!) is raised incorruptible in power and glory (vv. 42–43). That agriculture provides Paul with his guiding metaphor here (cf. vv. 35–38) is hardly surprising and suggests that the physical creation is by no means left behind in his eschatology (cf. Rom 8:21). Indeed, the exalted Christ is "the first fruits of those who have fallen asleep" (1 Cor 15:20; cf. v. 23).

A strikingly similar image is found in a dominical logion in the Gospel of John. Speaking of his own death and Resurrection, Jesus says: "Amen, amen, I say to you, unless a grain of wheat falls into the ground and dies, it remains alone; but if it dies, it bears much fruit" (Jn 12:24). Read within the context of John's theology of the Incarnation, this agricultural image is no mere metaphor. In the "flesh" of Christ, the Word has "tabernacled among us" (1:14), and in his death he has given this same "flesh" as "bread" to the world (6:51). Through his death and Resurrection his humanity has been "glorified" (12:16)—that is, it has been introduced into the heavenly glory that he had with the Father before the world came into being (17:5)—and the "temple of his body" (2:21) has become, like Bethel of old, the meeting place of heaven and earth (1:51; cf. Gn 28:12). This glorification of Christ's humanity also makes possible the sacramental life, by which those who "eat [his] flesh and drink [his] blood" possess eternal life even now and thus have hope of their own bodily resurrection (Jn 6:54; cf. 5:25–29). When it is a question of the fruit of the Ascension of the Son of Man, to say that "the Spirit is the life-giver [but] the flesh avails nothing" (6:62–63) must not be taken to signify that created realities cannot mediate God's life. On the contrary, "flesh" here refers to humanity in its state of weakness and mortality, just as it does in 1:14. The Word indeed assumed humanity in this "fleshly" condition but transformed it ("glorified" it) through the Paschal Mystery, so that the life-giving Spirit might be made available to the world (cf. 7:39).

This same theology of Incarnation and glorification is the proper context for understanding the parable of the true vine (15:1–6). The Old Testament background makes our starting point for interpretation inescapable: To say "I am the true vine" (v. 1) is to say "I am the true Israel." For Christ to call his disciples "branches" is to say that they are incorporated into Israel through their union with him. But to appreciate the force of these statements, we must have a correct hermeneutic. The evangelist is not simply adapting or reusing Old Testament symbols. He has not merely transferred the symbolism of the vine from Israel to Christ. Rather, this parable is better read as giving the *sensus spiritualis* of the Old Testament. That is, it is not so much the literary image itself, but the *res* to which that image refers, that "signifies" Christ. Christ recapitulates the living mystery of his people and their land. If the parable is read in this manner, Israel (people and land) is not left behind but is taken up into the mystery of Christ and glorified in him. The image of the vine expresses a similar sense of real continuity between the mystery of Israel and the mystery of Christ in an early Christian eucharistic prayer: "We thank you, our Father, for the holy vine of David your servant, which you made known through Jesus your servant" (*Didache* 9:2).

MARY AND THE LAND

The organic image of the vine may also lead us to reflect on the fact that the Word assumed a specifically *Israelite* humanity. Since many generations of Abraham's descendents had eaten the produce of the land and thus taken it up into their persons, the flesh he received from the Virgin Mary was literally drawn from the Holy Land. And of course, it continued to be nourished by the produce of that land throughout his life. Admittedly, John regards concern with the specifics of Christ's terrestrial origins as a distraction from what really matters: knowledge of his heavenly origin (cf. Jn 1:46; 6:41–42; 7:25–29, 40–43). At the same time, Christ's flesh-and-blood humanity has a special prominence in the fourth Gospel (cf. 1:14; 2:18–22; 4:6–7; 6:51–58; 11:35; 12:3, 7; 19:28, 34; 20:20, 22, 25–27), in which Mary also plays an important role as New Eve, mother of the Messiah, representative member of the renewed Israel, and mother of the Church (cf. 2:1–11; 19:25–27).[56]

As early as the second century, we find Irenaeus of Lyons drawing an explicit connection between the "virgin" earth from which Adam was formed and the Virgin Mary from whom Christ received his "enfleshment" (σάρκωσις).[57]

Jerome's free rendering of Isaiah 45:8 clearly indicates that this passage is fulfilled in the Incarnation.

> *Rorate caeli desuper et nubes pluant iustum,*
> *aperiatur terra et germinet salvatorem.*

> Drop down dew, O heavens, and let the clouds rain down the Just One;
> let the earth be opened and bud forth the Savior.[58]

Consistent with imagery found a few chapters later in Isaiah (55:10–11), the rain and dew are understood here to refer to the eternal Word descending from heaven, while the earth presumably refers to Mary and her virginal womb. This verse provides the opening lines for the famous *Rorate caeli* antiphon, which was more readily appreciated in the Middle Ages, when "the notion that a woman's body is like a field or a piece of earth" in which a man sows his "seed" was a commonplace.[59] A similar interpretation is sometimes given to Psalm 85 (84):11–13, which I cite here according to Jerome's *iuxta Hebraeos* translation of the Psalter.

> *Misesricordia et veritas occurrerunt, iustitia et pax deosculatae sunt,*
> *veritas de terra orta est, et iusticia de caelo prospexit,*
> *sed et Dominus dabit bonum, et terra nostra dabit germen suum.*

> Mercy and truth have met, justice and peace have kissed;
> truth has sprung from the earth, and justice has looked down from heaven.
> Moreover, the Lord will give the good, and our land will give its produce.

Here "our land" refers specifically to the land of Israel, which can spiritually signify Mary.[60] The fact that the phrase translated "its produce" (*germen suum*) can also mean "her embryo" makes this interpretation even more attractive.

But does the New Testament itself ever hint at a significant connection between Mary and the Holy Land? Possibly—in the words of Elizabeth: "Blessed are you among women, and blessed is the fruit of your womb!" (Lk 1:42). The second part of this macarism clearly alludes to the blessings that Israel will receive if they hearken to the voice of YHWH: "Blessed will be the fruit of your womb and the fruit of your land" (Dt 28:4; cf. 7:13).[61] Human reproduction and agricultural fertility are closely linked here (cf. 28:11, 18). The first part of Elizabeth's macarism makes a double allusion. First, it contains strong verbal echoes of blessings pronounced over two Old Testament heroines: Jael, wife of Heber the Kenite (Jgs 5:24), and the widow Judith (Jdt 13:18), each of whom courageously dispatched an enemy of Israel. Second, it alludes to the long series of formerly barren Old Testament women of faith who were enabled to conceive by a special blessing from YHWH: Sarah, Rebekah, Rachel, the wife of Manoah, Hannah, and the Shunemite woman.[62] This allusion is strengthened by the fact that the words "blessed are you among women" are spoken by Elizabeth, who was barren herself and was miraculously enabled to conceive (Lk 1:36–37).

Luke's infancy narrative is filled with such allusions to the Old Testament, and clearly he wishes us to read it as the beginning of the climax of salvation history. The Virgin Mary is "blessed" because the fruit of her womb is precisely the eschatological blessing that has come upon the faithful remnant of Israel.[63] The "great things" done for her (1:49) both recapitulate and transcend the miracles done in and through the daughters of Sarah. Before the hope of resurrection was revealed to Israel, the blessings of agricultural and reproductive fertility were essential to Israel's corporate personhood and identity and constituted a sort of immortality. As Ben Sira aptly puts it: "The days of a man's life are few in number, but the days of Israel are without number" (Sir 37:25). To bear children was to participate in the mystery of Israel and, by anticipation, in the eschatological blessings. It is fitting that the realization of the hope of eternal life should finally come to Israel through the fruit of the womb, which is also the fruit of the land.

THE EPISTLE TO THE HEBREWS

Finally, we turn to the Epistle to the Hebrews, which, according to both Davies and Janzen, represents a complete "abrogation" of the Old Testament's realistic promise of land, replacing it with the promise of a heavenly homeland and heavenly sanctuary that are "nonphysical eternal realities."[64] The grain of truth in this assertion is that Hebrews does indeed offer its readers a hope that far transcends the terrestrial land of Canaan or the restoration of the earthly city of Jerusalem. Wilken's attempt to deny this and to offer in its place a chiliastic interpretation, according to which Hebrews allegedly holds forth the hope of an earthly eschatological kingdom, is, in my opinion, entirely unconvincing.[65] Though Wilken's interpretation is in this respect almost diametrically opposed to that of Davies and Janzen, he seems to share with these two scholars the mistaken assumption that any proclamation of an "otherworldly" homeland would of necessity leave far behind the particularism and territorial realism of the Hebrew Scriptures. He is drawn to a chiliastic interpretation because he assumes that the only alternative is an interpretation by which Hebrews has transformed the Old Testament promise of land into "a spiritual concept that has no relation to the actual land of Canaan."[66]

All three scholars err in their interpretation of Hebrews because they overlook what the sacred author explicitly identifies as his "main point" (κεφάλαιον), namely, the sitting of the high priest Jesus "at the right hand of the throne of majesty in the heavens" (Heb 8:1). The notion that the Messiah, as both king and "priest forever," has "taken his seat" at the "right hand" of God is drawn from Psalm 110 (cf. Heb 1:13; 5:6; 7:17, 21). This affirmation occupies a central place in the solemn period with which Hebrews opens (1:1–4) and recurs at key points throughout the letter (8:1; 10:12; 12:2). It can be properly understood only in relation to Hebrews' incarnational Christology and soteriology, which I will summarize in the following paragraphs.

Christ is the preexistent Son of God, the "refulgence" of the Father's glory and "the very imprint of his being" (1:3 NAB). When he came into the world, the Son assumed the "body" that was "prepared" for him (10:5). This need not be taken in an adoptionist sense—as if the concrete individual humanity already existed in the Virgin's womb prior to the Word's descent—but it is worthwhile reflecting on the fact that God in a sense "prepared" Christ's humanity through the creation of the world, and of man in his own image, and specifically through the election of Israel *and their land*. The provision of a "body"—indeed, of *this body*—for Christ must have been in God's mind eternally.

By taking to himself a concrete humanity, the Son attained what the author of Hebrews discerns to be a fitting solidarity with the human race. As "son of man" he was "for a little while made lesser than the angels," in order that he might "taste death for all" (2:6–9). More specifically, he "partook" (μετέσχεν) in the "blood and flesh" of the "seed of Abraham," so that he might "in all things be made like his brethren" and thus serve as a merciful and compassionate high priest and "atone for the sins of the people" (2:14–17). In this passage, the phrases "seed of Abraham," "his brethren," and "the people" all refer specifically to Israel (cf. 13:12). According to the divine logic of salvation history, the incarnate Son obtains solidarity with the whole human race and a universally efficacious high priesthood *through* his union with his own people and atoning sacrifice on their behalf. The universal is achieved through the particular.[67]

The assumption of a body provides the Son of God with a concrete place and moment in history, and thus he is able to act in human freedom. It was "in the days of his flesh" that he offered prayers to the Father and "learned obedience" from his sufferings, and it is precisely in his humanity that he has been "perfected" forever (5:7–9; cf. 7:28). The priestly, sacrificial act by which he obtains our salvation has both an interior dimension and an exterior dimension. In an interior act of obedience, he chooses God's "will," but this interior act is realized in time and space through "the offering of [his] body once and for all" (10:10). The body is thus a sacrament of his human will, in that it makes his intention to obey the Father visible and gives it a concrete, historical realization, even while at another level the entire body-soul humanity of Christ serves as the "'sacrament,' that is, the sign and instrument, of his divinity" (*CCC*, no. 515).

Now, in order to demonstrate that the "heavenly calling" in which the addressees of Hebrews are "participants" (μέτοχοι; 3:1) is no mere "spiritual concept that has no relation to the actual land of Canaan"—which is my main purpose here—it will be necessary to consider next how the author views the relationship between Christ's earthly offering and his heavenly priesthood. Since Christ is a high priest, it was "necessary that he have something to offer" (Heb 8:3). Hebrews identifies this "something" as "himself" (7:27; 9:14) or his "body" (10:10), which it compares to a sacrificial animal that is "without blemish" (ἄμωμος; 9:14). Moreover, Christ makes this offering "by his own blood" (9:12), that is, by his death. How, then, is this death on earth effective in heaven?

The author of Hebrews generally eschews the traditional language of Resurrection (employing it only in 13:20), and his manner of viewing the Paschal Mystery is unique in the New Testament. In several passages he speaks of two distinct phases: an earthly offering and a heavenly exaltation (with the latter being variously described in terms of session, perfection, or glorification).

Having made purification for sins,
he took his seat at the right hand of Majesty in the high places. (1:4)

On account of the suffering of death,
[he was] crowned with glory and honor. (2:9)

He learned obedience from what he suffered
and [was] made perfect. (5:8–9)

He [offered a sacrifice for sins] once and for all when he offered himself . . .
[and he was] made perfect forever. (7:27–28)

Having offered one sacrifice for sins,
he took his seat forever at the right hand of God. (10:12)

But in other passages these two phases seem to merge into one, so that Christ's offering on earth is also an "event" in heaven. For example, as the author looks to the Yom Kippur ritual (Lv 16) to illumine its antitype, he claims that Christ "entered" the heavenly sanctuary "once and for all" through his own blood (9:12). This use of the word ἐφάπαξ ("once and for all") correlates with the frequent use of the same or similar terms elsewhere to insist that Christ's self-offering took place as a singular and definitive event (7:27; 9:26,

28; 10:10, 12, 14; cf. Rm 6:10; 1 Pt 3:18). We should probably not regard Christ's shedding of blood on earth and his entrance into the heavenly sanctuary "by his own blood" as two distinct events but as two dimensions of the same event, or as the same event in two modalities. At the same time, it is hardly necessary or advisable to obliterate the temporal distance between Good Friday and Easter Sunday. We can maintain the proper distinction between Christ's death and his Resurrection if we recognize that it is precisely through the glorification of his humanity that the "once and for all" event of his self-offering is transposed to the heavenly realm. Through his exaltation he brings into the Father's presence "all that he lived and suffered for us" (*CCC*, no. 519).

We might say, then, that the glorification of Christ's humanity mediates between his earthly offering and its heavenly efficacy. Because he "lives forever," he possesses a priesthood that "does not pass away," and he is thus able to "intercede for" and "save forever those who approach God through him" (7:24–25). This priestly intercession is not a second act added onto his once-and-for-all self-offering (v. 27); it *is* the latter, transposed to the heavenly realm. But it is especially through the notion of "perfection" that the author of Hebrews expresses the intimate relation between earthly offering and heavenly efficacy. "In the days of his flesh" (that is, when his humanity was still in its mortal state), Christ "learned obedience from what he suffered"; and this conformation (not reformation!) of his human will to the divine will already constituted an interior (moral and spiritual) perfection of his humanity (5:7–9; cf. 2:10). This perfection received its somatic counterpart through the Resurrection and Ascension (cf. 7:28), which conferred upon Christ's humanity "the power of an indestructible life" (7:16) and established him as "the source of eternal salvation" (5:9). This salvation is appropriated by "all who obey" Christ as he obeyed the Father (5:9), and who thus "advance to the perfection" that was unavailable under the Mosaic law and the Levitical priesthood (6:1; cf. 5:14; 7:11, 19; 9:9; 10:1, 14; 11:40; 12:23).

Naturally, we must bear in mind that all of this is entirely dependent on the Incarnation of the Word.

> Christ's human nature belongs, as his own, to the divine person of the Son of God, who assumed it. Everything that Christ is and does in this nature derives from "one of the Trinity." The Son of God therefore communicates to his humanity his own personal mode of existence in the Trinity. In his soul as in his body, Christ thus expresses humanly the divine ways of the Trinity. (*CCC*, no. 470)

Christ's self-offering "in the days of his flesh" is therefore already a heavenly act because it is a Trinitarian act. Through it the Son "expresses humanly" his eternal relational to the Father. Hebrews indicates this by means of a terse

Trinitarian formula: "How much more will the blood of *Christ*, who through the eternal *Spirit* offered himself without blemish to *God* [the Father], cleanse our consciences from dead works, to worship the living God" (9:14, emphasis added). Through the Incarnation, the eternal Trinitarian act has entered history and is most perfectly expressed in the historical act of obedience and love by which Christ laid down his life. Conversely, through the glorification of Christ's humanity, history has entered heaven. There is thus a mysterious interpenetration between the temporal and the eternal, and between the created and the uncreated.

At this point we must consider an element of the Epistle to the Hebrews's theology about which there has been no little confusion and disagreement, namely, the heavenly sanctuary.[68] Our author refers to it as the "true tent, which the Lord has set up, not man" (8:2) and distinguishes it from its "copy and shadow" on earth, that is, Israel's sanctuary (8:5; cf. 9:23). The latter is κοσμικός, which means "of the created order" (9:1), but the former is "not made with hands, that is, not of this creation" (9:11). The earthly sanctuary and its accoutrements are "antitypes of the true things," while the sanctuary that Christ entered is "heaven itself" (9:24).[69] These statements suggest that this heavenly sanctuary is in the first instance an eternal, uncreated reality. It would therefore be incorrect, without further qualification, to identify it as the glorified humanity of Christ.

At the same time, the sacred author's patent use of Platonic terminology (for example, "copy and shadow") should not lead us to conclude that his metaphysics is thoroughly or merely Platonic, nor should we assume that the heaven-earth polarity stands on its own as the only such differentiation operative in Hebrews. As Harold Attridge observes, "The earthly-heavenly dichotomy of the temple imagery intersects with, interprets, and is at the same time transformed by another dichotomy, that of new and old."[70] Thus, immediately after introducing the heavenly sanctuary in Platonic terms in 8:1–5a, the author of Hebrews quotes two Old Testament texts for support. The first recalls how Moses was instructed to follow the "pattern" shown him on Mount Sinai in constructing the wilderness tabernacle (8:5b; cf. Ex 25:40), and the second is the famous "new covenant" oracle from Jeremiah (Heb 8:8–12; cf. Jer 31:31–34). Together these two texts place everything Hebrews will have to say about the earthly and heavenly sanctuaries in chapters 9 and 10 within a framework established by the law and the prophets, to which Platonic categories are subservient. Indeed, the Platonic elements in Hebrews stand in the service of a comprehensive biblical view of reality, which includes not only the salvation-historical schema to which Attridge points ("new and old"), but also the biblical view of God and creation. Within this worldview, created realities possess a sacramental dimension. Remarkably,

Hebrews teaches that something has "taken place" in heaven and that this "event" involves the "entrance" of created realities into the heavenly sanctuary, beginning with the blood and flesh of Christ (see Heb 10:19–20).

Above we saw that in the Old Testament Israel's sanctuary is viewed as the earthly counterpart of YHWH's abode in heaven, and that while the former is derivative and mutable, the latter is transcendent and enduring. But the relationship between these two realities is not static, and the historical vicissitudes of the earthly temple lead up to an eschatological event. Whether this event is described in terms of YHWH's placing his own sanctuary in Israel's midst (Ez 37:26–28), or his "rousing Himself from his holy habitation" in heaven in order to dwell among Israel (Zec 2:15–17 [RSV 2:11–13]), or in terms of the exaltation and glorification of Jerusalem (Is 54:11–12; 60:1–22; 62:1–12; 65:17–25; Bar 5:1–4), it is always a question of a new union between earth and heaven. YHWH will "create new heavens and a new earth" by "[re]creating Jerusalem" (Is 65:17–18). Similarly, in Hebrews, the sharp distinctions between created and uncreated realities and between the Mosaic tabernacle and the heavenly sanctuary ultimately serve to indicate how a new union of earth and heaven has been effected through the removal of sins, and that this could never have transpired by means of the Levitical priesthood but only "through the offering of the body of Jesus Christ once and for all" (Heb 10:10).

The passage that is most decisive for Hebrews's understanding of the relationship between the earthly and heavenly realms is one that has received diametrically opposed interpretations.

> Therefore, brethren, since we have confidence of access into the sanctuary by the blood of Jesus, via the fresh and living way, which he has dedicated [ἐνεκαίνισεν] for us, through the curtain, that is, his flesh, and a great priest over the house of God, let us approach with a true heart in full conviction of faith, our hearts having been sprinkled from an evil conscience and our bodies having been washed with clean water. (10:19–22)

The verb ἐγκαινίζω ("create anew, dedicate") has a two-pronged Septuagint background, evoking here both the decisively "new" (καινός) event by which YHWH would transform and renew Israel (Jer 31:31–34 [LXX 38:31–34]; Ez 36:26–28; Is 43:19; 48:6; 65:17), as well as the "dedication" of the temple.[71] This leads to the central interpretive issue posed by this text. Clearly, Christ is presented here as both priest and sacrificial victim, as he is elsewhere in Hebrews. But is he in any sense also the new temple? Admittedly, this is far from explicit, but the language of this passage is suggestive. What Christ "dedicates" is a new *via sacra* into God's presence. To say that it is "fresh and living" (or "new and living") would be odd if the reference were simply to

heaven as an uncreated, eternal reality. The phrase might, then, quite appro-
priately be applied to the glorified humanity of Christ, which possesses "the
power of an indestructible life" (7:16).[72] The heavenly "tent" is "not of *this*
creation" (9:11), but it is of the *new* creation, which is eternally anticipated, as
it were, in heaven.

The identification of the temple curtain with Christ's "flesh" has suggested
to some that "the flesh of Jesus constituted an obstacle to God,"[73] but this idea
is alien to Hebrews and ill fits the context.[74] Whether or not we are to think
of the "curtain" of Christ's flesh being rent in two to provide access into
heaven (cf. Mk 15:38), the term "flesh" connotes mortality, and the conjunc-
tion of "blood" and "flesh" certainly evokes Christ's sacrificial death. But this
by no means requires the deduction that the author of Hebrews takes a pejorative view of Christ's humanity, even in its preglorified state. As we have
seen, the act of reverent obedience by which Christ achieved eternal redemption was made "in the days of his flesh" (5:7) and consisted in the offering of
his "body" as a sacrifice "without blemish" to the Father (9:14; 10:10). We
have also noted how closely linked Christ's death and exaltation are in Hebrews. We might even say that Christ's death is the formal cause of his glorification, inasmuch as the former confers upon the latter the character of a
priestly offering (even while the latter confers an everlasting efficacy on the
former). Christ's body is the sacrament both of his divinity and of his human
perfection, and it has this dual sacramental character both in the "once and for
all" history of "the days of his flesh" and in the glory that makes of that history a "once and for all" entrance into heaven of one who then "lives forever
to intercede" for "those who approach God through him" (7:25).

CONCLUSION

Taking its lead from the poems of Karol Wojtyła and his papal teaching as
John Paul II, this essay has viewed the land of Israel as a "sacrament" and
considered how it can be truly said that "man is the land." This mysterious
identification is rooted in the order of creation, manifests itself in the bond between the people and land of Israel in the Old Testament, and is truly present
in Christianity through the Incarnation of the Word and the glorification of
Christ's (Israelite) humanity. I have offered corrective nuances to the thesis
that Israel's "territorial realism" has been "spiritualized" in the New Testament. Properly understood, this spiritualization is not a matter of exchanging
physical realities for immaterial ideas. Already in the order of creation and in
Israel's covenant with YHWH, the land itself serves in a variety of ways as the
bearer of spiritual realities. There is a sort of sacramental union between the

material and the immaterial, whereby the invisible is made visible. This involves various transformations of the land—such as the manufacture of cultural implements and objets d'art, or the nourishing of the body with the land's bounty—but the material dimension is never left behind. And all of this is ultimately ordered to man's union with God. Thus spiritualization is sacramentalization. This sacramentalization of the land of Israel achieves a new level in the Incarnation and through the Paschal Mystery—it is even a quantum leap!—but still physical reality is not left behind. In a very real and physical sense the land of Israel has been taken up into the Christian mystery, and this spiritualization, while unique and unprecedented, is nevertheless fully in continuity with the Old Testament mystery of Israel's covenant with YHWH.

NOTES

1. Eugene Fisher, "A Commentary on the Texts: Pope John Paul II's Pilgrimage of Reconciliation," in Pope John Paul II, *Spiritual Pilgrimage: Texts on Jews and Judaism 1979–1995*, compiled by the Anti-Defamation League, ed. Eugene J. Fisher and Leon Klenicki (New York: Crossroad, 1995), 34.

2. Cf. *Catechism of the Catholic Church*, 2nd ed. (Vatican City: Libreria Editrice Vaticana, 1997), no. 1131. Hereafter cited as *CCC*.

3. *Lumen gentium*, nos. 1 (as cited in *CCC*, no. 775) and 48 (as cited in *CCC*, no. 776).

4. Pope John Paul II, *Spiritual Pilgrimage*, 34.

5. Pope John Paul II, *Spiritual Pilgrimage*, 34–35.

6. John Paul II, *The Place Within: The Poetry of Pope John Paul II*, trans. Jerzy Peterkiewicz (New York: Random House, 1982), 115, 114, and 118.

7. John Paul II, *The Place Within*, 115, 117, and 116.

8. John Paul II, *The Place Within*, 46–47. This poem seems to have been composed prior to the pilgrimage.

9. Pope John Paul II, *Spiritual Pilgrimage*, 63.

10. Pope John Paul II, *Spiritual Pilgrimage*, 141–42.

11. In the Latin Bible and the Western theological tradition the terms *mysterium* and *sacramentum* are closely associated, serving as alternative renderings of the Greek word μυστήριον. Cf. *CCC*, no. 774; and Avery Dulles, "Mystery (In Theology)," in *New Catholic Encyclopedia*, vol. 10 (New York: McGraw-Hill, 1967), 151–53.

12. Pope John Paul II, *Spiritual Pilgrimage*, 15. Similar statements about the Old Testament's "permanent value" or "intrinsic value" can be found in *CCC*, nos. 121 and 129.

13. Important recent contributions in English include: W. D. Davies, *The Gospel and the Land: Early Christianity and Jewish Territorial Doctrine* (Berkeley and Los Angeles: University of California Press, 1974); W. D. Davies, *The Territorial Dimension of Judaism, with a Symposium and Further Reflections* (Minneapolis: Fortress Press, 1991); Robert L. Wilken, *The Land Called Holy: Palestine in Christian History and*

Thought (New Haven: Yale University 1992); Waldemar Janzen, "Land," in *The Anchor Bible Dictionary*, vol. 4, ed. David Noel Freedman (New York: Doubleday, 1992), 143–54; Norman C. Habel, *The Land Is Mine: Six Biblical Land Ideologies* (Minneapolis: Fortress Press, 1995); and Walter Brueggemann, *The Land: Place as Gift, Promise, and Challenge in Biblical Faith*, 2nd ed. (Minneapolis: Fortress Press, 2002).

14. Wilken, *Land Called Holy*, 8. The phrase "territorial realism" is found on the same page.

15. Wilken, *Land Called Holy*, 56, emphasis added. Wilken holds that the term "chiliasm" is a "misnomer" (62), since the specific expectation of a *thousand-year* reign is not essential to the basic eschatological tradition shared by the various New Testament writers. It comes from the Book of Revelation, which represents an "idiosyncratic" form of the shared tradition (56). The New Testament tradition (according to Wilken) is, then, *broadly* "chiliastic" or "millenarian" in the sense of holding that upon his Second Coming Christ will establish his kingdom *on earth*.

16. Wilken, *Land Called Holy*, 65.

17. The charge may not stick to Janzen, who understands the Epistle to the Hebrews to speak of "nonphysical eternal *realities*." Janzen, "Land," 152, emphasis added.

18. Davies, *Territorial Dimension*, 93.

19. Janzen, "Land," 151–52; Davies, *Gospel and Land*, 366.

20. Unless otherwise indicated, biblical translations are my own.

21. John Paul II, *The Theology of the Body: Human Love in the Divine Plan* (Boston: Pauline Books & Media, 1997), 76.

22. John Paul's broadened use of the term "sacrament" is characteristic of much twentieth-century theology. For a sense of this context, see Raphael Schulte, "Sacraments," in *Encyclopedia of Theology: The Concise* Sacramtum Mundi, ed. Karl Rahner (New York: Seabury Press, 1975), 1477–85.

23. In a more absolute sense, of course, "all the earth" belongs to YHWH (Ex 19:5). But the land of Canaan becomes the special locus of his presence through the establishment of his covenant with Israel, which is prepared for and even inaugurated in his dealings with the patriarchs.

24. John Paul II, *Theology of the Body*, 76.

25. This is implicit throughout Dt 28, for example. Note especially the reference to YHWH's giving "your land's rain in its time" (v. 12).

26. Janzen, "Land," 147.

27. John Paul II, *Spiritual Pilgrimage*, 34.

28. The image of Israel as a fig tree per se is not found in the Old Testament, but it is suggested by several texts (Jer 8:13; 24:1–10; Hos 9:10; Mic 7:1) and finds expression in the New Testament in Jesus's prophetic cursing of the fig tree (Mk 11:12–14; Mt 21:18–19) and in his parable of the fig tree (Lk 13:6–9).

29. The story of Naboth's vineyard (1 Kgs 21) is probably to be read, on one level, as a parable. Note that it is set in Jezreel, which means "God sows" (cf. Hos 2:24–25 [RSV 2:22–23]). Other pertinent texts include: Is 3:14, 17:6; Jer 12:10; Ez 15:1–8, 17:1–24; Hos 9:10; Mic 7:1; Hab 3:17; and Zec 4:1–14.

30. Reading כבדו ("its glory") for Masoretic Text חסדו ("its love"); cf. Septuagint, Syriac, Vulgate, and 1 Pt 1:24.

31. The word זרע ("seed") can refer to semen (e.g., Lv 15:16) or offspring (e.g., Gn 13:15). It refers very often to human offspring but only rarely to animal offspring (e.g., Gn 7:3). The term צאצאים ("issue") can refer to the produce of the earth (e.g., Is 42:5) or to human offspring (e.g., Is 48:19). Note how the "dead" metaphor can be revived by being combined with a fresh simile: "And you will know that your seed (זרע) will be many, and your issue (צאצאים) *like the grass of the earth*" (Job 5:25).

32. For metals the Israelites seem to have been largely dependent on imports, though there is evidence of some local mining and smelting of copper and iron at various periods. Cf. B. S. J. Isserlin, *The Israelites* (Minneapolis: Fortress Press, 2001), 160–65.

33. The image of the land "giving birth" is also found in Heb 6:7–8, a passage which likewise employs "rain" as a symbol of the word of God and agriculture as an image for the appropriation of revelation.

34. This is not to suggest that literacy was especially widespread, much less universal, in Israel, but simply to point out that some Israelites who did write wrote extremely well. For literacy in ancient Israel, see A. R. Millard, "Literacy (Israel)," in *Anchor Bible Dictionary*, ed. Freedman, 4: 337–40.

35. For an overview of Israel's relationship to the nations as presented in the Old Testament, see Horst Dietrich Preuss, *Old Testament Theology*, vol. 2 (Louisville: Westminster John Knox Press, 1996), 284–307.

36. John Gray, *I and II Kings: A Commentary* (Philadelphia: Westminster Press, 1963), 455. T. R. Hobbs implausibly suggests that Naaman is motivated by "sentiment" and is asking for "a souvenir of Israel" (*2 Kings* [Waco, TX: Word Books, 1985], 60). Apparently unconvinced by his own hypothesis, Hobbs still finds Naaman's request "strange" and in "conflict" with the author's statement of universalism in verse 1 (66).

37. Wilken, *Land Called Holy*, 8.

38. Wilken, *Land Called Holy*, 9.

39. Wilken, *Land Called Holy*, 11.

40. Wilken, *Land Called Holy*, 10.

41. Wilken, *Land Called Holy*, 15.

42. Wilken, *Land Called Holy*, 14.

43. The closest he comes to acknowledging it is when he notes that "Ezekiel portrays Jerusalem as a cosmic mountain, a meeting place of heaven and earth." Wilken, *Land Called Holy*, 11; cf. 262–63, n. 26.

44. For an overview, see the twin articles on "Resurrection" by Robert Martin-Achard and George W. E. Nickelsburg in *Anchor Bible Dictionary*, ed. Freedman, 5: 680–91.

45. Davies, *Gospel and Land*, 367.

46. Davies, *Gospel and Land*, 367.

47. Davies, *Gospel and Land*, 368.

48. Davies, *Gospel and Land*, 179.

49. Davies, *Gospel and Land*, 190, 188.

50. Davies, *Gospel and Land*, 333.

51. Davies, *Gospel and Land*, 298, 367.

52. Davies, *Gospel and Land*, 162.

53. Davies, *Gospel and Land*, 366.

54. Janzen, "Land," 151–52.

55. Janzen, "Land," 152.

56. See Raymond E. Brown, *The Gospel According to John (I–XII)* (Garden City, NY: Doubleday, 1966), 107–9; and Raymond E. Brown, *The Gospel According to John (XIII–XXI)* (Garden City, NY: Doubleday, 1970), 922–27.

57. St. Irenaeus of Lyons, *On the Apostolic Preaching* [Ἐπίδειξις τοῦ ἀποστολικοῦ κηρύγματος], trans. John Behr (Crestwood, NY: St. Vladimir's Seminary Press, 1997), 61 (no. 32). When Adam was formed, the earth was still "virgin" because "God had not caused it to rain, and there was no man to till the soil" (Gn 2:5).

58. The Hebrew text speaks of "justice" (rather than "the Just One") and "salvation" (rather than "the Savior").

59. John F. A. Sawyer, *The Fifth Gospel: Isaiah in the History of Christianity* (Cambridge: Cambridge University Press, 1996), 69. According to Sawyer, this unscientific image promotes a degrading view of women, and he rejoices that the "image of the Virgin, and of women in general, as parcels of land . . . has mercifully little or no appeal today" (71).

60. Prosper Guéranger connects this passage to Is 45:8 and understands *terra* in both passages to refer to "the blessed Virgin Mary made fruitful by the dew of heaven" (*The Liturgical Year: Advent*, trans. Laurance Shepherd [Westminster, MD: Newman Press, 1948], 133). Jeremy Holmes provided me with this reference.

61. I have translated the Hebrew phrase פְּרִי בִטְנְךָ literally ("the fruit of your womb," as in the NAB), in order to make the allusion apparent. Because this promise is addressed to the *male* Israelite (the pronoun "your" is grammatically masculine in the Hebrew text), the phrase is often translated "the fruit of your body" (so RSV). The word בֶטֶן does sometimes clearly refer to the "abdomen" or "body" of a male (e.g., Jgs 3:21; Ps 31:10; Job 19:17), and the phrase פְּרִי בִטְנְךָ does seem to mean "the fruit of your (masc.) loins" in Ps 132:11 (cf. Mic 6:7). Alternatively, it is possible to understand the stock phrase פְּרִי בֶטֶן as functioning here somewhat in the manner of a compound noun ("womb-fruit"; as in Gn 30:2), in which case "your womb-fruit" might mean roughly, "the womb-fruit you have through your wife."

62. See Gn 17:16, 18:14, 21:1–2, 24:60, 25:21, 30:22–24; Jgs 13:2–3; 1 Sam 1:19–20, 2:20–21; 2 Kgs 4:14–17. Perhaps the memory of the widows Ruth and Naomi (Ru 4:13–15) and Sarah, daughter of Raguel (Tob 3:16–17, 6:18, 9:6, 10:11, 11:17, 14:3), is also evoked.

63. In Luke's infancy narrative, the Messiah and his herald come from the midst of the faithful remnant of Israel, namely, those who are "awaiting the consolation of Israel" and "the redemption of Jerusalem" (Lk 2:25, 38; a double allusion to Is 52:9). This remnant is embodied by three pairs of faithful Israelites, who together represent the *munus triplex* of Israel and its Messiah—Zechariah and Elizabeth (priestly), Joseph and Mary (royal), and Simeon and Anna (prophetic)—and in a particular way by Mary, who identifies herself as "the servant of the Lord" (Lk 1:38, 48), which is a prophetic title that expresses Israel's true identity and vocation (cf. Is 41:8, 42:1, 44:1, 45:4, etc.).

64. Janzen, "Land," 151–52.

65. Wilken, *Land Called Holy*, 52–55.

66. Wilken, *Land Called Holy*, 53.

67. Many a commentator has stumbled over the particularism of this passage. Most take "seed of Abraham" (v. 16) and/or "the people" (v. 17) as figurative ways to refer to Christians *simpliciter* (e.g., F. F. Bruce, *The Epistle to the Hebrews* [Grand Rapids: Eerdmans, 1964], 51; Hugh Montefiore, *A Commentary on the Epistle to the Hebrews* [London: Adam & Charles Black, 1964], 66–68; Harold W. Attridge, *The Epistle to the Hebrews*, ed. Helmut Koester [Philadelphia: Fortress Press, 1989], 94; Victor C. Pfitzner, *Hebrews* [Nashville: Abingdon Press, 1997], 68; and, with some hesitation over the first phrase, Paul Ellingworth, *The Epistle to the Hebrews: A Commentary on the Greek Text* [Grand Rapids: Eerdmans, 1993], 178 and 190). This tendency is symptomatic of a supersessionism that fails to appreciate the seriousness with which the New Testament authors take Israel's role in the economy of the new covenant. George Wesley Buchanan, on the other hand, while recognizing that the phrases "seed of Abraham" and "the people" refer to Israel *secundum carnem*, draws from this fact the erroneous conclusion that the author of Hebrews addresses a community consisting entirely of Jewish Christians and has no intention to apply his teaching to gentile Christians as well (*To the Hebrews: Translation, Comment, and Conclusions* [Garden City, NY: Doubleday, 1972], 36–38). In either case, the biblical principle of *the universal through the particular* proves to be a scandal for the post-Enlightenment mind.

68. Fortunately, Attridge has clarified a great deal in his fine excursus on this subject (*Hebrews*, 222–24) and throughout his commentary.

69. Here "antitype" (ἀντίτυπος) refers not to the greater reality but to that which is derivative. Cf. Walter Bauer et al., *A Greek-English Lexicon of the New Testament and Other Early Christian Literature*, 2nd ed. (Chicago: University of Chicago Press, 1979), 76.

70. Attridge, *Hebrews*, 224.

71. In the LXX, ἐγκαινίζω translates the Hebrew verbs חדש Piel ("renew, create anew": Lam 5:21; Sir 36:5 [RSV 36:6]; Ps 51[50]:12 [RSV 51:10]) and חנך Qal ("dedicate, rededicate": 1 Kgs 8:63; 2 Chr 7:5; 1 Mac 4:54, 57; 5:1). From the latter is derived the noun חנכה ("Dedication"), which as the name of the festival of 25 Chislev (i.e., Hanukkah) is rendered τὰ ἐγκαίνια in Greek (Jn 10:22). See Ceslas Spicq, *Theological Lexicon of the New Testament*, vol. 1, trans. and ed. James D. Ernest (Peabody, MA: Hendrickson, 1994), 396–97. Note also that the precise form ἐνεκαίνισεν ("he dedicated") occurs together with the phrase τὸν οἶκον τοῦ θεοῦ ("the house of God") in 2 Chron 7:5, just as in Heb 10:20–21.

72. The phrase "fresh and living" might simply contrast the newness and immediacy of access available to the Christian with the impotent symbolic rites of the old covenant, but in 7:16 "the law of fleshly commandment" is contrasted, not simply with what is new and immediate, but precisely with "the power of an indestructible life," that is, the power flowing from Christ's glorified humanity (cf. Eph 1:19–21; Phil 3:10, 21). Since the term πρόσφατος (here translated "fresh") can simply mean "new" or "recent" and is "common in Greek literature" (Attridge, *Hebrews*, 285, no. 27), we should not be surprised to find it used by so literate an author as ours and should not press its

meaning simply because this is its only use in the New Testament (the corresponding adverb is found in Acts 18:2 with no other nuance than "recently"). On the other hand, it might have been chosen over καινός ("new") in order to suggest the "powerful effects" and "incorruptible freshness" of this new *via sacra*. Cf. Christian Maurer, "πρόσφατος," in *Theological Dictionary of the New Testament*, vol. 6, ed. Gerhard Friedrich, trans. Geoffrey W. Bromiley (Grand Rapids: Eerdmans, 1968), 767.

73. *The New American Bible*, with Revised New Testament, Saint Joseph Edition (New York: Catholic Book Publishing, 1986), marginal note on Heb 10:20.

74. Friedrich, *Theological Dictionary of the New Testament*, 6: 767; Attridge, *Hebrews*, 287

Index

About the Contributors

Hadley Arkes is the Edward N. Ney Professor of Jurisprudence and American Institutions at Amherst College. An important figure both in academia and in the pro-life movement, he is the author of such influential books as *First Things*, *Natural Rights and the Right to Choose*, and *Beyond the Constitution*, among many others.

David G. Dalin is professor of history and political science at Ave Maria University and the Taube Research Fellow in History at the Hoover Institution at Stanford University. He has taught at the Jewish Theological Seminary and has been a visiting fellow at Princeton University's James Madison Program in American Ideals and Institutions. An ordained rabbi and prominent lecturer, he has authored and edited many books including *The Myth of Hitler's Pope*, *The Pius War: Responses to the Critics of Pius XII*, *Religion and State in the American Jewish Experience*, and *The Presidents of the United States and the Jews*.

Robert P. George is McCormick Professor of Jurisprudence and Director of the James Madison Program in American Ideals and Institutions at Princeton University. He is a member of the President's Council on Bioethics and formerly served as a presidential appointee to the United States Commission on Civil Rights. He was Judicial Fellow at the Supreme Court of the United States, where he received the Justice Tom C. Clark Award. He is the author and editor of many books, including *In Defense of Natural Law*, *Making Men Moral: Civil Liberties and Public Morality*, and *The Clash of Orthodoxies: Law, Religion, and Morality in Crisis*. Professor George is a recipient of many honors and awards, including a 2005 Bradley Prize for Intellectual and Civic

Achievement and the Stanley Kelley Jr. Teaching Award from Princeton's Department of Politics.

Matthew Levering is associate professor of theology at Ave Maria University. In 2006–2007 he held the Myser Fellowship at the Center for Ethics and Culture at the University of Notre Dame. He is the author of *Christ's Fulfillment of Torah and Temple*, *Sacrifice and Community*, and *Scripture and Metaphysics*. Most recently he has written *Ezra and Nehemiah* in the Brazos Theological Commentary on the Bible series and *Participatory Biblical Exegesis: A Theology of Biblical Interpretation* (both forthcoming). He has coedited such books as *Reading John with St. Thomas Aquinas*, *Aquinas the Augustinian*, and *Vatican II: Renewal within Tradition* (forthcoming). He is the founding coeditor of the quarterly journal *Nova et Vetera*.

Bruce D. Marshall is professor of historical theology at Perkins School of Theology at Southern Methodist University. He has authored and edited such books as *Trinity and Truth*, *Christology in Conflict: The Identity of a Saviour in Rahner and Barth*, and *Theology and Dialogue: Essays in Conversation with George Lindbeck*. He is a frequent contributor to numerous journals and ecumenical discussions.

David Novak is J. Richard and Dorothy Shiff Chair of Jewish Studies at the University of Toronto. He previously taught at the University of Virginia. A prolific writer and leader in Jewish-Christian dialogue, he is the author of such books as *The Jewish Social Contract: An Essay in Political Theology*, *Talking with Christians: Musings of a Jewish Theologian*, *Covenantal Rights*, *The Election of Israel: The Idea of a Chosen People*, and *Natural Law in Judaism*, among many others.

Michael Novak is the George Frederick Jewett Scholar in Religion, Philosophy, and Public Policy at the American Enterprise Institute. He has twice served as the U.S. ambassador to the United Nations Human Rights Commission, and once to the Conference on Security and Cooperation in Europe. He is the author of twenty-five influential books, translated into all major languages, including *The Spirit of Democratic Capitalism*, *On Two Wings*, *Business as a Calling*, *The Tiber Was Silver*, and *The Universal Hunger for Liberty*. He is a past winner of the Templeton Prize.

Gregory Vall is associate professor of theology at Ave Maria University. He previously taught at Franciscan University of Steubenville and Notre Dame Seminary in New Orleans. He has published articles in such journals as the

Catholic Biblical Quarterly, *Vetus Testamentum*, the *Thomist*, and *Nova et Vetera*.

George Weigel is a Senior Fellow of the Ethics and Public Policy Center. He is the author of *Witness to Hope: The Biography of John Paul II* and most recently of *God's Choice: Pope Benedict XVI and the Future of the Catholic Church*. His other books include *Catholicism and the Renewal of American Democracy*, *The Final Revolution: The Resistance Church and the Collapse of Communism*, *Soul of the World: Notes on the Future of Public Catholicism*, *The Truth of Catholicism: Ten Controversies Explored*, *The Courage to Be Catholic: Crisis, Reform, and the Future of the Church*, *Letters to a Young Catholic*, *The Cube and the Cathedral: Europe, America, and Politics tithout God*, and *Tranquillitas Ordinis: The Present Failure and Future Promise of American Catholic Thought on War and Peace*, among others. In addition to his books, Weigel has contributed essays, op-ed columns, and reviews to the major opinion journals and newspapers in the United States.